EXPERT SYSTEMS DEVELOPMENT

Building PC-Based Applications

Books and Training Products From QED

MANAGEMENT

Planning Techniques for Systems
  Management
Strategic Planning for Information Systems
Strategic and Operational Planning for
  Information Systems
Microcomputer Decision Support Systems:
  Design, Implementation and Evaluation
The State of the Art in Decision Support
  Systems
Management Evaluation of Software
  Packages
The Management Handbook for Information
  Center and End-User Computing
The Data Processing Training Manager's
  Trail Guide
The Practical Application of Expert Systems

SYSTEMS DEVELOPMENT

Effective Methods of EDP Quality Assurance
Handbook of Screen Format Design
The Complete Guide to Software Testing
A User's Guide for Defining Software
  Requirements
A Structured Approach to Systems Testing
Effective Methods of EDP Quality Assurance
Disaster Recovery: Contingency Planning
  and Program Analysis
Techniques of Program and System
  Maintenance
Expert Systems Development: Building PC-
  Based Applications

DATABASE

Data Analysis: The Key to Data Base Design
Diagnostic Techniques for IMS Data Bases
The Data Dictionary: Concepts and Uses
IMS Design and Implementation Techniques
DB2: The Complete Guide to Implementation
  and Use

DATABASE (cont'd.)

Logical Data Base Design
Managing Database: Four Critical Factors
Information Resource/Data Dictionary

TECHNOLOGY

Handbook of COBOL Techniques and
  Programming Standards
1001 Questions and Answers to Help You
  Prepare for the CDP Exam
1001 Questions and Answers to Help You
  Prepare for the CSP Exam
VSAM Techniques: System Concepts and
  Programming Procedures
The Library of Structured COBOL Programs:
  Concepts, Definitions, Structure Charts,
  Logic, Code
How to Use CICS to Create On-Line
  Applications: Methods and Solutions
CICS/VS Command Level Reference Guide
  for COBOL Programmers
Data Communications: Concepts and
  Systems

THE QED EASY LEARNING SERIES

PC Plus
dBASE III Plus Made Easy
DOS Made Easy
Typing Made Easy
Lotus 1-2-3 Made Easy
Typing Skill Builder
SQL As A Second Language

VIDEO TRAINING COURSES

Lotus 1-2-3 Proficiency
Lotus Macros & Advanced Functions
Managing Software Development
Building Production Systems with DB2

For Additional Information or a Free Catalog Contact

QED INFORMATION SCIENCES, INC. - P.O. BOX 181 - WELLESLEY, MA 02181
Telephone: 800 343-4848 or 617 237-5656

EXPERT SYSTEMS DEVELOPMENT

Building PC-Based Applications

Larry Bielawski
Robert Lewand

QED Information Sciences, Inc.
Wellesley, Massachusetts

Library of Congress Cataloging-in-Publication Data
Bielawski, Larry.
  Expert systems development.
  Bibliography: p.
  1. Expert systems (Computer science) 2. Microcomputer—Programming. I. Lewand, Robert. II. Title.
QA76.76.E95B54   1988   006.3'3   88-11473
ISBN 0-89435-239-3

Dedicated to
Beth and Malyce

Contents

vii

Preface

Most technologies have little value until they can be understood and applied by those who will benefit most from them. If you share this basic belief, then *Expert Systems Development* will be an important book for you. More than an introduction, survey, or overview of expert systems technology, the book offers practical advice on how to implement PC-based expert systems and will help you to choose from an abundance of tools and strategies that have become effective and popular in the marketplace.

Though much has been written about expert systems technology to date, and though there now exists an abundance of sophisticated PC-based products that rival those found in mainframe and minicomputer environments, there is still a need for a text that not only introduces practical artificial intelligence (AI) applications, such as expert systems, to experienced PC users and area experts, but also offers an effective method for building expert system applications that can open new pathways for improving productivity and replicating human expertise.

This book is also based on the belief that two very different kinds of expert system development tools or products exist in today's PC market: those aimed at an audience that is essentially nontechnical and application-oriented, and those designed specifically with programmers in mind.

Tools in the first category are, by their very nature, more general and easy to use, because they are designed specifically for individuals who are familiar with PC-based application programs, such as spreadsheet and database technologies. Such tools also build on the common experiences of PC users and incorporate development strategies and interfaces that are easy to master without prior programming experience. In fact, many PC-based expert system development tools use simple editors or menu-driven interfaces to ease the building process without compromising the level of sophistication that can be achieved.

The second type of development tool, which is aimed squarely at programmers, is sometimes more powerful and flexible but also much more difficult to use and requires a more extensive technical background on the part of the developer. In part, such tools are more complex because they are built on a programming "paradigm," or way of thinking, and are thus seen by developers as an "extension" of current AI-oriented languages, such as LISP and PROLOG. By design, these PC-based tools strive to offer the highest level of structure and flexibility to the developer of a complex expert system. But typical PC users or area experts do not begin to develop expert systems with this type of tool. Rather, expert systems programmers, sometimes referred to as knowledge engineers, quickly adopt such tools, for they see in them the capability that was traditionally available only on much larger systems. Furthermore, these tools, because they are directed at a different segment of the expert systems market, usually cost five to ten times more than products that are targeted at nonprogrammers.

Because we have targeted this latter audience of nontechnical expert system builders in this book, we have focused only on those PC-based tools that do not require programming experience, are easy to use, and are low enough in cost to allow a reasonable amount of experimentation with the technology. In fact, most of the tools covered in the book range from $100 to $500.

Additionally, we provide a staged approach to expert system development that we believe is highly effective in a PC-based environment. In presenting our approach, we offer in each of the development chapters a full discussion of the techniques used, a detailed set of examples, and an on-going case study that helps to illustrate key tasks in the building process. Our basic intent is to offer enough advice and examples so that our readers will be able to successfully implement a PC-based expert system. To this end, we have organized the book into two major sections that offer first an overview of the technology, and then provide a workable and effective method for the expert system building process.

Acknowledgements

We wish to thank Texas Instruments, Paperback Software, Softsync, 1st-Class Expert Systems, Knowledge Garden, and IntelligenceWare, whose representatives were all most helpful in getting materials to us and spending their time in conversations that led to detailed discussions of their products. We also want to thank individual expert system developers who were kind enough to let us use their systems for illustration. A special note of thanks goes to Zenith Data Systems, and particularly to Frederick Michael and Charlie Neiman, for allowing us to use the Z-EXPERT case study to exemplify the expert system building process. We also want to thank Edwin Kerr at QED for sharing our vision for this book. To our families, we owe the most for their patience and understanding during the writing of this book.

Section 1
An Overview of Expert Systems

Section 1 provides a general background on expert systems and their applications within the PC environment. Readers already familiar with these concepts may choose to proceed directly to Section 2, which describes how to actually build an expert system. Less experienced readers, however, should take the time to familiarize themselves with the concepts and terminology contained in the first two chapters of the book before moving on to the more practical side of expert systems development.

In chapter 1, "Expert Systems and the PC," we present a detailed rationale for PC-based expert systems. In doing so, we offer answers to seven important questions:

— What are PC-based expert systems?
— Why have PC-based expert systems become so popular?
— Who develops and uses PC-based expert systems?
— What kinds of expert systems can users or area experts develop on a PC?
— What is an appropriate area or problem for PC-based expert systems development?
— What kinds of expert system development tools are available for the PC?
— What is a reasonable, overall plan for building a PC-based expert system?

Chapter 2, "Expert Systems Concepts," describes the components and characteristics of an expert system. Here, we demonstrate the basic differences between expert systems and conventional programs, and we offer several examples for illustration. After investigating the notion of a "shell," an expert system development tool, we close the chapter with a glossary of key terms.

1
Expert Systems and the PC

As the world becomes more complex and technology more sophisticated, our dependence on computer tools continues to grow at an astonishing rate. Though in many ways we think that we are never going to catch up, we try to adapt to our technological surroundings and readily adopt whatever computing tools make our lives easier. Our established commitment to the personal computer coupled with word processing or spreadsheet software is but one example. Indeed, with such powerful information technologies, there is often no question: We know at practically the minute we experience such tools that we are clearly better off than before. Such is not the case with all technologies, however, and artificial intelligence (AI) and expert systems technology have historically fit into this category. But things are now beginning to change.

Though for years AI and expert systems work saturated our research institutes and universities, often little was found on the practical side. Personnel-intensive development environments, such as those involving large-scale computers and specialized programming languages like LISP, were often the norm in AI work, placing most applications outside the mainstream of many organizations and surely out of the hands of the experienced PC user.

Today, however, as a result of years of diligent AI and expert systems research and development, we have powerful tools at the PC level that can enhance productivity and replicate the knowledge and expertise of an organization's best workers. In effect, we can look at expert systems as a subset of AI technology in general, as indicated in Figure 1.1.

Since each of the subfields or areas of AI represented in the diagram may have additional subclassifications, we can see that AI is indeed a broad field. And though there have been great advances in robotics and natural language processing to date, expert systems represent by far the most mature area of AI research and development. This is mostly attributable to the fact that expert systems can be so widely applied within PC-based computing environments.

"Just as the affordable Model T popularized the automobile, inexpensive, PC-based expert system development tools are bringing artificial intelligence into mainstream corporate America," writes Marilyn Stoll in an article in *PC Week* (June 2, 1987). As expert system developers and teachers of the technology, we could not agree more. But this kind of technology transfer will not occur as widely as some forecasters might

3

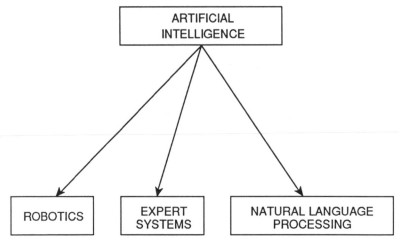

Figure 1.1. Major divisions of artificial intelligence.

think if would-be developers of expert systems do not know "how to" implement the technology in a PC-based environment. This is the goal and purpose of this book: to provide experienced PC users and area experts with an introduction to the world of expert systems and offer a carefully crafted approach to development that we have found useful, efficient, and cost-effective. But before we can proceed in offering our own advice on how to successfully build a PC-based expert system, we need to answer some important questions that will lead to a better overall understanding of the technology at this level.

WHAT ARE PC-BASED EXPERT SYSTEMS?

To answer the preliminary question, "What are PC-based expert systems?" we must first briefly define a generic expert system, which is nothing more than a software application that uses expert knowledge to solve problems or mimic human reasoning or expertise within a narrowly defined area or domain. So a PC-based expert system is one that runs on a PC, that is, on a "desktop" unit. This last fact is significant when we consider that, even at the PC level, we can now develop successful expert systems that can predict, diagnose, solve problems, plan, and aid us in many decision-making processes that require human expertise.

WHY HAVE PC-BASED EXPERT SYSTEMS BECOME SO POPULAR?

One obvious reason why PC-based expert systems have become popular is that they are closely tied to the virtues of the PC. When we consider

general PC factors such as desktop computing capability, versatility, ease
of use, and portability, the possibility for quickly integrating PC-based
expert systems into traditional computing environments becomes apparent.
According to Michael Burdick, a marketing manager for Paperback Software (the publisher of VP-EXPERT, an expert system development tool),
"The advantage of a PC-based [expert] system is you can get a hold of it,
get it into your company, use it in applications you're interested in, and
determine if that's a direction you want to take your company into as a
whole."

Moreover, expert systems technology is becoming easier to sell within
organizations today for a number of reasons. First, the marketing of the
technology is now better than ever before, demonstrating that expert systems are now acceptable in a variety of organizational applications, that
their costs have dropped dramatically at the PC level, and that better tools
and interfaces have simplified the expert system building process. And, as
more PC-based systems are fielded and validated for cost-effectiveness and
performance, there will be even less skepticism in general over the applicability of expert systems technology.

Also, the popularity of PC-based development "tools," sometimes referred to as expert system "shells," is a strong endorsement that expert
systems technology at the PC level has shown real potential for productivity. Such packages not only allow the experienced PC user to become
an expert system developer, but they substantially reduce the painstaking
tasks of capturing and structuring knowledge and expertise. Because these
tools are written with the experienced PC user in mind, they have become
very user- or application-oriented, adopting common "friendly" features
such as menus and spreadsheet or database-like interfaces. Also, as you
will discover later in the chapter, expert system tool developers have gone
to great lengths to automate as much of the expert system building process
as possible and to integrate existing databases from programs such as Lotus
1-2-3 or dBASE products. This integration feature alone can be quite
important when an existing data set must be used or modified often, and
expert systems technology can offer a cost-effective means for either ma-
nipulating or understanding that data. In fact, a whole new industry is
beginning to develop around what can be called "intelligent database applications" (discussed later).

WHO DEVELOPS AND USES PC-BASED EXPERT SYSTEMS?

Perhaps the most significant reason why PC-based expert systems have
become popular concerns those who now build and use them. According
to Tom Schwartz, a PC-based expert systems consultant and author of an

extensive report entitled *PC-Driven Expert Systems*, "Typically, it's your expert in various departments, who's gotten tired of answering questions all the time, who is responsible for the [expert] system." Schwartz's statement underscores two important facts:

1. PC-based expert systems are not always built by data processing (DP) or management information systems (MIS) professionals;
2. It is often the domain experts and experienced PC users themselves who are now building PC-based expert systems.

Paul Harmon, editor of the newsletter *Expert Systems Strategies*, provides additional support for this line of thinking: "The ideal person to develop a good domain-specific tool is a manager or consultant who understands the task and can create a tool that other managers facing a similar task will find easy and obvious to use" (*ESS*, No. 6, June, 1987).

In essence, what both Schwartz and Harmon are advocating for some applications are expert systems that can be developed by experienced PC users or area experts at the PC level. We agree and wish to emphasize the fact that, for such systems to be successful, they will have to be truly "easy and obvious to use." Not until expert systems are built with the kind of effective, human-machine interface that we find in programs like Lotus 1-2-3 will PC users widely adopt expert systems technology. As Harmon points out, we need to remember "that, in most cases, the developer was not a programmer and would not have developed the application if programming had been required. In other words, just as lots of managers who 'know nothing about programming' routinely develop and use electronic spreadsheets, those same managers will soon be offered [expert system] tools that will allow them to develop a wide variety of applications" (*ESS*, No. 6, June, 1987). That time is now!

When we look at expert system building tools from this perspective, we find that potential developers of PC-based expert systems form a vast and diverse group. Often, such developers are those individuals within an organization who recognize that "productivity" is a critical issue and that true expertise is often in short supply. Consequently, area managers, supervisors, and technical staff can become effective PC-based expert system builders in an attempt to gain the productive edge that the technology offers.

Sometimes such development does occur through the efforts of the DP or MIS staff within an organization. Because DP or MIS groups often control the selection and implementation of computing systems as well as the overall flow of information within an organization, such groups have historically been in a good position to take advantage of expert systems technology. Furthermore, DP and MIS groups within today's organizations stand to profit enormously if expert systems technology can be integrated with existing data and applications to offer greater productivity. For example, when we consider how much typical DP or MIS groups know about a given organization, including its day-to-day problems, needs, and procedures, we realize that they are already in command of much organizational knowledge and policy that can be put directly into an expert system. Such groups are also usually adept at costing computer systems, supplying training, and taking care of maintenance. And transferring technology to nontechnical staff is often touted as a great strength of such groups. So DP and MIS groups stand in a good position to aid in the development of expert systems, especially at the PC level, where the risks are low and the potential for high payoffs is relatively high.

In other organizational instances, there may be a critical shortage of experienced professionals, especially in areas that require diagnosis and problem-solving skills and where the cost and time of education and training preclude any quick solutions to staffing problems. Even more generally, pockets of expertise exist throughout all organizations, yet such experience and talent is usually never spread effectively throughout the company and is indeed sometimes lost through personnel turnover. So PC-based expert systems technology again offers at least a partial solution to this kind of problem.

WHAT KINDS OF EXPERT SYSTEMS CAN USERS OR AREA EXPERTS DEVELOP ON A PC?

For years, many AI researchers believed that workable expert systems could be derived through elaborate models that approximate human reasoning. Consequently, the discovery of fundamental laws of reasoning that could be put into machine form was the focus of much research and development. The product of this research was often found in programs such as computer chess games. By 1980, however, it became apparent to many AI developers that the power of an expert system did not necessarily rest in its reasoning power or its architecture, but rather in the structured knowledge that it contained. Thus, the term "knowledge-based systems" (KBS) became an apt description for many expert systems projects. In fact, since there is today a bias among some expert systems developers that true "experts" can rarely, if ever, be cloned in machine form, the new KBS terminology is sometimes favored over the more popular term "expert system." Texas Instruments, for example, has adopted the "knowledge-based systems" terminology as have other vendors. In this text, we will use the terms interchangeably.

Given this backdrop, what kinds of PC-based expert systems have been developed thus far? Not surprisingly, PC-based systems have been applied in most of the traditional areas of AI application: diagnosis, prediction, problem-solving, and decision support. In an article in *High Technology* (April, 1987), "Artificial Intelligence Goes to Work," Dwight Davis cites several case studies of expert systems at work, including those developed in a PC-based setting. Davis emphasizes in the article that "the systems profiled are not total solutions that can be left to operate autonomously. In all cases, they are treated as tools—very powerful tools—that assist people rather than replace them."

In some sense, it may be helpful to think of PC-based expert systems as "intelligent assistants," offering a partial solution to a particular problem. A good example is a PC-based expert system developed by the Ford Motor Company. The program, whose purpose was to diagnose sick robots, was implemented on an IBM PC, using Texas Instruments' Personal Consultant as the development tool. "The prototype system," says Davis, "contained about 100 rules [i.e., the system's knowledge] designed to take maintenance personnel, step by step, through the procedure of diagnosing and fixing an ASEA robot's problems." According to Morgan Whitney, Ford's director on the project, the knowledge base "probably covers about 20 percent of the rules that have to be written, but that's sufficient for 60–80 percent of the problems people typically run into." This is a very common goal for PC-based expert systems, since many are limited either by their size or sophistication, and often a working prototype is sufficient to test the original expert system idea and spawn further development work. In such cases, the expert system does not offer a total solution to the problem, but rather functions as an "intelligent assistant," leaving the true experts to the tougher problem-solving tasks.

In another case, a PC-based expert system was developed at the Argonne National Laboratory (the Department of Energy's Idaho Falls nuclear research facility) to improve plant safety and efficiency. At Argonne, "two expert systems are now being developed: one to diagnose problems and recommend the appropriate procedures in an emergency, and another to guide operators step by step through reactor startup procedures" (*PC Week*, June 2, 1987). Both systems are being developed using 1st-Class, an expert systems development shell published by 1st-Class Expert Systems, Inc. (discussed later in the book). According to Richard Lindsay, an Argonne systems engineer who found 1st-Class as easy to use as a spreadsheet, "We're trying to build a control system along with diagnostics that will out-control the human operator. This will allow the human operator to think about strategy rather than spend his time monitoring a thousand signals and trying to make sense out of them." Here again, we have another appropriate application of PC-based expert systems technology in which plant personnel are made more productive by reducing burdensome and mundane tasks. The fact that this particular system runs on a PC is, according to Lindsay, an added advantage: "The PC programs are nice because everyone around here has a PC on their [sic] desk." And again we see expert systems technology offering a partial solution to a given problem and functioning as an "intelligent assistant."

But perhaps the most effective area in which PC-based expert systems technology can be applied or experimented with (and often with minimal risk) is in conjunction with other application programs and databases. For example, when an expert system is linked with programs such as Lotus 1-2-3 or dBASE or with their data files, a "leveraging" effect is often realized.

To begin with, the data set is already in machine form and formulas have most likely been established for general calculation, "what if" analysis, and so on. An expert system development tool can then take the same data set to the next higher level where it can be transformed into knowledge within a predefined logical structure and thus used to give advice or solve problems (see chapters 2 and 4 on inductive tools). Such systems are low in risk because the expensive and time-consuming tasks of acquiring, structuring, and entering the data have already been completed. Furthermore, vendors of expert system development tools have recognized the effectiveness of integrating popular spreadsheet and database programs or specially formatted files with their packages and have provided within their tools "hooks," which can access commonly stored data or invoke procedures within other programs. This reduces the cost of specialized personnel to convert data from one form to another so that it can be used within the expert system.

When integrated with database programs in real time, expert systems can achieve an unusually powerful leveraging effect. Combining the two technologies often results in what are called "intelligent database applications," meaning that within the program some type of data manipulation or control mechanism exists that would usually require the intervention of an expert or trained operator. Common applications for such an integration strategy might be using expert systems as intelligent front ends or back ends to standard database applications so that data can be either entered or retrieved in an "intelligent" way (discussed more fully in chapters 4 and 5).

A more sophisticated integration of database and expert systems technologies involves adding procedural knowledge to a standard database application. That is, instead of just having data in some structured form, the integrated application may also contain rules that reflect organizational

EXCERPT FROM POLICY MANUAL 5.17.4

"Employees may use rental cars when traveling on company business to locations where air travel is allowed greater than 500 miles from the head office. Normal rental car expenses will be reimbursed at 95% for rates not to exceed $35/day. Rental car expenses between $35/day and $55/day submitted with justification will be reimbursed at 75%. Rental expenses above $55/day will be reimbursed at 50%. Employees with a rank of vice president or above will be allowed 95% of car rental expenses not to exceed $55/day and 70% of expenses beyond $55/day."

EXCERPT FROM KNOWLEDGE BASE (RULES)

```
If ( | car_rental_expenses | ).position is not vp
And    (car_rental_expenses).amount/(car_rental_expenses).duration is greater than 35.00
And    (car_rental_expenses).amount/(car_rental_expenses).duration is less than or equal to 55.00
Then car_rental_expenses_processed is confirmed
And 70 is assigned to ( | car_rental_expenses | ).rate
And ( | car_rental_expenses | ).rating is set to high
```

Figure 1.2. Policy statement and corresponding rule set. (Reprinted by permission, *AI Expert,* January 1988)

policy and decision-making. Take, for example, the written passage and the corresponding set of rules shown in Figure 1.2.

What is reflected in this simple example is a way to integrate procedural knowledge within a database so that not only is record-keeping achieved but also the data itself can now be used within the program for decision-making. Instead of only storing employee records that contain "fields" of information concerning car rental expenses and the distance traveled, the program can use these data elements (or "events" in some cases) to trigger a predefined action that is rule-based. What this example demonstrates is the degree of integration that can be achieved by combining expert systems with conventional database applications. The interesting fact about the example is that, if such a system were built, it would not have to be developed by an experienced expert systems programmer or knowledge engineer. Rather, the expert systems integration would be handled just as any other application program is. If the expert system and database tool vendors are the same, then one common type of interface for achieving this type of integration might exist. If not, then to help in this task of integration, most tool vendors try to use commands that correspond in name to those used in database packages such as dBASE. In fact, for most tools, more attention is given to dBASE than to any other database products.

WHAT IS AN APPROPRIATE AREA OR PROBLEM FOR PC-BASED EXPERT SYSTEMS DEVELOPMENT?

As we have suggested in the examples above, PC-based expert systems can be widely applied. In fact, to provide a table of specific areas or disciplines worthy of PC-based expert systems development seems limiting at best. Yet it is quite clear that certain kinds of tasks performed by experts lend themselves to PC-based expert systems technology better than others. Some general areas of PC-based expert systems application are as follows:

— intelligent information retrieval or manipulation
— diagnosis and problem-solving
— prediction and forecasting
— instruction or training

Yet, within any of these categories, the depth of the problem and the level of expertise or knowledge required to solve it can vary widely. So it is critical that the potential expert system developer knows when a project is implementable on a PC without the help of an experienced expert system builder, commonly referred to as a "knowledge engineer."

In an attempt to give novice builders a better sense of expert systems applicability overall, some writers and researchers have tried to classify applications of the technology into categories such as small, medium and large. The trouble with such classifications is that the categories often overlap and the criteria for classification are not always clear from a lay perspective.

A better classification approach is to think about the knowledge within an expert system in terms of how *simple* or *complex* it is.

At the simplest level, a good way to determine the feasibility of building a PC-based expert system is to discover whether or not the knowledge needed to solve a particular problem can be expressed in a series of "IF . . . THEN" rules that are understandable from a user's perspective. For example, one very simple rule might be:

IF the car's lights are weak, and IF the starter won't turn over, THEN either charge or replace the battery.

In a more complex situation, an expert may not be able to represent his or her knowledge in this way, but can easily provide some examples of his or her expertise at work. These examples could then be analyzed by a computer program (or yet another expert) in order to "induce" some general rules of thumb about the nature of that person's knowledge. A good example might be an expert loan agent, who, on the basis of individual cases, can demonstrate the sometimes flexible process of loan approval, but still be at a loss to come up with, say, 25 IF . . . THEN rules that capture the knowledge used.

In yet other instances involving an expert at work, there may be no apparent easy way to represent the knowledge being used simply because of its many interconnected elements or factors. For example, experienced stock market analysts who consistently predict accurate financial outcomes from a multitude of factors may find it extremely hard to describe the nature of their expertise at work either in IF . . . THEN rules or a complete set of examples.

What each of these situations suggests is that the more difficult the task and the more complex the knowledge, the higher the level of the expert system that will be needed to replicate this kind of expertise. And the more sophisticated the expert system, the more complex the development process will necessarily be.

But tool vendors and sophisticated expert system builders differ in their opinions on how to deal with the knowledge complexity issue. On the one hand, some believe that, as an expert system's knowledge becomes more complex, so should the development tool in terms of the features it offers and the way the developer uses it. More often than not, this means intricate and tedious procedures that call for a programming-oriented development strategy.

Others, however, believe that, as the knowledge to be embedded within an expert system becomes more complex, the tool must not only allow for a high level of knowledge structure and representation, but still keep the same degree of friendliness within the "developer interface." So, rather than employing a programming-oriented approach to expert systems development in order to achieve greater capability and flexibility, products that stem from this philosophy might combine several expert system methods within one system and include more intuitive, natural, and discovery-oriented features.

In other words, the more sophisticated the expert system to be built, the more help the inexperienced developer will need to be successful in the building process. Obviously, because we are targeting PC users and area experts in this book, and not knowledge engineers, we sympathize with this latter view on how to deal with the knowledge complexity issue when building expert systems. In fact, we have not included programmer-oriented tools in this book for precisely this reason, though we recognize that they are very appropriate for a more technical audience.

A good illustration of this kind of growing knowledge complexity and the subsequent expert system building process is Z-EXPERT, an example-based expert system developed by the authors for Zenith Data Systems (ZDS) and currently being used to configure computer products for potential customers. Normally, this task would require one-to-one personal interviews between knowledgeable ZDS sales representatives and potential customers with the intent of offering expert advice based on certain "rules of thumb."

Thus, a simple rule-based expert system could have been built that might represent the knowledge in rules like the one below:

IF the customer wants to do word processing, AND IF he or she will be working with large documents, THEN a Zenith computer with 640K memory and a hard disk would be a good match for these needs.

But when other items are introduced—such as more than one kind of software application to be used on the system, additional memory and disk requirements, and potential growth patterns—the expert system becomes rapidly more complex and its knowledge not as easily represented in a series of IF . . . THEN rules.

As it turned out, a better alternative for Z-EXPERT was to look at many past purchases and successful recommendations to see if a pattern for equipment selection could be "induced." Consequently, a development environment was selected that could accommodate this kind of example-based knowledge representation in an efficient way. We believe that by profiling Z-EXPERT and other PC-based expert systems throughout the book, we can not only show in a concrete way the building process at work, but also illustrate the various levels and application areas of expert systems that have been built by the typical PC user. In doing so, we also demonstrate how expert systems technology in general can and will continue to play a vital role in today's businesses, industries, schools, and government agencies.

WHAT KINDS OF EXPERT SYSTEM DEVELOPMENT TOOLS ARE AVAILABLE FOR THE PC?

Expert system software developers have carefully followed the trend toward PC-based expert systems and now offer a host of tools or shells that have made the entire building process as easy as many common PC applications. According to Paul Harmon, "If large numbers of managers are going to use small expert systems tools the same way that they use Lotus 1-2-3 or Wordstar, those tools will have to be designed to accomplish the specific tasks that these managers face" (*Expert Systems Strategies*, No. 6, 1987). Harmon's point is well-taken; it is probably unreasonable to think that managers or area specialists are going to build expert systems if they first have to come to grips with the intricacies of expert system technology or learn a programming language. PC users, we have learned, do not need to know "how it works" in order to know "how to work it." For this reason, Harmon concludes, "the market has shifted from a technology-driven market to a benefits-driven market." Thus, the emphasis from vendors today is on ease of use, access to commonly stored data, facilitating the knowledge acquisition process, and incorporating graphics, windows, menus, and natural-language features. So we will focus throughout the book on these concepts, features, and benefits of PC-based tools.

Basically, the PC-based tool market offers various products that take into account both the knowledge complexity issue in building expert systems and the needs of inexperienced developers. Despite the variety of product design, however, we can establish three broad classes of tools that are specifically targeted to meet the needs of inexperienced expert system developers or area experts:

— rule-based
— inductive
— hybrid

Because each of these technological approaches is discussed at length in other parts of the book, we will not go into detail here. However, the significant differences between these classes of tools are often application-specific.

As indicated earlier, rule-based systems are most appropriate when expert advice or knowledge can be expressed directly as a series of IF . . . THEN statements. In other instances, when several examples or "rules of thumb" are provided, sometimes in database or spreadsheet form, an inductive system is sometimes more appropriate, since such tools have the capability of "inducing" or generating rules directly from examples or known data. Also, when the knowledge to be embedded in the system is complex or some of its parts are not easily discernible, an inductive tool can be used in the knowledge acquisition process to actually "discover" the underlying structure or nature of the knowledge and then reveal this information in a visual form. In still other cases, it may be necessary to combine rule and induction methods within a single system to achieve the intended goal. In such instances, a "hybrid" tool that combines these methods would be appropriate. However, hybrid tools can combine more than just rule and induction methods, and many tend to be vendor specific. In chapter 4 we cover two such hybrid tools in detail in order to foster a better overall understanding of the hybrid approach.

The three types of systems and related tools cited above are well within the grasp and mastery of the experienced PC user. In fact, in many cases, they are no more difficult to use than spreadsheet or database software. We wish to emphasize, however, that the tools covered in this book are to be distinguished from other, more sophisticated tools on the market that are aimed specifically at programmers. For example, much excitement exists today over what are called "frame-based" expert system development tools for advanced PCs. But, as indicated in the Preface, such systems usually cost much more than tools directed at PC users and area experts, require some knowledge engineering experience to use them effectively, and build on a thorough understanding of programming languages such as LISP, PROLOG, or C. Therefore, we have not included in our discussions tools that fall into this class.

We would like to offer a concrete example that supports our basic point that expert system tools can indeed be directed to experienced PC users and area experts, and not to programmers. To do so, we need to take a brief look at Texas Instruments' first expert system development tool for the PC, Personal Consultant, and what developed from this product.

Several years ago, TI's Personal Consultant began as a rule-based program that could run only on TI machines. Then the company made the package available for the IBM PC and allowed it to evolve into a highly sophisticated, PC-based development tool and renamed it Personal Consultant Plus. But even the advanced version of Personal Consultant was not any more "friendly" to first-time expert system developers, which kept the product out of the hands of most PC users. In reaction, TI introduced a scaled-down version of the package, called Personal Consultant Easy, which incorporated only the simple rule-based portion of the tool and provided a much more "friendly" English-like developer interface. As its name suggests, Easy is in fact user oriented in a way that Personal Consultant Plus was never intended to be; the more sophisticated version was simply designed with knowledge engineers and programmers in mind.

More importantly, the introduction of tools like TI's Easy underscores another important point we would like to make with regard to development tools. We believe that TI introduced Easy specifically to meet the needs of a growing market of expert system developers who are experienced PC users or area experts. Thus, the introduction of this class of tool emphasizes the apparent fact that there is now a vast potential for PC-based expert systems development that did not exist only a few years ago.

WHAT IS A REASONABLE, OVERALL PLAN FOR BUILDING A PC-BASED EXPERT SYSTEM?

Building an efficient and effective PC-based expert system can sometimes be an intimidating task. But such efforts can be greatly facilitated by:

1. Adopting a flexible, staged approach to the expert system building process, and
2. Creating an optimal environment for expert system development.

These two key ingredients to successful expert system building are discussed below.

Adopting a Flexible, Staged Approach to the Expert System Building Process

The development approach that we offer in chapters 3 through 6 consists of four stages:

1. Problem and resource identification
2. Development tool selection
3. Prototyping and system building
4. Testing, validation, and maintenance

With the adoption of this staged approach, you will not only make the entire development process more manageable, but will also be better able to judge the overall effectiveness of the resulting expert system. This is especially true when you are "evaluating" the technology for yourself or trying to "sell" it to someone else within your organization. Because we have devoted a complete chapter to each of the development stages in Section 2 of the book, we will be very detailed in describing the building process itself and will offer many concrete examples that will foster a better overall understanding of the technology at the PC level. Each of the chapters in Section 2 begins with a discussion section, then offers examples of actual PC-based systems, and concludes with a portion of a case study on the Z-EXPERT project mentioned earlier.

Creating an Optimal Environment for the Expert System
Building Process

Related very closely to the adoption of an effective building methodology or approach is creating an optimal environment for expert systems development. As mentioned earlier, expert systems should not be thought of as a technology that displaces workers. Rather, expert systems can help people become more productive and rid them of unnecessary, routine, or mundane tasks that eat up valuable work time. They can, in many cases, simply become "intelligent assistants." Once this message is clearly understood within an organization, the better chance for less hostility toward the technology and hence the better the chance for its success.

Still, the biggest organizational stumbling block to expert systems development is the overall skepticism that exists concerning the usefulness of the technology, especially given its traditionally high costs with larger applications. In fact, the cost factor has often been a major determinant in how expert systems technology can or should be applied. When expert systems are implemented on a large scale, the initial costs for hardware alone can run anywhere from $50,000 to $100,000. When labor costs are added in, it may be possible to have systems that approach the quarter- to half-million dollar range. Thus, for such large expert systems to be deemed successful, they would have to bring a healthy return on investment.

This is why most large-scale software developers forcefully express their opinion that expert systems should be applied only where there is a very high potential payoff. Frankly, many argue, this is the only way that the traditionally high cost of the technology can be justified. But this is no longer the case with the introduction of PC-based expert systems, which offer minimal risk by comparison to earlier projects and yet still have the potential for a high payoff. According to Paul Harmon, "Since applications are being developed on existing PCs with tools that cost from $100 to $500, the costs and risks are modest while the potential increase in professional productivity can add up very quickly" (*Expert Systems Strategies*, No. 6, 1987). Thus, the key to building successful PC-based expert systems is often "experimentation" with inexpensive tools, and this is a major reason for our introducing a book such as this.

Still, despite their low cost, PC-based expert systems should be developed only when they are justified. That is, we should ask ourselves two important questions before we undertake an expert systems project, even at a PC-based level:

1. Is the expert systems project benefit-oriented?

Too often, when we speak of expert systems, we talk about them from a technological rather than organizational point of view. This stems, in part, from the newness of the technology and the fact that to date most building tools have emphasized features of the tool over its benefits or areas of proven applicability for the organization. So any definition of an expert system project should be stated in terms of outcome for the organization, even if that means thinking in terms of "return on investment."

2. Is the scope of the project within the realm of the experienced PC user?

If PC users are to have productive, user-developed expert systems, then they must be certain that the scope of the project is within the available resources, both technical and otherwise. Discovering if the knowledge within the system can be adequately represented in its complexity at the PC level is a good starting point. Then selecting an easy-to-use tool that fits the application will facilitate the overall building process. And finally, adopting the staged approach outlined above will ensure a positive outcome for the project.

In closing this chapter, we wish to emphasize one of our basic points: The applicability and productivity currently associated with PC-based expert systems technology can and should lead to an increase in highly useful applications or systems. Not only has expert systems technology been made accessible to experienced PC users and area experts through highly innovative and efficient tools, but we have begun to realize the potential for practical applications for this technology in general.

2

Expert Systems Concepts

In this chapter, we define and illustrate through several examples the concept of an expert system, and we describe its most significant features by contrasting it to a conventional computer program. Then we examine the architecture of a generic expert system, explaining how such a system might work and discussing the encouraging developments that have recently occurred in the production of expert system shells. Finally, we present a glossary of key terms in the field of expert systems for easy reference.

WHAT IS AN EXPERT SYSTEM?

To define an expert system, we must first ask: "What is an expert?" In our daily lives, we regularly consult people who have more experience than we in a particular area: the auto mechanic when we hear a strange noise coming from under the hood, the doctor when we experience an unfamiliar pain, the tax consultant when we want to be sure that we have not overlooked anything when filing our tax forms. These individuals are experts in their respective fields. On rare occasions, we may be privileged to consult with someone considered to be a leading authority in a certain area, but we don't always insist on this level of expertise. Rather, we expect of our consultants some of the following characteristics:

— Specialized training in a given area (formal education, apprenticeship, self-taught)
— Work experience in a given area
— Knowledge that exceeds our own in a given area
— Ability to give sound, reliable advice
— Willingness to offer a timely response

Here are some other characteristics that, though desirable, we don't usually insist upon in our experts:

— Extensive knowledge about fields outside the area of expertise
— More knowledge about an area than anyone else in the world
— Inexpensive fees

Now, think of an expert system as a "tool" that can offer expert-level advice in a specific area, a tool that can provide you with the same advice as the human expert. This is an expert system. A more formal definition might be:

An expert system is a program that simulates the performance of a human expert in a specific, narrow field or domain.

The term "expert system," however, may be misleading. The connotations of the word "expert" can lead us to expect *infallible* performance which we do not insist upon in those we call experts. Is there a medical doctor who has never misdiagnosed a disease? Does there exist a stockbroker with no regrets? Where is the chef who has never experienced a culinary disaster? We really should not demand more of our expert systems than we ask of human experts (though, as we will explain later, an expert system may indeed outperform a human expert in some areas). As mentioned in chapter 1, some expert system developers have reacted to this criticism by referring to this technology as "knowledge-based systems." This terminology not only reduces the sometimes unrealistic expectations suggested by the word "expert," but also points to the differences between such systems and conventional programs.

DIFFERENCES BETWEEN EXPERT SYSTEMS AND CONVENTIONAL PROGRAMS

Though an expert system is developed and run on a computer, several important differences exist between expert systems and conventional computer programs. Some argue that these distinctions are so significant that an expert system cannot really be considered a computer program at all. What are some of these differences?

Most computer programming courses emphasize the concepts of "semantics" and "syntax" of a language, the structure of its data, and the development of efficient algorithms or sequences of instructions. Once an individual has a grasp of a computer language, the idea is to define appropriate data structures and procedures to solve a problem. A typical conventional program, then, is run on a *complete set of data* with the expectation of a *unique solution* to the problem. In contrast, an expert system frequently runs on an *incomplete set of data* and may well produce *many solutions* to a problem, each with varying degrees of confidence.

To illustrate this difference, consider the problem of calculating the average of a list of numbers. Give a correct conventional program all the numbers to be averaged and out pops the (unique) solution. If we fail to supply the program with all the numbers, we are given an incorrect answer.

On the other hand, if the program is provided with the *complete* set of data, the program returns not several answers, but a single answer. This type of problem is ideally suited for a conventional program; using an expert system to calculate averages would be inappropriate.

But what if the problem were to find pertinent books in the reference collection of a library dealing with some obscure person? An experienced reference librarian would ask some basic questions about the subject from the inquirer and then, on the basis of this incomplete information, make the best possible recommendations. Note that, in all probability, there is no unique solution to this problem; several books are likely to be helpful, some more than others. This type of problem calls for an expert system.

Whereas a conventional program is *algorithmic* in nature and requires a *complete* set of data to produce a *unique* solution, an expert system is *conceptual* in nature, can function with an *incomplete* set of data, and may produce *several* solutions.

One point to emphasize is that, assuming a correctly written program, one feels that the outcome or result produced by the conventional program is certain; the recommendations produced by expert systems may *not* be. With reference to the last example, even expert librarians' advice may prove to be *uncertain*. Chances are they will couch their recommendations in phrases such as "You *might* find the information you are looking for in . . ." or "You'll *probably* find that information in . . ." Similarly, most expert systems include the facility for determining and displaying their confidence in the advice they offer. In conventional programs, this feature is generally neither present nor important.

Finally, expert systems are distinguished from conventional programs by their method of development. Most software engineers have adopted a top-down approach to software development: The project is broken down into several smaller projects, each of which may in turn be further modularized. An effective methodology, the top-down approach requires a vision of the overall structure of the problem at hand and an awareness of the relationship among the various modules that work together to solve the problem. In expert systems development, this vision is often blurred. Frequently, it is not until all the expert's knowledge is entered into the system that the structure of the knowledge becomes evident. An expert may be able to offer advice without consciously being aware of the organization of the knowledge he possesses which enables him to give the advice. For this reason, the top-down approach to expert system development is often less effective than it is in the development of conventional software.

The chart in Figure 2.1 summarizes the basic distinctions between expert systems and conventional programs.

CONVENTIONAL PROGRAM	EXPERT SYSTEM
Requires a complete set of data	Can function with an incomplete set of data
Uses algorithms	Uses heuristics or rules of thumb
Produces a unique solution	May produce several solutions
Generates results that are certain	May generate uncertain results
Lends itself to a top-down approach to development	Accommodates a bottom-up development methodology

Figure 2.1. Differences between conventional programs and expert systems.

ARCHITECTURE OF AN EXPERT SYSTEM

What does an expert system "look like"? What are its general characteristics? First note that, just as no unique set of traits defines a human expert, not every expert system has the same architecture. But certain generic attributes appear in most of these systems. To help understand these characteristics, we first examine a human expert, in this case, an auto mechanic.

A customer drives her car over to the garage one morning and is immediately impressed with the greeting she receives. The mechanic reveals his friendly disposition through some small talk, and then starts asking the customer questions about the problem she is experiencing with her car. Based on the answers to these questions, the mechanic has a pretty good idea of what's wrong with the car. He has heard these symptoms described before. He has learned the probable causes of these problems and, in fact, he recently serviced another car with precisely the same trouble. He then informs the customer that the problem is probably due to one of two possible malfunctions; but, nine times out of ten, the problem can be solved by replacing a single part. The customer leaves the shop, secure in the expertise that the mechanic has demonstrated. When she returns to the shop later that day, she is all the more impressed that the mechanic hit

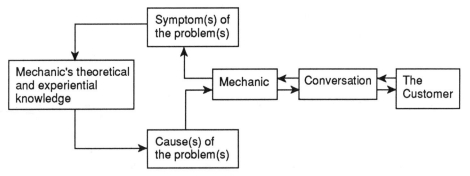

Figure 2.2. A customer-mechanic encounter.

the problem right on the head, quickly repaired her car, and, throughout the entire episode, maintained his good-natured manner. He is the ideal expert.

If we wanted to abstract the scenario above for the purpose of identifying its essential components, we might represent it as in Figure 2.2.

In conversation with the customer, the mechanic learns of the symptoms of her car's problem. He then considers these symptoms in the context of his knowledge about cars and, as a result, suggests causes of the problem. Though he may be thinking of both the symptoms and the causes in highly technical terms, the mechanic then describes the causes to the customer in a manner that makes sense to her.

Also note that when another customer drives into the shop later that day, the encounter modeled in Figure 2.2 is unchanged. That is, the *scheme* remains the same. What *does* change, however, is the information in the "Symptoms" and "Causes" boxes: different problems, different causes. What may also change is the content of the box on the far left, the mechanic's knowledge. Based on his experience with the first customer, the mechanic may revise, for example, his estimate as to how frequently the part he replaced causes the problems she described. Instead of 9 times out of 10, he may now feel that 95 times out of 100 is a better estimate. Furthermore, on his lunch hour, the mechanic may have looked over some repair manuals and learned something new. This new information is then added to his experience and is available for the benefit of future customers.

In order to discuss the model above in the general context of expert systems, it would be convenient to label some of the components in Figure 2.2. The collection of knowledge is generally referred to as a knowledge base, while the data base contains the facts that are input and output (i.e., the symptoms and the causes in the car-repair problem). The conversation that occurs between the expert and the client is called the human interface.

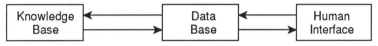

Figure 2.3. The general encounter model.

Omitting reference to the particular expert and the particular customer, then, the encounter model could be represented as in Figure 2.3 above:

These are the essential components of an expert system: a collection of knowledge, a collection of data, and the human interface. But something is still missing from Figure 2.3. When the mechanic felt he knew the symptoms of the customer's problem, he was able to deduce probable causes by using his knowledge. But how? By guessing? By reviewing every single fact he learned in school and through his years of experience? Probably not. Rather, the mechanic was somehow able to recall from his accumulated knowledge only the information pertinent to the problem at hand. This is an extremely complex process!

Let us represent this process in our general scheme by including one more box and labeling it the "inference mechanism" (Figure 2.4).

The inference mechanism performs the complex task of combining elements from the "data base" with elements from the "knowledge base" to produce new information in the form of advice.

For the builder of an expert system, an important question concerns the nitty-gritty of the inference mechanism and the representation of knowledge in the knowledge base. How does the novice begin to approach the problem of an inference mechanism? When it comes time to actually write or develop a knowledge base, how does one represent this information in a PC? Before answering these questions, we must first examine the components of an expert system more closely.

To illustrate these concepts, consider an expert system whose function is to classify the common vehicles described by these nine simplified statements:

1. An aircraft is a vehicle that travels through air.
2. A helicopter is an aircraft with rotors.
3. A plane is an aircraft with wings.

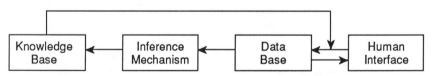

Figure 2.4. Architecture of a generic expert system.

4. A jet is a plane with no propellers.
5. A boat is a vehicle that travels on water.
6. A motor vehicle is a vehicle that travels on land.
7. A motorcycle is a motor vehicle with two wheels.
8. A truck is a motor vehicle with four wheels that is used primarily for commercial purposes.
9. A car is a motor vehicle with four wheels that is used primarily for transportation purposes.

This list of definitions of vehicles is not intended to be exhaustive (bicycle and hot-air balloon, for example, are not included), but it serves to introduce the concept of "knowledge representation."

The Knowledge Base

The nine definitions above make perfectly good sense to us. The structure of these facts in the form of sentences is both comprehensible and natural. Computers, however, do not yet handle English sentences very well. For this reason, if we want a computer to process the information contained in these definitions, an alternative structure must be devised, one which the computer can be made to understand. This problem, one of the most elusive in artificial intelligence, is known as the knowledge representation problem.

Several schemes for knowledge representation exist and more are being developed as researchers become more sophisticated. Two of the most common methods for PC-based expert systems are decision trees and rules.

A decision tree is a structure that pictorially represents relationships among various objects in a certain class.

Figure 2.5 depicts a decision tree that captures the classification of vehicles in our previous example. The items in boldface are referred to as the *results* or *goals* (the vehicles that are to be identified). The items in uppercase are the *factors* (which serve as the defining criteria for the vehicles), while the other components (Air, Water, Land, Yes, No, 2, 4, Commercial, Transportation) are *values* of the factors for specific vehicles. While these seem like explicit terms, they are not yet standard. Other authors, for example, would use the word *attribute* or *parameter* to refer to the criteria that distinguish the vehicles.

The pictorial nature of a decision tree makes it easy to extract the definition of a particular vehicle and to observe the relationships among the vehicles in our example. For example, line (12) of Figure 2.5 indicates

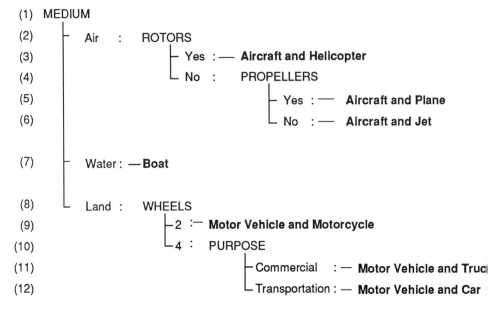

(1) MEDIUM
(2) ├ Air   :   ROTORS
(3) │   ├ Yes : — **Aircraft and Helicopter**
(4) │   └ No :   PROPELLERS
(5) │   ├ Yes : — **Aircraft and Plane**
(6) │   └ No : — **Aircraft and Jet**

(7) ├ Water : — **Boat**

(8) └ Land :   WHEELS
(9)   ├ 2 :— **Motor Vehicle and Motorcycle**
(10)   └ 4 :   PURPOSE
(11)   ├ Commercial   : — **Motor Vehicle and Truc**
(12)   └ Transportation : — **Motor Vehicle and Car**

Figure 2.5. Decision tree representation of vehicles.

that if a vehicle is land-based, has four wheels, and is used for transportation, then it is both a motor vehicle and a car. Line (3) suggests that a helicopter travels through the air and has rotors.

The second representation scheme we will consider is the rule-based system (sometimes called the production rule-based system).

In a rule-based system, the knowledge representation takes the form of a collection of conditional statements, statements of the form "IF . . . THEN."

The rules describing our collection of vehicles might look like this:

1. IF the vehicle travels through air THEN the vehicle is an aircraft.
2. IF the vehicle travels on land THEN the vehicle is a motor vehicle.
3. IF the vehicle travels on water THEN the vehicle is a boat.
4. IF the vehicle is an aircraft and the vehicle has rotors THEN the vehicle is a helicopter.
5. IF the vehicle is an aircraft and the vehicle has wings THEN the vehicle is an airplane.

6. IF the vehicle is an airplane and the vehicle has no propellers THEN the vehicle is a jet.
7. IF the vehicle is a motor vehicle and the vehicle has two wheels THEN the vehicle is a motorcycle.
8. IF the vehicle is a motor vehicle and the vehicle has four wheels and the vehicle is used for commercial purposes THEN the vehicle is a truck.
9. IF the vehicle is a motor vehicle and the vehicle has four wheels and the vehicle is used for transportation purposes THEN the vehicle is a car.

Though less graphic than the decision tree representation scheme, the rule-based representation does come closer to resembling the definitions of the vehicles. The important point, however, is that there are several equivalent ways to represent knowledge. The method to use depends largely on the software employed to build the expert system. We will elaborate on this topic later in this chapter and again in chapter 4.

Although some expert system developers feel strongly that not every application can have its pertinent knowledge captured in a sequence of IF . . . THEN statements, the rule-based approach is nevertheless the most popular in PC-based expert systems development. In fact, at the Third Artificial Intelligence Satellite Symposium sponsored by Texas Instruments in April 1987, of the many expert systems discussed and illustrated during the four-hour session, all were rule-based!

For the example above, nine rules seem to capture the essential knowledge concerning our vehicles. You can imagine that a more realistic or pragmatic expert system would require many more rules in its knowledge base. MYCIN, for example, an expert system developed at Stanford University for the purpose of diagnosing infectious blood diseases, is a rule-based system with about 500 rules in its knowledge base. Though developed on a large computer, the architecture of MYCIN serves as a model for several PC-based systems available today and for this reason is historically significant. Equally significant is XCON, a rule-based expert system produced for the Digital Equipment Corporation, which offers advice on the configuration of appropriate computer equipment to satisfy a customer's needs. Its knowledge base contains over 3,300 rules! Depending on its complexity, the knowledge base of a typical PC-based expert system would probably not exceed 500 rules.

We hasten to add, however, that the problem of knowledge representation is not one that you must consider in order to develop an expert system. As you will discover later in this book, most expert systems produced on a PC today are developed with the assistance of off-the-shelf software which determines the format of the knowledge representation.

We now turn our attention to the second component of an expert system.

The Global Data Base

All the rules in the knowledge base will be worthless if the system has no facts on which to operate. The global data base serves as the expert system's repository for facts gathered from two sources: (1) information supplied by the user in response to questions asked by the system, and (2) information inferred or deduced by the system's inference mechanism working on the knowledge base. To illustrate the differences between these two sources of facts, we return to the garage where the mechanic is interviewing a customer about the problem she is having with her car.

Mechanic: What seems to be the problem?
Customer: Whenever I pull out of my parking space, I notice that I leave a puddle of fluid behind. There is some sort of a leak from under my car. (This is volunteered information.)
Mechanic: Does the fluid smell like gas?
Customer: No, it doesn't. (This is information elicited from the user.)
Mechanic: It could be a cooling system leak. (This is information inferred.)

The point is that, in order for an expert system to use its knowledge base, it needs some starting point, some indication of which rules pertain to the problem. In the context of the vehicle classification example above, if the user wants the system to identify a certain vehicle, the system will be helpless to do so until it is given some facts (e.g., whether the vehicle travels through air, on land, or on water). Facts such as these are stored in the global data base. As the session between the expert system and the user proceeds, the global data base grows in size as new facts are added and, finally, contains the conclusion of the session (the problem is a cooling system leak or the vehicle is a boat).

While collecting information supplied by the user of the system into the global data base is fairly straightforward, deducing new information from old is more subtle. This responsibility belongs to the third major component of an expert system: the inference mechanism.

The Inference Mechanism

The inference mechanism compares information supplied by the user with the knowledge contained in the knowledge base and deduces whatever conclusions may logically follow. If, for example, the user has volunteered that a vehicle travels on water and the knowledge base contains the rule: "IF a vehicle travels on water THEN the vehicle is a boat," the job of the inference mechanism is to deduce that the vehicle is a boat. In a rule-based expert system, there are several methods of performing this task, the two most common being *backward-chaining* and *forward-chaining.*

Backward-Chaining

In backward-chaining, the inference mechanism guesses at a conclusion and then attempts to prove that its guess is correct by—

a. finding a rule whose THEN part is the same as its guess, and
b. establishing the condition(s) contained in the IF part of the rule.

Using the Vehicle Identification System as an example, let us suppose that we are looking at a single-propeller airplane and we want the system to identify the vehicle. The inference mechanism may first guess (erroneously) that the vehicle is a jet plane. In an attempt to prove that its guess is correct, the inference mechanism observes that Rule 6 contains its guess (jet) in its THEN part.

Rule 6:
IF the vehicle is an airplane and the vehicle has no propellers THEN the vehicle is a jet.

So, in order to verify that its guess is correct, the inference mechanism tries to establish the conditions in the IF part of Rule 6, namely—

a. the vehicle is an airplane, and
b. the vehicle has no propellers.

Once these two conditions are established, the mechanism can conclude from Rule 6 that the vehicle is a jet.

But how does it go about establishing conditions (a) and (b)? Consider first condition (a): the vehicle is an airplane. Notice that Rule 5 contains the conclusion "airplane" in its THEN part:

Rule 5:
IF the vehicle is an aircraft and the vehicle has wings THEN the vehicle is an airplane.

So, in order to verify that the vehicle is an airplane, it would be sufficient to establish—

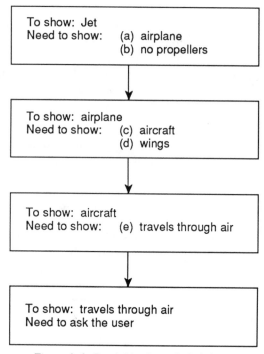

Figure 2.6. Partial backward-chaining.

   c. the vehicle is an aircraft, and
   d. the vehicle has wings.

Rule 1 indicates when a vehicle is an aircraft:

Rule 1
IF the vehicle travels through air THEN the vehicle is an aircraft.

Thus, all that needs to be done to establish that the vehicle is an aircraft is to verify that it travels through air. But notice that the knowledge base contains no rules whose THEN part contains the conclusion "travels through air." At this point, the system prompts us for information by asking, "Does the vehicle travel through air?" Since we are looking at a single-propeller aircraft, we respond, "Yes." The system accepts our answer and uses Rule 1 to conclude that the vehicle is an aircraft. Condition (c) has been established.

   Let us review the process up to this point by examining Figure 2.6.

   Once we respond "Yes" to the question of whether the vehicle travels through air, the inference mechanism deduces condition (c) from Rule 1: The vehicle is an aircraft. It next tries to establish condition (d): The vehicle has wings.

Because no rules in the knowledge base contain the conclusion that the vehicle has wings, the system again asks us for this information. When we respond "Yes," Rule 5 is applied and the system concludes that the vehicle is an airplane. This information is added to the global data base. The system has verified condition (a): The vehicle is an airplane.

Continuing to justify its guess that the vehicle is a jet, the system next attempts to show condition (b): The vehicle has no propellers. As before, the inference mechanism scans the knowledge base trying to find a rule whose THEN part contains its goal, namely, that the vehicle has no propellers. Failing to find such a rule, the system asks us for this information. Since the vehicle in question *does* have a propeller, we supply this information to the system.

Because having no propellers was essential to the system's guess that the vehicle was a jet, the system now acknowledges that its first guess was incorrect and immediately formulates another. This time, it may attempt to prove that the vehicle is an airplane. But the global data base already contains this information. So the system confidently reports back to us: "The vehicle is an airplane." Despite one false start, the system has indeed demonstrated its expertise in the area of vehicle identification.

The session described above is summarized in Figure 2.7.

The diagram in Figure 2.7 is called a *tree* and each of the rectangles in the tree is a *node*. In the inference mechanism described above, the goal appears in the top node: to prove that the vehicle is a jet. All other nodes represent subgoals, facts that need to be established in support of the main goal. In our particular example, because fact (b) could not be established, the goal of proving that the vehicle was a jet could not be realized. But all the information accumulated along the way (the vehicle travels through air, is an aircraft, has wings, has propellers) paid off when the expert system made its second guess.

In summary, the idea behind a *backward-chaining* inference mechanism is to take a guess concerning vehicle identification, and then to try to establish the presence of the conditions necessary to support that guess. This is the type of reasoning that humans generally employ in a diagnostic setting. Once a customer describes her car's problems to the mechanic, he formulates a guess concerning the cause of the problem and tries to verify his guess, perhaps by performing a series of tests. If the test results confirm his diagnosis, the job is finished; otherwise, the mechanic formulates another guess and goes about trying to prove that this second guess is correct. The process continues until the problem is solved. This

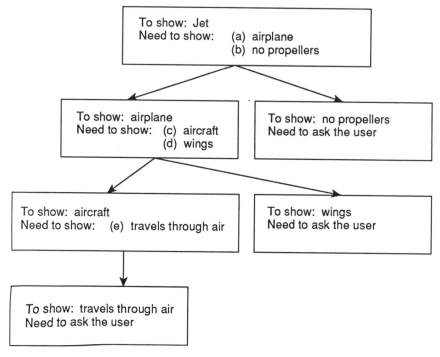

Figure 2.7. Complete backward-chaining.

technique of backward-chaining, starting from the goal and working towards the conditions sufficient to establish that goal, contrasts with the other primary type of inference mechanism, *forward-chaining*.

Forward-Chaining

In *forward-chaining*, the inference mechanism compares the information in the global data base (initially supplied by the user, but expanded by the system's deductions) not with the THEN part of a rule in the knowledge base, but rather with its IF part. Should the comparison reveal a match between information in the global data base and the IF part of a rule, that rule "fires"; that is, the THEN part of that rule is added to the global data base. This process repeats until no matches occur between facts in the global data base and the IF parts of rules in the knowledge base.

To illustrate forward-chaining, we return to the Vehicle Identification System, now assumed to have a forward-chaining inference mechanism, and suppose that we are again looking at a single-propeller airplane and asking the system to identify the vehicle as such.

Initially, the global data base is empty, so the system asks us to supply information to get started. We may be asked, for example, whether the vehicle travels through air, on land, or on water. We, of course, answer "travels through air." The system adds this fact to the global data base and then may ask us to supply information concerning wings, rotors, propellers, etc. Equipped with this data, and noting that "travels through air" matches the IF part of Rule 1, the system fires that rule.

Rule 1:
IF the vehicle travels through air THEN the vehicle is an aircraft.

The fact that the vehicle is an aircraft has been established and added to the global data base. Now Rules 4 and 5 are observed to have "aircraft" in their IF parts.

Rule 4:
IF the vehicle is an aircraft and the vehicle has rotors THEN the vehicle is a helicopter.

Rule 5:
IF the vehicle is an aircraft and the vehicle has wings THEN the vehicle is an airplane.

Because we earlier responded "No" when asked if the vehicle had rotors and "Yes" to the question concerning wings, these responses reside in the global data base and enable the inference mechanism to fire Rule 5. The system records that the vehicle is an airplane.

But "airplane" appears in the IF part of Rule 6. The system will attempt to fire Rule 6 but first needs to check the global data base to determine whether the vehicle has propellers.

Rule 6:
IF the vehicle is an airplane and the vehicle has no propellers THEN the vehicle is a jet.

Since we initially volunteered that it does not, the system realizes that it has exhausted all the applicable rules in the knowledge base and scans the global data base to inform us of its conclusion: "The vehicle is an airplane."

This forward-chaining session can be depicted as in Figure 2.8.

A loan officer studying a mortgage application is likely to exercise a forward-chaining method in reaching his decision. He knows the criteria

Actual Vehicle: Airplane

Question	Response	Global data base
Does the vehicle travel through air, on land, or on water?	Travels through air	Vehicle travels through air.
Does the vehicle have rotors?	No	Vehicle travels through air. Vehicle has no rotors.
Does the vehicle have wings?	Yes	Vehicle travels through air. Vehicle has no rotors. Vehicle has wings.
Does the vehicle have propellers?	Yes	Vehicle travels through air. Vehicle has no rotors. Vehicle has wings. Vehicle has propellers.
		Vehicle travels through air. Vehicle has no rotors. Vehicle has wings. Vehicle has propellers. Vehicle is an aircraft. (Rule 1) Vehicle is an airplane. (Rule 5)

Figure 2.8. Forward-chaining.

that are necessary for a loan approval (for example, a certain minimum income, job stability, etc.), and he compares the applicant's data against these criteria. Suppose, for example, that one of the loaning institution's rules is: "IF the applicant earns less than $15,000 THEN do not approve a loan in excess of $50,000." If an applicant for a $75,000 loan reports an income of $14,400, the IF part of the rule matches this information, resulting in this rule being fired and the loan application denied.

In summary, in *backward-chaining,* a conclusion is guessed and then supported (or not supported) by working *backward* through the rules (from the THEN part to the IF part); a *forward-chaining* inference mechanism first establishes facts and then deduces new facts by working *forward* through the rules (from the IF part to the THEN part).

Which is the better method?

A more appropriate question would be "What conditions favor the selection of one chaining mechanism over the other?" The rule of thumb is this: If the problem to be solved contains only a few possible conclusions but involves a large number of facts to be generated, backward-chaining is more appropriate. Recall that backward-chaining begins by assuming that a certain conclusion is correct and then attempts to justify the conclusion by establishing the pertinent facts. If thousands or even hundreds of possible conclusions exist, this method could lead to a large number of false starts and wasted time. If, on the other hand, only a few possible conclusions exist, chances are that the system would reach the correct one in a short time. Forward-chaining, on the other hand, begins by trying to establish all the necessary facts before a conclusion is established. If the problem under consideration contains a very large number of facts, this technique may consume more time than necessary. So, although our rule of thumb is not absolutely cut-and-dried, it can be stated as follows:

If a problem involves significantly more conclusions than facts, forward-chaining is preferred; if the problem involves significantly more facts than conclusions, backward-chaining is probably more appropriate.

A backward-chaining inference mechanism is sometimes described as "goal-driven": a goal or result contained in the expert system is selected at the start, and the system seeks information to support that goal. A forward-chaining mechanism, in contrast, may be described as "data-driven," because such a system first gathers all the facts that pertain to the problem and then considers the rules in light of this data collection.

As with the case of knowledge representation, the task of selecting an inference mechanism for your purposes is largely related to your choice of software for developing your system. Chapter 4 goes into detail on this subject.

Explaining Conclusions

Virtually all well-written PC-based expert systems in use today include the capability of explaining their conclusions. Recall from Figure 2.8 that, by the time the session ended, the global data base contained this information:

Vehicle travels through air.
Vehicle has no rotors.

Vehicle has wings.
Vehicle has propellers.
Vehicle is an aircraft. (Rule 1)
Vehicle is an airplane. (Rule 5)

By keeping track of this information, an expert system can have the attractive feature of being able to explain or justify its conclusions to the user. After receiving the answer that the vehicle was an airplane, the user might ask the system how it reached its conclusion. The system could then reply:

You said the vehicle travels through air.
If a vehicle travels through air then it is an aircraft.(Rule 1)
You said that the vehicle has no rotors.
You said that the vehicle has wings.
If an aircraft has wings then it is an airplane.(Rule 5)
You said the airplane has propellers.

Other systems might display the pertinent branches of their decision trees in response to a user's request for an explanation. In this way, users need not take on faith the conclusions of an expert system; rather, they can examine the reasoning process performed by a system and then decide whether they are willing to accept its conclusions.

This explanation facility of expert systems is particularly important if the users are skeptical of the advice offered by the system or if the stakes involved in accepting the system's recommendations are particularly high. No conscientious medical doctor, for example, would accept a diagnosis or prescription produced by an expert system if the doctor did not understand and agree with the reasoning the system used to reach its conclusion. By being able to query a system concerning how it reached its conclusions or why it is asking a certain question, the user is likely to have more confidence in the system's advice.

Certainty Factors

Frequently, an expert in a particular field may know that a given set of conditions will cause a certain effect some but not all of the time. The mechanic, for example, may feel that an odorless leak from under the front of an automobile signifies problems with the cooling system nine out of ten times. Failure of the air conditioning system may, in 98 percent of the cases, be attributable to an inadequate amount of freon in the system. Similarly, a good expert system should have some "feel" for how certain its knowledge is. For this reason, the rules in the knowledge base of an expert system frequently contain an indication of their degree of certainty. Sometimes on a scale of 0 to 100, sometimes a scale from 1 to 10, or sometimes from −1 to 1, a number called a certainty factor (CF) may be associated with a rule. For example, on the scale of 0 to 1, the two rules above might appear in the knowledge base as:

IF the leak is from the front of the car and the fluid is odorless THEN check the water pump (CF = 0.9).

IF the air-conditioner is not working THEN check the freon level (CF = 0.98).

In addition to chaining through rules and updating the global data base, another job of the inference mechanism is to keep track of the certainty of the advice that the system is going to ultimately make.

When several rules are used to reach a conclusion (as is most often the case), and when these rules have different certainty factors associated with them, a difficult task is to combine these certainty factors in such a way as to produce a meaningful and significant level of confidence in the system's final conclusion. There is no want of techniques for doing such. The February 1987 issue of *Statistical Science*, a review journal of The Institute of Mathematical Statistics, devotes no fewer than 40 pages to this controversial question. The *Proceedings of the Workshop* on *Uncertainty in Artificial Intelligence* (July 1987) numbered 428 pages! Here are three examples of how this process works in some systems:

EXAMPLE 1

Consider these two rules and their associated certainty factors:

IF it is winter THEN the high temperature on a given day is < 32F (CF = .8).
IF the high temperature on a given day is < 32F THEN it will snow (CF = .3).

In other words, suppose that on a winter day we are 80 percent confident that the temperature will remain below freezing, and we are 30 percent confident that on a day when the temperature remains below freezing, it will snow. A natural question would be: "How confident are we that it will snow on a given day in the winter?"

One approach to this problem is to multiply the certainty factors of the two rules involved. In this example, this would result in the rule:

IF it is a winter day THEN it will snow (CF = .24).

In a general setting, this system for propagation of uncertainty can be summarized by saying:

If one rule is of the form IF A THEN B (CF = x),
and another is of the form IF B THEN C (CF = y),
then these combine to yield a third rule of the form
IF A THEN C (CF = xy).

EXAMPLE 2

Now suppose we have the following two rules and certainty factors:

IF there is more than 8 inches of snow THEN the airport will close (CF = .9).
IF the visibility is < 1 mile THEN the airport will close (CF = .8).

What certainty should be assigned to the airport's closing if there is more than 8 inches of snow and the visibility is < 1 mile? A commonly employed technique is to add the certainty factors of the two rules above and then subtract their product: $.9 + .8 - (.9 \times .8) = .98$. So this technique would produce the rule:

IF there is more than 8 inches of snow AND the visibility is < 1 mile THEN the airport will close (CF = .98).

In general, this uncertainty propagation technique works this way:

If one rule is of the form IF A THEN B (CF = x),
and another is of the form IF C THEN B (CF = y),
then these combine to yield a third rule of the form
IF A AND C THEN B (CF = x + y − xy).

EXAMPLE 3

A third technique combines the certainty factor associated with a rule with the confidence expressed by the user of the system to determine an overall level of confidence.

From experience, the manager of a hotel has observed this rule:

IF a guest is satisfied with the room THEN on his next trip to this city the guest will again patronize this hotel (CF = .75).

Assume now that the manager (the user of the system) estimates with a certainty of .9 that a particular guest was satisfied with the room.

One common means of evaluating the likelihood of this guest's returning to this hotel on his next trip to the city is to multiply the certainty factor associated with the rule (.75) by the confidence identified with the fact (.9). In this example, the result would be:

This guest will return to this hotel on his next trip to the city (CF = .675).

In general: If a rule is of the form IF A THEN B (CF = x), and if the user's confidence in fact A is y, then the confidence in fact B is xy.

Two points should be made here:

First of all, not all expert system builders are comfortable with the three techniques for propagating uncertainty illustrated above. Researchers are still looking for a system for assigning a measure of certainty to the expert system's advice which is at once significant, mathematically sound, and implementable.

Secondly, most software available for developing expert systems on a PC come with a built-in uncertainty propagation algorithm; in general, this is not an issue you have to confront except to understand the significance of the certainty associated with an expert system's final result.

The Interface

The fourth and final major component of an expert system is the interface. Though it is impossible to say that one component of an expert system is more important than another, the interface, being the only component visible to the user, stands apart from the others. The knowledge base, the global data base, and the inference mechanism are all transparent; though the system's builder takes great pains to ensure that these components are correct and efficient, the user takes no direct notice of them. The user interface, in contrast, enables the user to interact with the expert system through a dialogue.

How much software has been written which, in the eyes of its author or developer, is extremely powerful, useful, and elegant, but which is never used by others because it is simply too difficult to deal with? Even the most powerful expert system will go unused if it takes too much effort on the user's part. For this reason, it is obviously important to make the interface as friendly as possible. This implies the need to identify who the user of the system is likely to be. If the users are themselves something of experts (as was the case for many of the earlier expert systems), the interface needn't be as painstakingly friendly as would be required in a system whose users are absolute novices. Whereas an expert might want to skip over the instructions and other background information and get right down to the session, a novice would want to be led more deliberately through the session. This point was not lost on the developers of Dipmeter, an expert system used by geologists. Over 42 percent of the code that makes up this expert system is devoted to the interface!

Designing an appropriate interface to an expert system is an art that requires a great deal of trial and error as well as a willingness to painstakingly clarify for the user what might be completely obvious to the developer of the system. Because of the variety of interfacing techniques available today (natural language, menus, pull-down windows, mice, light pens, graphics, etc.), expert system developers have plenty of options for building friendly interfaces, even at the PC level. The challenge is to tailor the interface to the targeted users.

EXPERT SYSTEM DEVELOPMENT TOOLS

Because of the referential nature of this chapter, you may feel at this point that you know what goes into an expert system, but that you are no closer to being able to build one than you were before reading this book. This section of the chapter should convince you that the process is not really as difficult as it may at first seem.

The critical aspect of writing an expert system is being able to match patterns or strings of words.

When facts in the global data base are compared to either the IF or THEN parts of rules in the knowledge base, a rule gets fired if a match occurs. For example, if the global data base contains the fact "The vehicle travels on water," and if one of the rules in the knowledge base is "If the vehicle travels on water then the vehicle is a boat," it is important for the program to recognize that the fact in the global data base matches the IF part of the rule so that the rule can be fired. Because certain programming languages such as LISP or PROLOG are ideally suited for pattern-matching, these have been the languages traditionally chosen for writing expert systems. But despite claims by many artificial intelligence researchers that these languages are easy to learn and use, LISP and PROLOG still are not widely used by the average PC user. As a simple illustration, consider the problem of adding the values of two variables, X and Y, and storing the answer in the variable Z. In LISP, the statement to accomplish this task is

$$(SETQ\ Z\ (+\ X\ Y)).$$

Although this statement seems entirely natural to one experienced in the use of LISP, it appears complicated to others.

Fortunately, for those who are unfamiliar with LISP or PROLOG and are unwilling or unable to take the time and make the effort to master one of these languages, an alternative exists: "Expert System Development Tools" or "Expert System Shells," which allow the construction of expert systems without requiring knowledge of any traditional, high-level programming language. Although some of these tools may require the developer to learn a few keywords and syntactical conventions, in general the tools are simple to use.

What Is an Expert System Development Tool?

When using a shell, you don't need to think about how you are going to program an inference mechanism, knowledge base, or global data base. You needn't be overly concerned about the questions of knowledge representation, chaining, or propagation of uncertainty. The inference mechanism has already been written, and all that remains for you, the developer, is to customize an interface and to add and structure the knowledge that is specific to your particular domain. Even this turns out to be simple, because the tool leads you through the details of adding knowledge (usually in the form of examples or rules). While these shells have been available for larger systems for years, it has not been until recently that they have been written to work effectively on PCs and that they have been made affordable. As indicated in chapter 1, several PC-based shells can be purchased for between $99 and $500. As an example of how these shells work, we now step through the process of building a knowledge-based system using a generic, PC-based shell.

Using a Development Tool

Let us return to our automotive repair example and, using the mechanic as our expert, develop an expert system that captures his knowledge about cars that will not start. According to the mechanic, the factors he considers when a car won't start include (a) condition of the battery, (b) condition of the fuel filter, (c) whether the gas tank is empty, (d) condition of the cables, (e) the sound that occurs when you try to start the car, and (f)

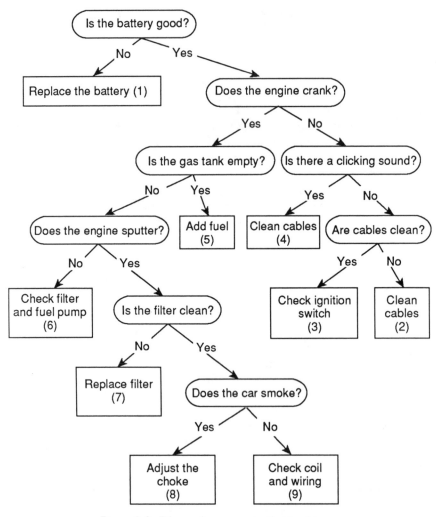

Figure 2.9. Diagnosing a car starting problem.

whether the car emits smoke. The flow chart in Figure 2.9 describes the mechanic's approach to the problem. In this figure, the text contained in the ovals represents a question that the mechanic asks himself; the text in the rectangles is his diagnosis. The rectangles have been labeled 1 through 9 for reference.

Most expert system development tools on the market fall into three general categories:

1. Rule-based tools (those that require you to enter the rules in IF . . . THEN form)

2. Inductive shells (those that allow you to enter a descriptive set of examples from which the tool will construct a decision tree or set of rules)
3. Hybrid tools (those that combine rules and induction and add other unique features to help structure knowledge)

Chapter 4 describes many of the tools currently available and indicates which category each falls into. Let us consider each of these three categories in turn.

Rule-Based Tools

A typical rule-based tool requires you to be able to formulate expertise or knowledge as a collection of IF . . . THEN rules and to associate with each rule a certainty factor, say a number between 0 and 1, which expresses the degree of confidence we have in the rule. For the auto diagnosis problem depicted in Figure 2.9, for example, we could write our first rule:

RULE 1: CF = 1
IF the battery is not good THEN replace the battery.

Setting the certainty factor (CF) to 1 in this case indicates that we are absolutely certain of this rule.

The second rule of this system is a bit more complicated because several conditions must exist before the advice in rectangle (2) is appropriate. Nevertheless, the rule that matches this particular branch of the tree in Figure 2.9 might be written as:

RULE 2: CF = 1
IF the battery is good AND the engine does not crank AND there is no clicking sound AND the cables are not clean THEN clean the cables.

Again, the certainty factor of 1 suggests our confidence concerning this rule.

Similarly, the rule corresponding to the advice in rectangle (3) could be written:

RULE 3: CF = .8
IF the battery is good AND the engine does not crank AND there is no clicking sound AND the cables are clean THEN check the ignition switch.

By setting the certainty factor to .8, we are implying that we are reasonably sure of this particular rule but not absolutely certain that the problem lies in the ignition switch.

RULE 1   CF = 1
IF the battery is not good THEN replace the battery.

RULE 2   CF = 1
IF the battery is good AND the engine does not crank AND there is no clicking sound AND the cables are not clean THEN clean the cables.

RULE 3   CF = .8
IF the battery is good AND the engine does not crank AND there is no clicking sound AND the cables are clean THEN check the ignition switch.

RULE 4   CF = .9
IF the battery is good AND the engine does not crank AND there is a clicking sound THEN clean cables.

RULE 5   CF = 1
IF the battery is good AND the engine cranks AND the gas tank is empty THEN add fuel.

RULE 6   CF = .8
IF the battery is good AND the engine cranks AND the gas tank is not empty AND the engine does not sputter THEN check the filter and fuel pump.

RULE 7   CF = 1
IF the battery is good AND the engine cranks AND the gas tank is not empty AND the engine sputters AND the fuel filter is not clean THEN replace the fuel filter.

RULE 8   CF = .75
IF the battery is good AND the engine cranks AND the gas tank is not empty AND the engine sputters AND the fuel filter is clean AND the car smokes THEN adjust the choke.

RULE 9   CF = .9
IF the battery is good AND the engine cranks AND the gas tank is not empty AND the engine sputters AND the fuel filter is clean AND the car does not smoke THEN check the coil and wiring.

Figure 2.10. The knowledge base for diagnosing car-starting problems.

Each node in the tree in Figure 2.9 corresponds to a rule with one or more conditions listed in the IF part and one conclusion in the THEN part. The complete set of rules for this example appears in Figure 2.10.

Chances are that the mechanic does not have a slip of paper containing these nine rules; they are probably so well-known that he would probably find them strange to look at in the form appearing in Figure 2.10. But this is very likely the structure required by the inference mechanism and, as long as they correspond to the mechanic's strategy for diagnosing starting problems, they embed his knowledge into an expert system.

So the idea behind using shells of this type is to translate the knowledge of an expert into a form that makes sense to the inference mechanism, namely the form of IF . . . THEN rules. This process of interviewing an expert to capture his knowledge into a systemized set of rules is referred to as knowledge engineering or knowledge acquisition and is discussed further in chapter 5.

Inductive Tools

Some expert system development tools provide an alternative to explicitly formulating and entering IF . . . THEN rules into a knowledge base. These shells will generate a decision tree or a set of IF . . . THEN rules for *themselves* after you provide a sufficient number of examples. Tools such as these are called *inductive*.

Induction is particularly useful when the developer is inexperienced in building an expert system or when the knowledge that is being captured resists easy expression as a collection of IF . . . THEN rules. To illustrate tools in this category, we return to our now familiar automotive repair example.

Based on the flow chart in Figure 2.9, the eight specific *questions* that the mechanic considers in diagnosing car-starting problems are:

1. What is the condition of the battery (good or bad)?
2. Does the engine crank (yes or no)?
3. Is there a clicking sound (yes or no)?
4. What is the condition of the cables (clean or dirty)?
5. Is the gas tank empty (yes or no)?
6. Does the car sputter (yes or no)?
7. What is the condition of the fuel filter (clean or dirty)?
8. Does the car emit smoke (yes or no)?

The eight different *diagnoses* the mechanic could make are those listed in the rectangles of Figure 2.9 and repeated below:

1. Replace the battery.
2. Clean the cables.
3. Check the ignition switch.
4. Add fuel.

5. Check the filter and fuel pump.
6. Replace the filter.
7. Check the coil and wiring.
8. Adjust the choke.

In using an expert system development tool that requires examples, the developer lists for each of the diagnoses the answers to whichever of the eight questions above are pertinent. For example, as indicated in Figure 2.9, the diagnosis "adjust the choke" would be made if the questions were answered as follows:

1. What is the condition of the battery?	Good
2. Does the engine crank?	Yes
5. Is the gas tank empty?	No
6. Does the car sputter?	Yes
7. What is the condition of the fuel filter?	Clean
8. Does the car emit smoke?	Yes

Notice that questions 3 and 4 do not pertain to this particular diagnosis. Some shells require you to answer such questions with a special symbol (an asterisk, for example) to indicate that the question is not pertinent. Adopting this convention, a complete example for the "choke adjustment" diagnosis might look like Figure 2.11.

This example, of course, is equivalent to RULE 8 of Figure 2.10:

RULE 8 CF = .75
IF the battery is good AND the engine cranks AND the gas tank is not empty AND the engine sputters AND the fuel filter is clean AND the car smokes THEN adjust the choke.

Whereas the mechanic might find trying to capture his knowledge in the form of a collection of IF . . . THEN rules contrived, supplying the developer with examples may seem a lot more natural. The developer can then leave it to the inductive shell to construct a decision tree or rule set.

A complete set of examples to correspond to Figure 2.9 appears in Figure 2.12. The corresponding decision tree is in Figure 2.13.

Some inductive tools produce *trees* such as the one in Figure 2.13; others produce a list of *rules* from examples (as in Figure 2.10); some shells are capable of inducing both decision trees and rules. What all these inductive shells have in common, however, is the ability to *generalize* from a set of examples the underlying structure of the knowledge that the examples represent.

(1)	What is the condition of the battery?	Good
(2)	Does the engine crank?	Yes
(3)	Is there a clicking sound?	*
(4)	What is the condition of the cables?	*
(5)	Is the gas tank empty?	No
(6)	Does the car sputter?	Yes
(7)	What is the condition of the fuel filter?	Clean
(8)	Does the car emit smoke?	Yes
Diagnosis:		Adjust the choke
Certainty Factor?		.75

Figure 2.11. Example for adjusting the choke.

Perhaps you have noticed the remarkable similarity between the appearance of Figure 2.12 and that of an electronic spreadsheet such as Lotus 1-2-3. Certain example-driven expert system shells take advantage of this similarity by allowing you to enter your examples into spreadsheet form and then "import" them into the shell. This is a great time-saver, especially if you are familiar with spreadsheets and already have extensive data in spreadsheet form. But this feature of importing data from a spreadsheet into an expert system also makes possible using the data in a more knowledgeable, intelligent, and powerful manner. No data collection is very useful unless one can discern its underlying patterns. And this is precisely what happens when a shell converts examples to rules or a decision tree. This aspect of expert systems, referred to as "leveraging" data, is more closely examined in chapters 4 and 5.

Hybrid Tools

Hybrid tools are those expert system development shells that cannot be categorized neatly as either rule-based or inductive systems, yet draw extensively on these techniques. In addition to combining these basic knowledge acquisition and representation approaches, hybrid tools offer more flexible and powerful building environments. Because the methods

	Ex. 1	Ex. 2	Ex. 3	Ex. 4	Ex. 5	Ex. 6	Ex. 7	Ex. 8	Ex. 9
(1) What is the condition of the battery?	Bad	Good	Good	Good	Good	Good	Good	Good	Good
(2) Does the engine crank?	*	No	No	No	Yes	Yes	Yes	Yes	Yes
(3) Is there a clicking sound?	*	No	No	Yes	*	*	*	*	*
(4) What is the condition of the cables?	*	Dirty	Clean	*	*	*	*	*	*
(5) Is the gas tank empty?	*	*	*	*	Yes	No	No	No	No
(6) Does the car sputter?	*	*	*	*	*	No	Yes	Yes	Yes
(7) What is the condition of the fuel filter?	*	*	*	*	*	*	Dirty	Clean	Clean
(8) Does the car emit smoke?	*	*	*	*	*	*	*	Yes	No
(9) Diagnosis:	Replace Battery	Clean Cables	Check Ignition Switch	Clean Cables	Add Fuel	Check Filter and Fuel Pump	Replace Fuel Filter	Adjust Choke	Check Coil and Wiring
Certainty Factor:	1	1	.8	.9	1	.8	1	.75	.9

An * indicates that the question does not apply.

Figure 2.12. Examples for Diagnosing car-starting problems.

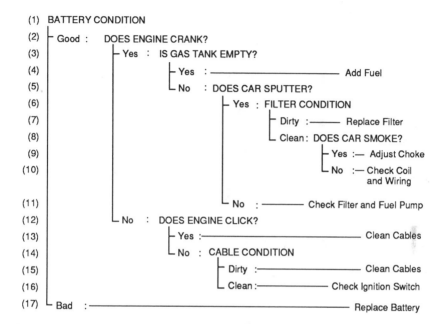

Figure 2.13. Decision tree for diagnosing car-starting problems.

that hybrid tools use to accomplish this flexibility and power vary from vendor to vendor, it becomes difficult to talk about such tools generically.

The hybrid tools we have selected for inclusion in this book, however, do have some common features: they are both touted as end-user (not programmer) oriented tools and are both low in cost. Furthermore, each comes with a separate front-end module that assists the developer in the knowledge acquisition process. Thus, the hybrid tools discussed in this book do not differ as much in kind or type as they do in implementation.

The obvious advantage in selecting a hybrid tool is that greater development flexibility is achieved through combined methods. Most tools in this category offer additional features as well (for example, more versatile system control and output). One should keep in mind, however, that, as a tool becomes more flexible and powerful, it will often become more difficult to use. This usually translates into more keywords to remember and strict adherence to syntactical rules. How difficult are hybrid tools to use? In the case of the tools discussed in this book, the vendors have identified their products as appropriate for the experienced PC user or area expert.

The discussion of hybrids in chapter 4 and the examples in chapter 5 are intended to help the reader better understand the nature and complexity of these tools.

USING THE EXPERT SYSTEM

Aside from the question of customizing a user interface, the system is ready to be used once the knowledge has been entered as examples or rules. Here is a typical exchange between the automotive repair expert system and a user:

User:	Run Repair
Computer:	WELCOME TO THE AUTOMOTIVE REPAIR EXPERT SYSTEM!
	Please respond to the questions which appear on the screen.
	What is the condition of the battery? (Good, Bad)
User:	Good
Computer:	Does the engine crank? (Yes, No)
User:	No
Computer:	Does the engine click? (Yes, No)
User:	No
Computer:	What is the condition of the cables? (Dirty, Clean)
User:	Clean
Computer:	I am 80% certain that the problem is the ignition switch.

Take a moment to compare the above session with Figures 2.12 and 2.13. You will realize that the computer is merely processing its embedded knowledge.

PROS AND CONS OF AN EXPERT SYSTEM SHELL

Before the emergence of expert system shells, the process of building an expert system was a formidable task, as Figure 2.14 illustrates.

Stage 1, establishing the structure of the expert system, was a laborious, skill-intensive process which involved using LISP, PROLOG, or some other high level programming language, designing appropriate data structures for the knowledge base and inference mechanism, devising a method of keeping track of the certainty factors of the rules, and writing procedures to handle the explanation facilities. An arduous task indeed, and one really outside the realm of all but experienced programmers.

Today, an alternative to laboring through Stage 1 is available: Use an expert system shell. When you purchase a shell, you bypass all the work of Stage 1. You essentially buy the architecture of an expert system. With-

STAGE 1: Establish the Structure of the System.

    (a) Learn a high-level programming language.
    (b) Design a knowledge base and an inference mechanism.
    (c) Devise a method of handling uncertainty.
    (d) Implement explanation facilities.

STAGE 2: Capture the knowledge.

    (a) Interview the person whose knowledge you intend
        to duplicate.
    (b) Fill the knowledge base with rules.

STAGE 3: Develop an interface.

Figure 2.14. The stages of building an expert system.

out having to design and program an inference mechanism, knowledge base, or global data base, you can concentrate on the task of supplying the knowledge to the shell (Stage 2) and tailoring an effective interface (Stage 3) using its editing facilities.

Shells represent a considerable savings of both time and effort, and make expert systems technology available even to someone with no programming experience. In many ways, using a shell to build an expert system is analogous to using word processing, spreadsheet, or database software for individualized needs. Few of us would even dream of writing our own word-processing software when so many commercial packages are available. We simply purchase the software that comes closest to our requirements. We can now do the same for building expert systems.

But, just as our word processing package may not do exactly as we wish, whatever expert system development tool we purchase may not either. Some shells may only chain forward; some only backward. Some shells are strictly rule-based when we might prefer an inductive system for a particular application. Some may not allow the design of the interface to be as friendly as we would wish. In other words, it is just as unreasonable to expect one particular shell to serve everyone's needs as it would be to look for one word-processing package that suits everyone. The best we can do is to study the features that particular tools have to offer and to choose the one that comes closest to meeting our requirements and applications. Chapter 4 contains guidelines and examples to assist you in selecting an appropriate expert system shell.

GLOSSARY

Artificial Intelligence. The branch of computer science that investigates machines which exhibit human-like intelligence.

Attribute. See *Factor.*

Backward-chaining. An inferencing strategy in rule-based expert systems that begins with a goal and attempts to establish the conditions sufficient to reach the goal.

Certainty Factor. A measure of the confidence or degree of belief in the information contained in the knowledge base or global data base of an expert system.

Confidence Factor. See *Certainty Factor.*

Consultation. The process of a user interacting with an expert system.

Decision Tree. A structure that pictorially represents definitions of and relationships among various objects in a certain class.

Developer Interface. The component of an expert system shell which is visible to the system developer.

Expert System. A computer program which simulates the performance of a human expert in a specific field or domain.

Expert System Development Tool. See *Shell.*

Factor. A determinant used to discriminate among the possible results offered by an expert system.

Firing. The process of adding information to the global data base as a result of matching the conditions of a pertinent rule in the knowledge base.

Forward-chaining. An inferencing strategy in rule-based expert systems that compares information in the global data base with the IF part of the rules in the knowledge base.

Global Data Base. The component of an expert system that contains the established facts.

Induction. The process of formulating rules starting with a set of examples.

Inference Mechanism. The component of an expert system that compares information supplied by the user to the knowledge contained in the knowledge base and deduces whatever conclusions logically follow.

Interface. See *Developer Interface* and *User Interface.*

Knowledge Base. The component of an expert system that contains the knowledge of the expert which it emulates.

Knowledge Engineering. The process of transferring knowledge from a human to an expert system.

Knowledge Representation. The structure and organization of the knowledge embedded in an expert system.

Leveraging Data. The process of increasing the value of data by discovering its underlying structure and patterns.

LISP. A high level programming language commonly used in the field of Artificial Intelligence.

Parameter. See *Factor.*

Production Rule. See *Rule.*

PROLOG. A high level programming language commonly used in the field of Artificial Intelligence.

Rule. A statement of the form IF . . . THEN or IF . . . THEN . . . ELSE.

Shell. Computer software that facilitates the development of expert systems.

User Interface. The portion of an expert system visible to the end user.

Variable. See *Factor.*

Section 2
Building a PC-Based Expert System

In Section 1, we offered an overview of the nature of expert systems and their applications at the PC level. Specifically, we examined *what* an expert system is and *why* this technology is becoming increasingly prominent in a variety of organizations. Building on this foundation, Section Two details the *who* and *how* of PC-based expert system development. In particular, we outline in this section a four-stage process that captures the essential tasks involved in building an expert system.

Chapter 3, "Problem Identification and Resource Assessment," suggests questions that should be answered before the decision is made to build an expert system, questions that concern the suitability of the proposed problem and whether the developer has the resources to be successful with the project.

Chapter 4, "Tool Selection," offers a methodology for selecting an appropriate shell for a defined expert systems project and then describes six popular PC-based expert system development tools that are representative of the market today.

Chapter 5, "System Prototyping and Building," offers a guide to acquiring knowledge, transferring it into an expert system, and dealing with uncertainty. Also included in this chapter is a discussion of the characteristics of an effective expert system user interface, including explanation of a system's reasoning.

Chapter 6, "Testing, Validation, and Maintenance," concludes the section by defining the concept of system validation and by describing a procedure for system maintenance and updating.

Each of the four chapters in this section contains background material, working examples of tools and/or systems, and a portion of a case study involving Z-EXPERT, which illustrates the steps involved in developing a PC-based system.

3
Problem Identification and Resource Assessment

As with any software development project, maintaining a cautious approach from the outset is highly appropriate. Before beginning an expert systems project, a developer ought to carefully study the problem and appraise the available resources as a precaution against investing time, effort, and money into a venture with little chance of success. The three questions that the developer should ask are these:

1. Is the proposed problem suitable for an expert systems approach?
2. Is the proposed problem worth solving?
3. Are there resources available for solving the problem?

This chapter addresses these three questions.

IDENTIFYING AN APPROPRIATE PROBLEM

Identification of an *appropriate* problem is an extremely important first step in developing an expert system. As indicated in chapter 2, a suitable problem is not one that is *computational* in character, but rather a situation that requires *cognitive* expertise. Expert systems are particularly good at solving problems involving diagnosis, classification, analysis, or teaching skills. Because they are intended to process knowledge, they are often of less value for data processing applications. To get a better sense of the notion of cognitive problems, consider the following examples:

1. *Equipment configuration.* As mentioned in chapter 2, one of the earliest successful expert systems was XCON, whose purpose was to configure Digital Equipment Corporation computer systems. Later in this chapter, you will read about Z-EXPERT, a PC-based expert system that recommends a specific model of a Zenith Data Systems computer based on the user's needs. Configuration of equipment is most often a task handled exclusively by technicians or individuals knowledgeable about the product line and talented in matching products with user requirements. In other words, equipment configuration is a cognitive process and, therefore, an appropriate domain for expert systems technology.

2. *Scheduling.* When scheduling daily activities, a dispatcher takes into account factors such as the number of deliveries to be made, the physical volume of the merchandise to be delivered, the destinations, and the available personnel and equipment, and then combines this information to produce a plan for the day's deliveries. Scheduling is not done by performing a series of mathematical computations, but rather by relying on some general principles and rules of thumb developed through experience. So scheduling is another suitable task for an expert system.

3. *Insurance Underwriting.* An auto insurance company agent writing an automobile policy for an individual might consider, among other factors, the client's age, address, driving record, and year and model of the vehicle to be insured. Using this information, the agent performs a risk assessment and then determines the policy premium. In doing so, the agent consults tables formulated on the basis of the company's past experiences. Not a number-crunching problem, this process can probably be described by the agent and is therefore a suitable candidate for an expert system approach.

4. *Filling Prescriptions.* Certain drugs are known to perniciously interact. When a doctor prescribes medication or when a pharmacist fills a prescription, both must be certain that the drug will not interact adversely with other medication which the patient is taking. Currently, most doctors and pharmacists rely on their training and memory to avoid these potentially dangerous conflicts. This, too, is a cognitive activity and an appropriate problem for an expert system.

Precisely Formulate the Problem

Equal in importance to the selection of a suitable problem for developing an expert system is the ability to *articulate* or define that problem. Too often, an individual or a team embarks on the solution with an incomplete or vague notion of the specific question being addressed. All who are party to the development of an expert system should understand and be able to precisely express the problem.

In building an expert system for weather forecasting, for example, the developer or development team must have a clear understanding and consensus on the factors considered critical in weather prediction as well as the goals of the system. Will the system be used locally or nationally? Will it address the question of wind prediction or be used only as a temperature and precipitation forecaster? If questions like these are not answered early in the planning stage, the development process will be highly disadvantaged because of the vagaries of the concept.

Start Small

One final thought on the process of identifying a suitable problem: Some prominent individuals in the field of expert systems urge developers to tackle huge and extensive problems to make the project worthwhile. In our experience, we have found that addressing relatively easy problems, at least in the early stages of expert system development, is a better strategy from the perspectives both of learning the technology as well as reducing the frustration level.

For example, an expert system to diagnose all varieties of automobile problems would be a rather broad and unmanageable task for the novice developer. A preferable plan would be to build a system which addresses, say, problems relating to the electrical system alone. With the experience of this smaller project, one would have a broader background and might then tackle the cooling system. In this way, a complete automobile diagnostic expert system would evolve in a bottom-up fashion, with less chance of bewilderment. With experience, the developer can work on more involved and complex projects. Our advice, then, is to start small.

Here is an example which illustrates the difference between an appropriate and an inappropriate problem:

EXAMPLE

A small retail computer outlet carries a variety of software as well as several lines of hardware. The manager of the store employs three people: a salesperson, a technician, and a bookkeeper.

Due to increased business, the manager finds that his employees, perfectly competent though they are, are overworked. Morale is falling and, along with it, productivity. Until confident that his business success is not merely fleeting, the manager is reluctant to add people to assist each of his three employees. He has heard about expert systems and how they might help in situations such as his, so the manager decides to investigate this technology. Is he on the right track? Yes and no. Let us consider the nature of the responsibilities of the three employees.

First, the salesperson. Her job involves making potential customers feel at ease, answering their questions concerning the product lines, and gently convincing them to make a purchase. Lately, however, she finds that while she is trying to answer all a customer's questions, other potential customers are losing their patience in waiting to be helped and are leaving the store disgruntled and without having made a purchase. Can an expert system help here? We feel the answer is YES. Not that an expert system can welcome a potential customer with the same warmth and grace as a salesperson, but the system can certainly offer the same advice to the customer as she. This is a cognitive skill. The salesperson listens to the customer explain his system specifications or intended areas of application, asks questions to clarify the customer's requirements and, taking all this information into consideration, deduces a suitable system configuration for this individual. Her job is an analytic one and, as such, lends itself to an expert systems approach. The manager can assist his salesperson by having in place an expert system which mimics her, one that contains all of her knowledge and expertise and leads customers to the same system configuration as she would herself. Such a system would free her to handle the more personal side of her job: setting the customer at ease, adding a component of warmth to the customer-vendor relationship, and, finally, ringing up a sale. While she is attending to these aspects of her job with one customer, another customer may be getting his questions answered by the expert system.

What about the technician? Because of the heavy volume, he occasionally falls so far behind in his repair work that customers become irritated. The manager may know how to replace parts but, because he cannot troubleshoot, he is of little assistance. Diagnosis is the bottleneck within this operation, and diagnosis happens to be one of the strengths of expert systems. If there were such a diagnostic expert system in place, the manager could input the symptoms of a hardware malfunction and receive a recommendation on how to correct the problem.

This brings us to the bookkeeper. Could an expert system be developed that performs cash flow analysis and produces a report? Not really. Tabulating receipts and expenditures is not cognitive in nature; it is computational. She needs a program that will speed up her calculations, not one that captures her knowledge. An expert system will not help here.

The manager should introduce two expert systems into his operation: one to assist in sales (analysis) and one to serve in the shop (diagnosis). Both of these areas are cognitive, the knowledge involved is rather procedural, and the two systems would be relatively easy to develop. Should the manager decide at some point to hire an apprentice technician, the diagnostic system in the shop could also be used to train the assistant (teaching) and eventually increase her expertise. This leads to the next consideration in expert system development: assessing the worthiness of the project.

ASSESSING THE WORTHINESS OF THE PROJECT

The fact that the nature of a particular problem lends itself to an expert systems approach does not, in itself, justify initiating such a project. Some decision, classification, diagnostic, or teaching problems are *so* easily solved that the effort required to build an expert system as a solution would outweigh the benefits. Consider, for example, an expert system that recommends which of two routes should be taken to get to work in the morning. It might be great fun to identify the critical factors that would need to be considered in order to build such a system (day of the week, weather, road conditions, accidents, traffic lights, time of the day, etc.), but the cost/benefit ratio of this system would be much too high. After listening to the radio for a few minutes in the morning, we can usually plan our route mentally and instantaneously, based on experience, without the use of an expert system. Indeed, it would take longer to turn on the computer and interact with a completed expert system than it would to mentally process all known data and accordingly decide on a specific route. So the expert system you build should have at least the potential for a high payoff. While not contradicting the advice offered above ("start small"), we urge you to consider as a project only those problems with solutions worth the effort that building an expert system requires.

Cost/Benefit Ratio

One method of assessing a project's worthiness is the time-honored cost/ benefit analysis. Tally up the expenses involved in developing the expert system and compare them with the money that the system will ultimately save. Two problems immediately surface when you consider this approach: one dealing with cost, and the other, with benefit.

The cost associated with building an expert system is notoriously difficult to estimate. In researching this subject, we came upon many articles which offered conflicting guidelines concerning cost estimates of developing a "small" expert system. One article advised that you should expect to spend between $10,000 and $50,000. Another considered the range to be $25 to $50,000, while a third suggested that the cost should not exceed $100,000.

Equally perplexing were the estimates of the amount of *time* that goes into building a small system. Some authors indicate that you could develop such a system in three months; others suggest allocating up to five years for the project. Clearly, there are too many variables at work here to offer precise estimates. The scope and complexity of the project as well as the experience of the developers are critical factors in the amount of time system development involves. About the only assertion that can authoritatively be made concerning cost is that you will have to consider (a) hardware, (b) software, (c) salaries, and (d) overhead. If you already have a PC, and if you are going to develop the system yourself in your spare time, you have even less expense. Most likely you *will* have to invest in software (probably between $100 and $500), but keep in mind that the software can be used repeatedly, so its cost should be amortized over its lifespan. Our experience is that the development of a PC-based expert system takes months (not years) and costs hundreds (not thousands) of dollars. Figure 3.1 summarizes the cost factors associated with developing an expert system.

On the benefit side, a common predicament is that the value of an expert

Hardware
Software
Salaries
Overhead

Figure 3.1. Sources of expense for expert system development.

system is not always monetary in nature. How do you assess the financial worth of a system that reminds doctors or pharmacists of adverse drug interactions? What value do you put on a system that confirms a medical student's diagnosis of a bacterial infection? While many expert systems do enhance productivity and consequently save a measurable amount of money, often the value of expert systems lies in their ability to reassure, remind, or corroborate. These functions are more difficult to evaluate.

Availability of the Knowledge

A second hallmark of a worthy project is that the knowledge or expertise that it contains is either scarce or not always available. The realization that some of its most respected aircraft designers and tool-design engineers were on the verge of retiring motivated the Boeing Aerospace Company's adoption of expert systems technology. So as not to let the expertise of these long-time employees depart with them, Boeing embarked on a project of capturing their knowledge in a series of expert systems. Using computer assisted design (CAD) workstations, these systems graphically indicated the methods of the senior engineers and proved to be useful in training the next generation of designers and engineers. So successful was this and other projects that Boeing has established its own Artificial Intelligence Center.

Locations of the Knowledge

A third consideration that relates to the worthiness of a project concerns the number of locations where knowledge is simultaneously required or useful. Human experts cannot be present in more than one place at a time, but their knowledge can. Capturing an expert's knowledge in a PC-based expert system can either proliferate an individual's expertise or simply make it more widely available. Consider, for example, APHASIA, a PC-based expert system used to classify aphasia from clinical findings. Developed by neurologist Douglas Katz using an inductive shell, this expert system is now available to all who have access to a PC, from another neurologist sitting in his office in a sophisticated urban hospital, to the general practitioner in the backwoods of some underdeveloped nation, to the medical student preparing for an examination. In response to the questions that the system poses, the user enters the clinical findings and receives in return Dr. Katz's diagnosis.

Some problems are more worthy of an expert systems approach than others. The developer must choose a project that will be worth the effort, at least by some standard. The following example suggests what we consider to be a worthwhile project.

EXAMPLE

The Goucher College Biographical Reference Advisor is a PC-based expert system built by the authors to identify appropriate biographical reference sources. The system works during all the hours the library is open; the two Goucher College reference librarians do not. Using this system, students can take advantage of the reference librarians' expertise even when the librarians are not physically present.

But even when the librarians are present, the Advisor is up and running and accommodates the majority of routine queries which students would otherwise pose to the librarians. This enables the reference librarians to devote time to the more interesting aspects of their jobs and to help students with more difficult problems. Looked at from this perspective, the Goucher College Biographical Reference Advisor increases the productivity of the library staff.

Should there come a time when another position is added to the reference librarian staff, the Advisor stands ready to introduce the new member to the biographical reference collection of the library and to familiarize that person with the operating mode of the current staff.

Teacher, productivity enhancer, knowledge proliferator, the Goucher College Biographical Reference Advisor was clearly a justifiable expert systems project, and its overall cost was less than $500.

ASSESSING THE RESOURCES

Assuming that a problem has been identified whose nature lends itself to an expert systems solution, the next preliminary phase of the expert system building process involves evaluating the personnel, hardware, and time resources available to develop the system.

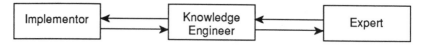

Figure 3.2. The development team.

Personnel

Three distinct tasks are involved in building an expert system and, prior to the introduction of shells, these usually required a team of at least three distinct people: the expert, the knowledge engineer, and the implementor. Figure 3.2 suggests the interaction among these three.

The expert, of course, is the individual or group of individuals possessing the knowledge or expertise that the system is intended to replicate. Experts must not only exist, but should be cooperative, unthreatened by the prospect of having their knowledge captured in a machine, and willing to make the effort to assist in the construction of the system. They need not be computer literate, but they should understand the nature of an expert system and be sympathetic to the goal of developing the system.

The knowledge engineer asks suitable questions of the expert and formulates the expert's knowledge in accordance with the requirements of the software. Ideally, the knowledge engineer knows something about the field of expertise under consideration; but, more importantly, he or she must be familiar with the structure of the knowledge demanded by the expert system development tool. This person must also be capable of transforming the knowledge from the human expert into machine form. (Chapter 5 addresses more concretely the task of knowledge engineering.)

Finally, someone has to actually write the expert system and incorporate into it the knowledge of the expert as provided by the knowledge engineer. The chief characteristic of the implementor, therefore, is familiarity with the development software.

In the not-so-distant past, say ten years ago, expert system development teams of fewer than three people in number (the expert, the knowledge engineer, and the implementor) were unheard of. Today, primarily due to the availability of PC-based expert system development shells, more and more expert systems are being built by individuals. What has changed? Surely the expert remains indispensable. No expert, no expert system. But shells, which have recently become so easy to use, enable experts themselves to act as their own knowledge engineers and implementors. No longer do you need to be a programmer in order to implement an expert system. You simply need to be familiar with a PC and the development software. Although there remain three distinct skills required to build a

PC-based expert system, today's typical development teams range in size from one to about four people.

Hardware

The second resource that needs assessment is hardware. Considerations here include (a) the requirements of the expert system shell, (b) the hardware available for development, and (c) the target hardware (the equipment on which the finished product will run). Expert systems generally require a lot of memory and mass storage to accommodate the knowledge they contain. As a reader of this book, you most likely already have access to a personal computer, so you may not have to invest in additional hardware. You will need to survey the shells which are available for your equipment (see chapter 4 for help with this task).

Earlier in the history of knowledge-based systems, the practice of developing the system on one type of machine with the intention of running it on another was not uncommon. Often, the development environment would include a sophisticated LISP-based workstation or mini-computer, while the delivery or run-time environment might not. This difference accounted for problems of transition or portability between the two environments and complicated the development and deployment cycles. Today, this issue is not as prominent, since several expert system development shells run on even the low line of personal computers and so, in most cases, the development and delivery environments are identical.

Time

Finally, before embarking on an expert systems project, you will need to consider the available time. While one person using a shell can develop a primitive expert system in less than one day, more realistic and sophisticated systems may require a much longer period of time. Exactly how much longer depends on such factors as cooperation of the expert(s), skill of the knowledge engineer, efficiency of the implementor, complexity of the expert system software, and the very scope of the project. Keep in mind that a one-person team will circumvent interpersonal conflicts which may otherwise flare up and delay a successful completion of the project.

Furthermore, rarely is an expert system ever really completed. Usually, the system requires some maintenance in response to discoveries of errors in the knowledge, new knowledge to be added to the system, and the need to improve the user interface. But, putting aisde the issue of maintenance (see chapter 6 for a discussion of this topic), our experience has been that a typical small system can be developed in a matter of a few months.

What is important is commitment. A project that begins without the commitment of time and effort on the part of all involved is a project doomed to time and cost overruns and, quite possibly, failure due to unrealistic expectations.

For an illustration of resource assessment, consider the following example:

EXAMPLE:

When we developed the Goucher College Biographical Reference Advisor, our team consisted of four people: two reference librarians (the experts) and the two authors, who served as both knowledge engineers and implementors.

The librarians were enthusiastic about the project and thought that the work ahead of us would be justified by the amount of time they thought the system would ultimately save them. The vision was that this system would handle the majority of students' routine queries and thus enable the librarians to devote more time to the more interesting and difficult cases students sometimes presented.

While one of us kept busy investigating and becoming more familiar with the shell we elected to use, the other had extensive conversations with the librarians aimed at discovering the factors they considered when recommending reference works to students and the reasoning process they used to reach their conclusions. Once these questions were answered, the project picked up steam and, consequently, at times it took two of us to enter the knowledge at the pace at which the librarians were providing us with information.

The question of which hardware to use was one to which we devoted a great deal of thought and discussion. The two finalists were a Zenith Data Systems desktop computer (IBM compatible) and Digital Equipment Corporation's MicroVAX workstation. Both systems had their advantages and disadvantages. We finally convinced ourselves to work with the desktop system when we considered the possibility of this system's being deployed at colleges other than Goucher. Other academic libraries would be more likely, we thought, to have access to personal computers than to VAX workstations.

The Goucher College Biographical Reference Advisor consumed the part-time efforts of four people over a span of five months before it became sufficiently useful; this was about two months longer than anticipated by the team.

Figure 3.3 lists some questions that you should consider in assessing the proposed problem and resources available for an expert systems project.

On the following pages of this chapter, we introduce a case study that serves to further illustrate the concepts presented in chapter 3. The case study will be continued in chapters 4 through 6.

THE PROBLEM

ASSESSMENT

* Is the problem suitable for an expert systems approach?
* Is the problem worth solving?
    - Will the system result in a savings of time?
    - Will the system improve productivity?
    - Will the system increase profit?
    - Will the system preserve endangered knowledge?
    - Will the system proliferate knowledge?
    - Will the system be used as a training device?
    - Will the system be used in a hostile environment?
* Is the problem manageable?

THE RESOURCES

PERSONNEL

* Does there exist a source of knowledge (an expert)?
* Is there someone who can transfer the knowledge into the system?
* Can someone implement the system?

HARDWARE

* What hardware is or can be made available?
* What are the requirements of the development tool?
* Are the development and the delivery environments compatible?

TIME

* Can all involved commit sufficient time to the project?
* Can someone take responsibility for maintenance of the system?

Figure 3.3. Checklist for problem and resource assessment.

Z-EXPERT CASE STUDY—PART ONE
Problem Identification and Resource Assessment

Zenith Data Systems (ZDS) has grown extensively from its humble beginnings to a company that now grosses over $1 billion annually. The company's success is attributable to a number of factors, including its ability to deliver a quality product, to meet or exceed IBM standards for its line of compatible PCs, and to develop an aggressive marketing strategy targeted at specific clientele. One of ZDS's niche markets is its direct sales program within higher education, where the company has been ranked second to IBM in supplying PC-based products to colleges and universities across the United States.

Such rapid growth, however, did not come without some difficulties. Keeping pace with increasing direct mail orders, providing technical support to a broad clientele, and having enough inventory on hand were among some early problems identified. But perhaps one of the biggest problems from the user/buyer point of view was providing enough pre-sales support so that customers, whether individuals or schools, would purchase the right machines that meet their current needs and offer growth potential.

This general problem was made even more difficult by a number of related circumstances. For one, ZDS, like almost all high-tech companies, simply did not have a large enough sales force to cover the newly-expanded clientele base and had to suffer the unusually high turnover rates associated with sales personnel in the PC industry. Also, by developing a direct sales program in higher education, ZDS had to abandon its dealer/distribution approach to sales support and begin to deal with customers directly, even if that meant a one-to-one relationship. Although Dealers of Record were established for service and warranty work, the sales burden was relegated to either student representatives on college campuses or left to sales literature, complete with mail order forms. An experienced ZDS sales representative could really only afford to get involved with the "big" customers (i.e., the schools themselves), thus lessening the amount of direct interaction with individuals.

A related problem that ZDS discovered early on involved the ZDS products themselves. As a maker of IBM compatibles, ZDS had to produce a diverse set of products that would be both cost- and performance-competitive. This in turn led to a highly stratified product line that would allow the bundling of certain products, yet leave enough overlap among systems for a customer to select a price category without compromising functionality. The result is that ZDS currently offers a large array of preconfigured systems, with the possibility for still other systems to be put together or "configured" by individual sales reps or customers. The result of this strategy is that, in order for the casual or unsophisticated user to buy a ZDS system, a number of significant decisions have to be made before an appropriate system can be either selected or recommended. One can easily imagine the difficulty in such decision-making, especially when the products involve advanced workstations with a variety of memory, graphics, and speed and storage capabilities. In addition, most purchase decisions are influenced by the need to consider the enhancement and upgrading of a computer system over time.

One can also easily see that immediately expanding the sales force across the country would not only have been difficult in terms of recruitment and training, but also costly for the company in both time and money. A better solution was to look to PC technology itself as a way of expanding the sales force. And, in particular, using the help of an expert system, which would later become known within the company as Z-EXPERT.

Appreciating the nature of its pre-sales customer support problem, (that is, clearly understanding the expertise needed and recognizing the limited domain of the problem) ZDS could quickly embrace expert systems technology as an attractive and cost-effective remedy to its current problem. The potential of an expert system solution was brought to Zenith's attention at the June '87 COMDEX show in Atlanta, where Charles Neiman, sales manager for ZDS's southeast region, was able to review an expert system developed at Goucher College in Baltimore, Maryland, for the purpose of assisting in library research. During the demo of this prototype expert system, Neiman and the co-developers of the library system jointly saw the possibility of building a similar system to advise customers on system purchases. In fact, Neiman and others at ZDS were enthusiastic enough about building Z-EXPERT that they established a development contract to build the expert system as quickly as possible.

The following is an account of the first phase of the process of building Z-EXPERT: problem and resource assessment.

Appropriateness of the Problem

Although the overall problem that Z-EXPERT would presumably solve seemed clear to the expert system developers from the start—that is, the lack of an extensive ZDS sales force in the higher education market—a number of aspects to the problem had to be defined. For example, it was not clear at the outset whether Z-EXPERT was to replace a ZDS representative in the field or simply offer some degree of pre-sales support that would later be verified by an experienced salesperson. Also, it was unclear as to whether or not Z-EXPERT would include pricing information, since this factor had been identified early on as important to buyers of ZDS products.

What was finally determined, however, was that the true problem resided in the extensiveness of the ZDS product offerings and, specifically, in the matching of user needs to a particular system configuration. This meant that factors such as the size and capability of a Zenith PC, as well as disk storage and video options, were the most critical in equipment selection. So the problem was expressed as follows:

A breakdown occurs in the buyers' decision-making process because they do not know how to match their needs to the capabilities of currently available ZDS products.

This overall problem was made even more clear by the fact that most users' needs could only be expressed in very general terms (for example, "I want to do word processing or graphics"), while the products themselves were described in specific technical terms (such as, 768K memory and 20 MB Winchester disk). Furthermore, it is usually the salesperson who bridges this gap in matching the customer's needs to the product, so it became clear that Z-EXPERT would be playing, to some degree, the role of knowledgeable ZDS representative in matching the ZDS products to customers' needs.

Having the expert system task well understood, and seeing within the system some reasonable difficulty, the developers began to look at the type of expertise they would be replicating within the system. This task was accomplished through several interviews with ZDS sales representatives, who were asked how they made certain judgments and equipment recommendations concerning a customer's computer needs. From these interviews, several important facts were uncovered.

First, the sales reps generally agreed as to how they came up with system recommendations. Without much variation, they all would begin by inquiring into a user's application needs to get a general sense of how the ZDS system would be used. Then they would probe more deeply to get information that would lead to more precise system sizing and capability information. And finally, they would conclude their inquiry by a question or two regarding future use of the machine and preferences among many systems that might fit customer needs. Then the typical Zenith sales representative would "infer" from what he or she was told a certain category or class of machine. From here, it was a short step to arrive at a precise system configuration for the potential buyer.

The process at work was essentially a matching task, where the expert sales representative could "translate" a generally expressed need (such as, "I do a lot of high level programming") into a central system requirement (such as, "This user needs an advanced machine such as a Zenith Z386"). This means that only cognitive skills were used in this task, drawing on extensive experience in dealing with customers having similar needs. The sales rep's recommendation also reveals the important fact that there would be general agreement on proposed solutions among the experts and that these solutions (i.e., specific system configurations) could be clearly articulated.

Worthiness of the Project

To determine if Z-EXPERT was worth building, both the developers and Zenith staff had to answer a number of tough questions concerning how the expert system would ultimately be used. It was difficult, for example, to assess how much potential business might have been lost because of the lack of a trained sales representative offering pre-sales support. But being able to provide additional sales expertise in machine form was desirable from a management point of view at Zenith, despite not knowing in advance any real payoffs.

Also, there was no effective way to determine if customers were satisfied with their ZDS system in terms of the application for which it was purchased, let alone know how the system allowed them to grow over time. So again, if more pre-sales support were available, even in machine form, the company would not only do better in terms of sales, but customers would more likely be satisfied over time.

Yet, despite this overall vision for the product, would Z-EXPERT be bundled with every demo machine that ZDS sent out? Would potential buyers who had access to a PC be offered the expert system on disk to try out? Or would only dealers and campus representatives be given the package to augment their pre-sales support? One fact was obvious: With ZDS requiring pre-sales expertise in many locations at once, Z-EXPERT should be placed in the hands of as many potential customers as possible, especially in those locations where trained sales representatives were less accessible.

But the potential for a big payoff from Z-EXPERT did not stop here. It became obvious during the initial field-testing of the package that the expert system could also serve as a training device for new ZDS representatives, allowing them to profit from the expertise that was embedded within the system. Also, using expert systems technology for this kind of personnel problem was quite attractive to ZDS from a public relations point of view. And working cooperatively with individuals from the academic community was an added plus in terms of the ZDS corporate image and marketing strategy within higher education.

Still, it should be pointed out that a dollar-and-cents payoff from the current version of Z-EXPERT could not be predetermined until the package had been out in the field for a few years. For example, Digital Equipment Corporation's expert system for product configuration (X-CON) took a number of years to be recognized as a true success. But one needs to keep in mind that X-CON was in many ways a pioneering effort in expert systems technology, and that now the gestation time for an expert system to show a payoff, especially at the PC level, has been greatly reduced.

Resource Assessment

To build Z-EXPERT, the developers had to assess what resources were immediately available and what skills would be required. Since Z-EXPERT was destined not to become an extremely large or overly complex expert system from the very beginning, the developers were able to easily convince both themselves and ZDS officials that they had the necessary expertise to build the system in a reasonably short period of time. Also, technical resources were not a problem, since Z-EXPERT, if it were to be successful, had to run on all ZDS PCs, meaning that the package in its run-time version had to be scaled so that it would run on PCs with the least capability. This meant that the portability of Z-EXPERT from machine to machine would not be a problem and that the package could be widely distributed in all environments.

Desiring portability, however, did not mean that Z-EXPERT should be built on the least capable ZDS machine. In fact, quite the opposite. A higher power, advanced PC was provided by Zenith for the development of the project.

A much more problematic resource for the development of Z-EXPERT was the ability to effectively acquire knowledge from ZDS sales representatives for incorporation into the system. Because Z-EXPERT was being built precisely to augment the available expertise in the field, it would necessarily follow that this same expertise would be in short supply when it was time to build the expert system itself. Fortunately, one of the developers of the project had significant exposure to the ZDS product line and was able, through the help of product information sheets, to use his own understanding of PC users' needs to function as a ZDS representative throughout the initial prototype stages. This initial development strategy proved to be fortunate for both ZDS and the developers, for it demonstrated nicely that developers of PC-based expert systems can be, and often are, area experts as well.

Still, there was a need to represent broader expertise in Z-EXPERT than could be extracted from one individual, especially since this person was not an experienced ZDS sales representative. So, to accomplish this task, the developers released a preliminary copy (prototype) of the expert system so that all ZDS representatives would have something concrete to measure against their own experience. In doing so, the developers were able to attain a better initial "proof of concept" than would have resulted if the representatives had only been queried on the feasibility of such an expert system project. Thus, the project was allowed to evolve through real examples to the point where the developers could mold the software with each successive revision into a product that would eventually yield a complete system that met the customer's needs.

Such a development methodology, sometimes referred to as an "example-based approach," is common in PC-based expert systems building. The commitment to the project has a chance to build as the system develops from past experiences, and the up-front costs are deferred until a working model of the system can be field-tested. Such an approach also reduces the overall risk of the project, since the project can develop at a rate that is consistent with the amount of available resources, personnel or otherwise.

4
Tool Selection

In chapters 1 and 2 we introduced the idea that, from a user's perspective, expert system tools can be classified roughly into three broad categories: direct rule-based, inductive, and hybrid tools. The basis for this classification scheme is how the tools allow the experienced PC user or area expert to acquire and structure knowledge within the expert system building environment. We want to reiterate at this point that each class of tool is suited to a particular kind of problem and differs greatly from the others in the way the developer interacts with it. The basic knowledge representation methods that we focus on in this book are rules and induction; however, these approaches may be combined in hybrid environments along with still other techniques.

We also wish to emphasize that we are primarily focusing on tools that use rule-based and induction techniques because most PC-based expert systems can be built with such tools. But great differences may exist in efficiency within the building process, overall system performance, and ease of use from the end user's perspective. Some tools, for example, offer elaborate methods for dealing with rules once they are known or defined, but offer little in the way of discovering or inducing new rules from past situations or known data. Other tools offer adequate induction methods, but are internally limited in their ability to express knowledge directly in rule form or to deal adequately with situations involving uncertainty.

What is most important, however, is that the expert system developer become knowledgeable enough to recognize which tool is most appropriate to the expert system goal, which fits within existing resources, and which is suited to the background of the developer. In fact, some experienced expert system developers and tool vendors argue justifiably that a developer may have to work doubly hard when a tool is not well suited to the expert system problem, forcing the developer to "get around" the inherent limitations of a tool. This is precisely why we have placed significant emphasis on the applicability of tools in chapter 2 and will again in this chapter discuss tools in light of this important criterion.

We have identified five criteria for tool selection which are important from both the user and developer points of view:

1. Fit of the tool to the problem
2. Effectiveness of the developer interface
3. Effectiveness and friendliness of the user interface

4. Integration capability with existing programs and databases
5. Run-time licensing for delivered systems

Each of the categories is detailed below ·and then used to discuss six representative tools on the market today. We wish to emphasize from the outset that we are not "evaluating" the tools discussed in this chapter. Nor are we endorsing any one particular product. Rather, we have chosen to discuss a select group of tools and related expert systems applications because they help to define the overall market and demonstrate important differences in capability, ease of development, and end-user friendliness of the products that are available. Also, we wanted to take an approach that was as up-to-date as possible and not focus, as many other books have done, on early developments in expert systems technology. For a more complete list of tools currently available that are appropriate for experienced PC users or area experts, see Appendix A.

We also present at the close of this chapter a continuation of our detailed case study involving Z-EXPERT, the Zenith Data Systems expert system introduced in chapter 1 and discussed in its first phase in chapter 3. In this particular segment of the case study, we detail our own experiences in selecting an appropriate expert system development tool.

FIVE CRITERIA IN EXPERT SYSTEM TOOL SELECTION

1. Fit of the Tool to the Problem

The first and unquestionably the most important characteristic of an expert system tool is its overall suitability to the expert system building process. In particular, what must be assessed is how the tool acquires, represents, and structures the knowledge within the system and how it handles uncertainty. For example, most PC-based expert system building tools can express knowledge as a series of IF . . . THEN rules. With other tools, however, it may be difficult or nearly impossible to directly input the knowledge in this form, and so examples might be used to acquire the knowledge. Also, some tools only express rules in a basic IF . . . THEN form, while other packages use a graphic decision tree format to reveal a rule- based structure. In still other cases, knowledge acquisition may not be a problem, but representing the confidence level associated with the rules entered into the system may be a more formidable challenge.

Three distinct categories of tools exist which fit a variety of PC-based expert systems applications, are aimed at experienced PC users and area experts, and are low in cost:

1. Rule-based systems
2. Inductive systems
3. Hybrid systems

Since each of these system categories has already been discussed in detail in chapter 2, we offer at this point only a summary checklist for determining the overall applicability of the tool.

For Rule-Based Tools

1. Is the knowledge to be captured well known, "procedural" in nature, or easily expressed in rules?
2. Can a set of predefined rules in the form IF . . . THEN be directly input into a system and then combined to lead to a GOAL or recommendation?

For Inductive Tools

1. Can a set of examples be established that demonstrates either knowledge or experience at work, or that represents past practices or events?
2. Can the system's factors and their corresponding values be easily identified and put into a tabular or spreadsheet-like form?
3. Is the overall structure or classification of knowledge within the system unknown?

For Combination or Hybrid Tools

1. Does the application call for both rule- and induction-based techniques?
2. Does the application require greater flexibility in knowledge representation or structure than can be achieved through either rule or induction methods alone?
3. Does the problem call for knowledge that is not easily definable or structured?

What the above checklists suggest is a significant difference in tool applicability. When knowledge can be expressed in a direct IF . . . THEN form, then *rule-based systems* that use either an editor or menus for knowledge entry should be used for reasons of efficiency. But when the GOALS and the system factors, variables, or parameters may be known, but not the specific rules or their interaction, then an *inductive tool* might better fit the application. Such inductive tools not only provide a vehicle for knowledge acquisition or representation, but sometimes offer the chance for discovering new factors and visualizing their interaction within the knowledge base. And when a combination of these and other methods and techniques is necessary to acquire or represent knowledge, then a *hybrid* tool might best fit the application area.

2. Effectiveness of the Developer Interface

In order to develop effective PC-based expert systems in an efficient way, a tool's "developer interface" must not only be easy to use, but flexible enough to accommodate the growing sophistication of the developer. With this in mind, we have defined below five subcategories that will aid developers in their evaluation of a particular tool.

Documentation, On-Line Help, Tutorials

An important aspect affecting tool selection is the quality of the overall documentation and training materials provided by the tool vendor. We cannot overemphasize the importance of this factor, since PC-based expert system tools differ greatly in both their approach and execution, and the documentation is often the first place for developers to turn when trying to understand the overall applicability of the tool and the way in which they interact with it.

Typical documentation for expert system shells or tools comes in three basic forms: printed reference materials, on-line help, and tutorials. In some cases, the initial success in using the tool may stem from how well the developer understands how the tool acquires and structures knowledge. Inductive tools, for example, often use a special software program or algorithm to "induce" knowledge, so it may be important in some applications to understand in a general way how this induction process works.

On-line help usually includes a summary of the more critical or important system commands or features and is designed to "jog" the developer's memory concerning matters of syntax or command usage. Reference manuals, on the other hand, provide an in-depth look at all of the system features and usually offer examples that show the tool's features at work. And tutorials give the inexperienced developer an introduction to the capabilities of the tool (usually through a demonstration) and identify the various tasks and skills needed to build a basic system.

Recognizing the importance of tutorials, many tool manufacturers have gone to great lengths to offer the best instructional materials possible. Some vendors devote the first portion of their manuals to a tutorial or instructional guidebook, while others provide an entire separate volume for this purpose. Some vendors have done such a good job at training the expert system builder that the critics have suggested that they release their tutorials as separate products. One vendor, in fact, has done so.

As the developer becomes more experienced with the tool, however, the reference manual will perhaps be the most important resource. So a basic idea to keep in mind when selecting a tool is to consider the quality of the documentation provided. In our review of the tools covered in this book, we found some differences in documentation quality and length, but we are pleased to report that, overall, most of the documentation we encountered was not only authoritative but well written.

Knowledge Entry and Command Functions

Editors   A text editor offers the most basic and direct method for entering knowledge into a system either in the form of IF . . . THEN rules or data to be used as examples. However, many tools use a tailored or "intelligent" editing utility to aid in entering data or rules. For example, the editor may prompt the user for factual information and automatically check for syntactical errors. Some editors have an "integrated" feature that allows the developer to move quickly back and forth between testing and debugging the system and editing the knowledge base once an error or undesirable recommendation has occurred. Most editors will have a command list somewhere on the screen at all times, identifying which keys are tied to specific editing functions. Another common feature is a familiar editor command structure, such as Wordstar, which helps to transfer previously learned skills to the expert system building task.

Menus   Other tools adopt a menu-oriented approach for knowledge or data entry. Most often, such tools are tightly structured and do not allow any other means of data entry or knowledge base manipulation beyond the menu interface. That is, they may not offer both a menu and editor at the same time. But some tools do offer the possibility of circumventing the rigid menu approach by allowing the developer to "import" an ASCII file containing a knowledge base that was created by another system or editor. The positive side of a menu-driven system is that the inexperienced developer is kept on course by tight control and is consistently prompted for important information. The negative side, however, is that if the developer already understands the underlying structure of the knowledge and can express this structure in the form of rules or examples, then it may be more efficient to simply input such information directly through an editor and not be encumbered by a complex set of menus.

Visualization of Knowledge Structure and Tracing

Another important factor affecting the ease of development in using an expert system shell or tool is its ability to visually display the underlying logic of the system or, more basically, the structure of its knowledge. This feature is often critical in developing and debugging an expert system, for it depicts how a particular problem will be solved or how a consultation will be conducted. In fact, according to some tool vendors, this feature alone may be responsible for the success of their products, because as a typical rule-based system becomes more complex, the developer can often "get lost" in the logic and no longer see how the different pieces of knowledge are interconnected by looking at what seems like an endless series of IF . . . THEN statements.

The most popular implementation of this "visualization" feature is a decision tree that reveals how the factors, variables, or attributes are used within a system to get to a particular goal or offer advice (see chapter 2 on decision trees). What is basically displayed is a hierarchical arrangement of key words that represents the interaction of the rules within the system. A decision tree can be read from the bottom up or from the top down to see how the system will work logically. In some shells, a tree may represent the entire knowledge base; in others, it may provide only a "trace" option, where a particular pathway used to get to a goal or result is displayed. This graphical feature is often tied to a tool's ability to explain its reasoning.

Later in this chapter, we reproduce screens for those tools which have some type of capability for visualizing a knowledge base.

Uncertainty-Handling

Basic uncertainty-handling within an expert system is often crucial to reaching a valid conclusion or result, especially if the knowledge used is overly complex or unclear. But we need to distinguish here between true *probability* and *certainty* or *confidence factors* as they are handled by expert system tools or shells. Probability factors are calculated on the basis of complex statistical inferences that show relationships between factors or variables. Confidence or certainty factors, on the other hand, are simply numerical weights that can be attached to certain facts, rules, or user responses to suggest an overall degree of certainty within the system.

Most PC-based expert system tools incorporate only confidence or certainty factors, though the terminology of probability theory may arise in particular tools. In fact, some of the tools we discuss later have extremely elaborate mechanisms for calculating compound uncertainties. Also, confidence factors can be expressed both by the developer and expert when building the system rules and by the user when providing a response during a consultation. Though there is a distinction between *expert confidence* and *user confidence*, the system may internally combine the two types of confidence through certain calculations to reach a GOAL or result with an overall confidence factor.

We must also point out that not all tool manufacturers have incorporated uncertainty handling in their expert system development products. Some argue, in fact, that uncertainty can weaken the entire advice or recommendation process. For example, when one says that he or she is 60 percent sure that someone else will like something 75 percent of the time, it becomes difficult to immediately perceive with precision what is actually being said. So, some developers argue that a better strategy is to be as explicit as possible in representing the knowledge and querying the user, rather than being more general and using uncertainty calculations to account for the lack of confidence that is either expressed by the user or associated with the rule base.

Graphics-Handling and Integration

Graphics handling and integration is also an important component of expert system tools, especially now that graphics in general have become very sophisticated and easily available on the PC. Within expert systems, graphics can be used in a variety of ways:

— To represent the structure of the knowledge within the system
— To trace the logic of a particular consultation
— To provide critical information to users in the form of on-screen windows
— To capture and display visual images necessary to conduct a consultation or illustrate a result

Since each of the graphical capabilities varies from tool to tool, we will not try to discuss common features here but treat each tool's graphics handling capabilities separately. We would only add that our experience has demonstrated that, more than a frill, graphics can perhaps do more than any other feature to increase the user friendliness of a system and offer a delivered system that has a polished, professional look.

One type of graphics implementation that deserves additional attention is *windowing*. Windows can offer a powerful means for visualizing the relationship between units of information within the system, especially when we think of a window on a screen as being a particular subset of the information contained in that screen. At the user level, windows are often critical to the successful use of the system by providing on-line help or other relevant information that relates to either a question or system recommendation. At the developer level, they can provide reference information for system development and performance, or offer an "inside" view of the system's reasoning process.

3. Effectiveness and Friendliness of the User Interface

The success of a PC-based expert system will often lie in the effectiveness and friendliness of the user interface. No matter how good the logic of the system or how complex its knowledge, if the user cannot effectively interact with the software, then the expert system will not achieve its primary goal of replicating human expertise. This is precisely why many tool vendors have made significant investments in trying to come up with system development features that keep the needs of the end user in mind. The result is that we currently have tools that make extensive use of graphics, windows, and natural-language interfaces.

Three criteria can be used to evaluate the effectiveness and friendliness of the user interface: user response format, replay capability, and explanation of reasoning. These are discussed below.

User Response Format

Since most PC-based expert systems use a question/answer format during a consultation, how the end user is prompted and responds will be critical to the system's overall success. Following are the most common kinds of input formats:

— Typed response with ENTER key to accept
— Light bar controlled by cursor keys with ENTER key to accept choice
— Command list on-screen with function keys for input
— Mouse interface for selecting graphical options

Of these user interaction formats, clearly those with the fewest key strokes are the most efficient. Also, the more "visual" the choice, the easier the system will be to use. But this means that all of the possible choices or responses have to be offered to the user at one time, which may limit the overall flexibility of the system.

A better but much harder interface to implement is one that uses natural language (NL) as the primary means of user interaction with the system. A simple version of an NL interface may be a one- or two-word response from the user that is looked up in the system's "dictionary" and then interpreted as a valid response to a given question. But in cases when a sentence or phrase can be entered by the user, the effectiveness of most NL interfaces may break down considerably due to system resources at the PC level. Natural-language interfaces often require extensive CPU power and disk space, so typically at a PC level they will be limited in both their capability and flexibility. Recognizing this fact, tool vendors have tried to incorporate only low level natural-language features, such as more explicit English-like translations of rules, into their products.

Another dimension of user input concerns the ability of the user to indicate the amount of uncertainty tied to a particular response. As indicated earlier, most tools will allow certainty or confidence factors to be associated with rules within the knowledge base, but not all offer the ability for the user to input the degree of certainty associated with a response. Such systems either allow responses that are 100 percent certain or assigned the value "unknown" by entering a "?" as a valid user response. Only some of the tools covered in this book accommodate user uncertainty. In such instances, the user usually has the option of entering a numeric value associated with a response, or of moving a lighted bar along a number line with the cursor keys to suggest relative certainty.

The last and perhaps most critical element of the user interface is the way the system communicates the end user the essential information needed to either understand a question or interpret the recommendation it offers. In other words, the logic and reasoning of the system will be useless if the user cannot make sense of what the system is asking for in its questions or what it is saying in its advice. This is precisely why simply revealing rules that were fired during a consultation or providing a logic trace is of little value to the end user; such information cannot be readily understood. A better method, then, is to try to communicate with users in an intuitive and natural way so that understanding is achieved and the user has as much input and control of the system as possible. Among the more popular methods of accomplishing this kind of communication are the following:

— Simple text on the screen
— Natural-language translations
— Windows for embedded/hidden text or graphics
— Hypertext for nonlinear information retrieval
— Tailored/selected report generation

Since these methods are often tool-specific and are implemented differently by various vendors, it becomes difficult to talk generically about this component of the user interface. In fact, in any given expert system, a combination of these methods and others may be used to ensure that the expert system is communicating effectively with the end user. To give you a better sense of what various communication strategies look like, we describe the communication method within the user interface section for each of the tools covered in this book. Our hope is that, by seeing a variety of communication methods at work, you will be better able to choose one that fits your particular needs.

Replay Capability

A second feature to look for in the user interface is its ability to "replay" or "rerun" a particular consultation without requiring the user to answer again all of the system's questions. Typically, this feature is invoked when users want to rerun a consultation in a "what-if" situation. That is, they may simply want the new RESULT or GOAL that is associated with a change in one or more values of the system's factors, variables, or parameters. Ultimately, what is achieved through a replay feature is better efficiency in either developing or using the system.

Most tools have some sort of replay command. Some tools also offer the opportunity to create "answer files" which can then be used as test cases in replaying a consultation. Often, the test case can take the form of a simple ASCII file that contains the answers to the questions asked during a previous consultation. To have this capability, the tool usually must be able to run in a "batch" mode, or in some other fashion where the input for user responses does not come from the keyboard. The net result of using a test case approach is a much quicker way of rerunning or experimenting with the expert system.

Explanation of Reasoning

Most expert system development tools on the market today have some sort of capability for explaining the reasoning behind a particular consultation. In general, this feature is often tied to the tool's ability to let the user ask two important questions in retracing the system's reasoning: (1) "HOW" a particular RESULT or GOAL was reached, and (2) "WHY" a particular question was asked during a consultation. Not all tools, however, will allow the user to ask both questions; in some, the means for revealing the system's reasoning may not be achieved through HOW and WHY questions at all.

A clear distinction exists between how a developer might use a reasoning-explanation feature to further develop or fine-tune a system, and how the end user might profit from having such system-reasoning information to help understand how a valid RESULT or GOAL was reached. Unfortunately, in most tools the explanation facilities that are available to the developer are the same ones that are employed by the end user, so the developer must make certain that when an explanation of reasoning is being presented to the user, it will be understandable by that person. In some systems, the developer may be able to incorporate either an external program or draw on the system's communication features discussed earlier to design a more tailored explanation facility.

4. Integration Capability with Existing Programs and Databases

Of all the features of expert system tools, the ability to integrate an expert system application with an existing program or database may contribute more than any other factor to the wide-scale development and adoption of expert systems technology at the PC level. The reason for this potential outcome, as indicated in chapter 1, is that often a leveraging effect is realized when expert systems technology can offer gains in productivity as a result of being incorporated with an existing application program or database. For example, an expert system can use the data within an existing database to discover or induce rules or patterns which can then be used to solve new problems. In a different situation, an expert system may function as an "intelligent" front end to a spreadsheet or accounting program to keep data entry personnel from inputing out-of-range data into the system or generating inaccurate reports. (We provide an example of this type of application in chapter 5.)

Method of Integration

Recognizing the potential for this kind of integration, every tool discussed in this book (and almost every tool on the market today) has some sort of feature or utility program that provides integration capability. Generically, this capability is referred to as a "hook" to other programs or databases. Furthermore, this integration function often takes a similar form within most of the tools on the market.

The favored approach seems to be the use of key words within the expert system shell that can either call an applications program directly or read and write data to a specially formatted file. Often these key words are the same as those used in common applications programs in order to make the integration process more familiar to the developer.

Compatibility with Other Programs

Most tools can directly access files in ASCII, Lotus 1-2-3, and dBASE formats. So, when evaluating a tool for compatibility and integration capability, it is best to look for familiar key words and to make sure that their function is what is desired for the application. To offer our readers a better sense of how this important feature is implemented and where it might be applied, we have provided in chapter 5 some examples of this integration process at work.

Portability Issues

One important tool feature that has captured significant interest is the ability to make a developed expert system more portable, that is, easily movable from one system to another. Sometimes this type of feature takes the form of a "code generator" that actually translates a knowledge base into a conventional program like Pascal or C. In other instances, a tool may have the capability of producing a tailored rule-set that can be directly "imported" or used by yet another expert system tool or shell. In fact, since many tool vendors have offered some kind of importing feature, it may be safely said that if any expert system's rules are in some sort of structured IF . . . THEN form with English-like syntax, then with minor modifications they will most likely be portable to other expert system development tools or environments. This is an especially important feature if the developer intends to "move" a PC-based expert system to mainframe or minicomputer environments. As with graphics, we will cover this important feature more in depth as it relates to specific tools on the market.

5. Run-Time Licensing for Delivered Systems

Policy and Cost of Run-Time Versions

Most expert systems offer some type of run-time version of their packages so that a developer can publish and distribute knowledge bases to end users who might not have purchased the development tool. Most vendors offer either a specially discounted run-time version or, better yet, a royalty-free policy regarding distribution of the run-time program. However, it has only been recently that PC-based expert system developers have delivered enough systems to take advantage of this type of licensing. Most of the less expensive tools on the market simply assume that the user is either going to be the developer or that users would buy the entire package.

Delivery and Copyright Issues

Another issue related to licensing is copy protection. Most of the tools available on the market are not copy protected, but strict licensing procedures must be observed. Most often what happens is that, while expert systems technology is being explored in a company, a tool might be purchased for exploratory purposes and then be passed among several individuals to determine if it will meet the needs of various expert system problems. Then, once a particular tool is adopted, several copies may be purchased and an in-house training/support infrastructure will begin to develop around the chosen tool at a modest cost. Demo versions are also available from most tool vendors for the purpose of evaluation.

SUMMARY OF CRITERIA FOR TOOL SELECTION

1. Fit of the tool to the problem

2. Effectiveness of the developer interface
   Documentation, on-line help, tutorials
   Knowledge entry and command functions
   Visualization of knowledge structure and tracing
   Uncertainty-handling
   Graphics-handling and integration

3. Effectiveness and friendliness of the user interface
   User response format
   Replay capability
   Explanation of reasoning

4. Integration capability with existing programs and databases
   Method of integration
   Compatibility with other programs
   Portability issues

5. Run-time licensing for delivered systems
   Policy and cost of run-time systems
   Delivery and copyright issues

TOOLS EXPLORED

In the following section, we provide an overview of expert system tools from six vendors. Of course, this is only a small sampling of the tools available for the PC which are targeted at the experienced PC user or area expert. In fact, over 30 PC-based expert system tools exist on the market today, and more are on the way. So, rather than be comprehensive in our review of tools (a job better left to trade journals, which can be updated regularly), we have provided in this section what we feel is a representative view of the tools available which are accessible to the experienced PC user. In particular, we have focused on rule-based, inductive, and hybrid tools.

Two tools are discussed in each category in order to ensure a better overall understanding of the tool class. The tools profiled in this section are all touted as products that are appropriate for an inexperienced expert system developer and offer unique features that will be attractive to this audience. One additional reason we have selected the tools represented here is their low cost. With the exception of an enhanced version of one product, the highest price tool covered in this section is $500. We believe that this price range goes along with our general philosophy that expert systems projects at the PC level should start out small.

The tool discussion section closely follows the format of the criteria for tool selection established earlier in the chapter. However, since products differ widely, we have tried to be as flexible as possible in our discussions and have therefore avoided checklists and have adopted a prose style for commenting on the features of various tools. Also, we have avoided making comparative judgments about the overall effectiveness of particular tools, which is a task better left to reviewers. It is quite possible that some tool vendors may have recently updated their products significantly. In other cases, because the field of expert systems is rapidly changing, there may exist new methods or approaches that go beyond rule, induction, or hybrid systems and are still appropriate for a nonprogramming-oriented audience. We therefore suggest that you contact the vendors directly before committing yourself to any one product. For this purpose, we provide a list of current PC-based expert system tool vendors and their addresses and telephone numbers in Appendix A.

TOOL DISCUSSION BY CATEGORY

Rule-Based Tools

The two tools that we have selected as representative of the rule-based category (Texas Instruments' EASY and Paperback Software's VP-EX-PERT) have a common feature: They are both primarily *general purpose*, rule-based expert system tools with similar inferencing mechanisms. That is, the knowledge they contain is expressed directly in rules with IF . . . THEN form, and the primary control mechanism for the system's reasoning process is backward-chaining. Both tools, however, have specific, distinct approaches for dealing with knowledge acquisition and improving the development and delivery processes. Our overall intent in presenting these tools is that you understand as thoroughly as possible what rule-based systems are and that you discover how at least two different manufacturers have implemented this concept at the PC level.

PC EASY
Texas Instruments, Inc.

1. Fit of the Tool to the Problem

Texas Instruments' Personal Consultant EASY is a rule-based tool that has many additional features that make it appropriate for the experienced PC user or area expert, and its cost is less than $500. This means that EASY is particularly well suited to applications that use procedural knowledge or to other situations in which knowledge can be directly expressed in the form of IF . . . THEN rules. The primary control mechanism within the inference engine is backward-chaining, indicating that EASY can be used for GOAL-driven applications. EASY uses the term PARAMETER to mean a factor or variable with a rule, while a finished system's results or recommendations are called GOALS.

As mentioned in chapter 1, TI's EASY is actually a smaller subset of a higher power expert system development tool, Personal Consultant Plus (PC Plus), which is more programmer-oriented and therefore not included here. EASY does have, however, complete compatibility with the more sophisticated PC Plus, which a developer may consider later if PC EASY is selected as the initial tool. Texas Instruments has also recently released a new product, Procedure Consultant, which generates decision trees for domain-specific work.

2. Effectiveness of the Developer Interface

Documentation, On-Line Help, Tutorials

EASY's documentation is among the best that can be found in expert system tools currently available. Because TI has been in the expert systems business a long time, the company has learned how to acquaint novices with expert systems techniques and concepts. Given this background and experience, TI actually provides two manuals with its EASY product: a *Getting Started* volume that contains a step-by-step walk-through of the building process, and a very detailed *Reference Guide*. The manuals are professionally done, incorporate extensive graphics, and are organized and indexed effectively. On-line documentation is also available with the system, but is considerably briefer. The *Getting Started* manual is keyed to demo knowledge bases on disk, so it functions like a tutorial, stepping the user through the various building stages.

Knowledge Entry and Command Functions

Instead of using an editor for entering rules, EASY uses a highly structured menu system that prompts the developer for needed information and then stores it in a rule-based form. Even the individual rules themselves must be constructed in menu fashion: The user is first asked for the IF part of the rule, and afterwards the related THEN expression. Spaces must be used between parameters, values, and special symbols, and a parameter in EASY is the same as a factor in other expert system tools. EASY has 65 reserved words and some syntactical constraints within statements or expressions, so building more extensive systems with the tool will require spending some time learning the package and becoming familiar with the reference manual. TI has even defined the language used within EASY as ARL (Abbreviated Rule Language), which, although still a programming "language" to a degree, remains easy enough for the inexperienced expert system developer to use.

An additional feature that makes EASY appropriate for the beginning expert system builder is its integrative use of natural language to express in detailed form the nature of the system's GOALS and parameters. Consequently, each time a new parameter or factor is added to the system, a "translation" prompt appears, asking the developer to express in English what the parameter actually means. According to TI, these translations can be used later to refer to a particular parameter, serve as user prompts in some cases, and, most importantly, be invoked for HOW and WHY consultations during either development or use of the system (see next section on "Effectiveness and Friendliness of the User Interface"). A translation that refers to a parameter might look like the following:

Parameter: PARK
TRANSLATION: the park you should visit

This same translation can then be used later in a consultation to offer advice, as in the following example:

Then it is definite (100%) that the park you should visit is Grand Canyon.
[where Grand Canyon is the value for the parameter "park"]

More will be said later about EASY's translation capability in the next section dealing with the user interface. It should be noted, however, that translations are not required in EASY and they can be added or edited later.

Visualization of Knowledge Structure and Tracing

Though EASY does include a valuable translation feature for rules, the tool does not provide any overall graphical capability for a visualization of knowledge or rule structure, though the program does handle graphics quite well, as will be shown later. TI simply chose not to include a facility for looking at a knowledge base in the form of a decision tree. EASY does, however, provide an excellent vehicle for locating a particular rule, parameter, or fact simply by calling up that system element from one of the various menus.

Also, EASY will reveal the rules used or fired during a particular consultation as a means of tracing the system's logic. The tracing feature, when activated, provides a textual (not graphical) record of the flow of logic and actually works backwards from a recommended GOAL, printing each rule that was used. By examining the values of the parameters associated with fired rules, the developer can identify the reasoning pattern used during a consultation (i.e., how the values of the parameters affected the firing of the rules toward a GOAL). This feature is also used with the HOW and WHY commands to further help reveal the system's reasoning for the end user (covered more fully in chapter 5). Figure 4.1 is an example of a typical rule screen in EASY.

Uncertainty-Handling

EASY handles two different kinds of certainty or confidence:

— Confidence attached to facts or rules
— Confidence attached to a user response

The tool accomplishes this through the use of a "certainty factor range" (CF range), whereby the developer can assign a numeric value (-100 to 100) to both the IF and THEN parts of a rule. Furthermore, the user can indicate the confidence or certainty level of a particular response by moving a bar graphical along an imaginary number line, as shown in Figure 4.2.

The program then calculates the overall confidence involved in the consultation by using each of the confidence factors associated with individual rules and responses. Also, EASY will allow the developer to combine

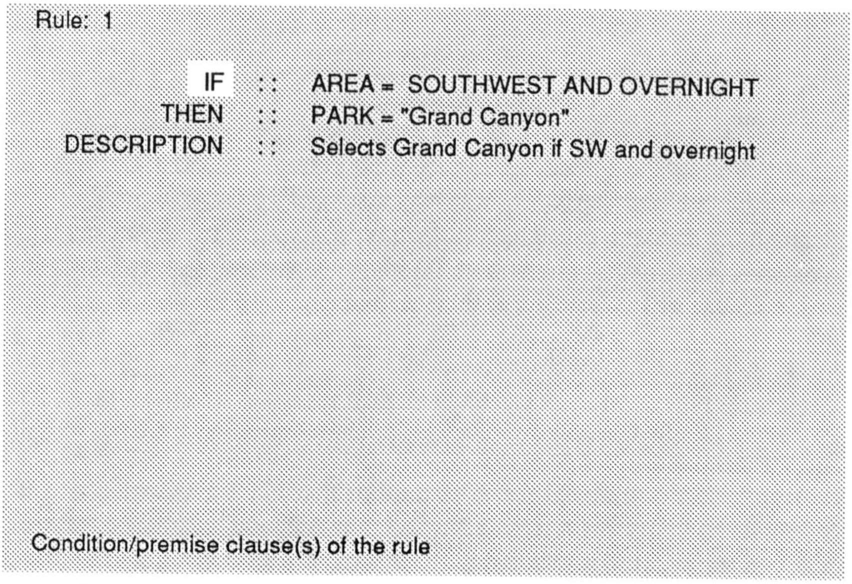

Figure 4.1. Typical rule screen in TI EASY (Courtesy of Texas Instruments, Inc.).

confidence factors from a previous rule or result with those associated with the current parameter or question being asked. Since the formulas used for uncertainty calculation are sophisticated in EASY, the tool offers a great deal of flexibility in dealing with uncertainty overall. Keep in mind, though, that understanding complex calculations which combine a number of confidence factors may require some knowledge of statistics and probability theory.

Graphics Handling and Integration

EASY supports one type of graphics integration through its SNAPSHOT utility. In effect, SNAPSHOT allows the developer to "capture" graphics screens that are created with almost any type of graphics editor, such as Dr. HALO (which TI says it has tested). Since SNAPSHOT is loaded into memory before a picture or graphic is created, the utility allows the developer to "frame" a portion of a screen that will be captured. These graphic images are compressed and stored in a file on disk. Then, when needed, they can be retrieved and displayed in a variety of ways. EASY allows graphics to be associated with knowledge bases or parameter properties, or to be called by the THEN part of a rule through a special graphics command. Below is a rule that will display a picture on the screen.

IF   8BIT-DATA AND PARITY = ODD AND
             BAUD-RATE = 9600

THEN   SWITCH-SETTING = SET257 AND PRINT
             "Set switches 2, 5, and 7." AND
             PICTURE "SWITCH257"

```
                    MONEY MARKET FUNDS ADVISOR
   What is the direction of short-term interest rate movements?


              Yes
       . . . . . . . . . .    UP
       <.>. . . . . . . . .   FLAT
       <.>. . . . . . . . .   DOWN




   1. Use an arrow key to indicate your degree of certainty.
   2. To select only one item, with 100% certainty, press CTRL-right arrow.
   3. After making selections, press RETURN/ENTER to continue.
```

Figure 4.2. Indicating user confidence in TI EASY (Courtesy of Texas Instruments, Inc.).

Notice how the PRINT command will print out text, while the PICTURE command will display switches 2, 5, and 7 from the file "SWITCH257."

Overall, EASY incorporates this one type of graphics capability well, but the package does not allow for creative screen design through windowing techniques. EASY does, however, support a variety of screen attributes through its :ATTR command, and since the program will call external programs, a developer can use other screen control programs for custom displays.

3. Effectiveness and Friendliness of the User Interface

User Response Format

As with the developer interface, EASY's user interface is also menu-oriented, guiding the user through the questions and offering on-line help and explanations along the way. Most responses can be controlled through the cursor keys using a "light bar" for selection. Other commands are handled through special function keys (for example, F1 for help). EASY also allows the user to associate uncertainty with a response. As mentioned earlier, this feature is implemented graphically by allowing the user to indicate relative certainty in a response by using the arrow keys. Figure 4.3 shows a typical user response screen in TI EASY.

Replay Capability

EASY provides two ways to replay a particular consultation without having the user respond again to the system's questions. The REVIEW command provides a summary list of user responses, and when invoked offers the user the option of rerunning the consultation as is, or of altering any of the original answers. REVIEW only works if the knowledge base has not been taken out of memory. If the knowledge base has been removed from memory (such as when the user quits the program or loads a new knowledge base), and if the user still wants to rerun a previous session, the PLAYBACK command must be used, which will write to a "playback file" all of the user's responses for a given consultation session.

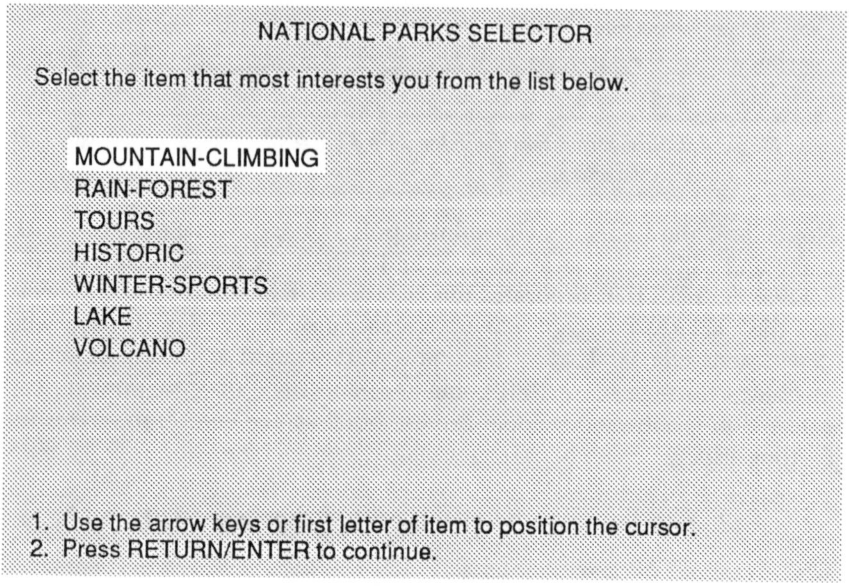

NATIONAL PARKS SELECTOR

Select the item that most interests you from the list below.

MOUNTAIN-CLIMBING
RAIN-FOREST
TOURS
HISTORIC
WINTER-SPORTS
LAKE
VOLCANO

1. Use the arrow keys or first letter of item to position the cursor.
2. Press RETURN/ENTER to continue.

Figure 4.3. Typical EASY user response screen. (Courtesy of Texas Instruments, Inc.).

This way, a user (or developer) can run similar successive cases through the expert system using answer files created with the PLAYBACK command.

Explanation of Reasoning

Because of its English translation capability mentioned earlier, EASY is particularly good at helping the user understand the program's reasoning during a consultation. Primarily, this is achieved through HOW and WHY questions which are invoked by pressing F2 and then selecting from a menu, as shown in Figure 4.4.

When the WHY question is asked by the user, the system offers a developer-initiated statement as to why the question is needed or is being asked, and then the system displays the rule in which the question is used. In contrast, when the HOW question is asked, EASY lists all the parameters used (i.e., those that have values) to reach a valid goal. But these parameter values are not only those entered by the user, but also those contained in the THEN statements of the rules that were fired during a

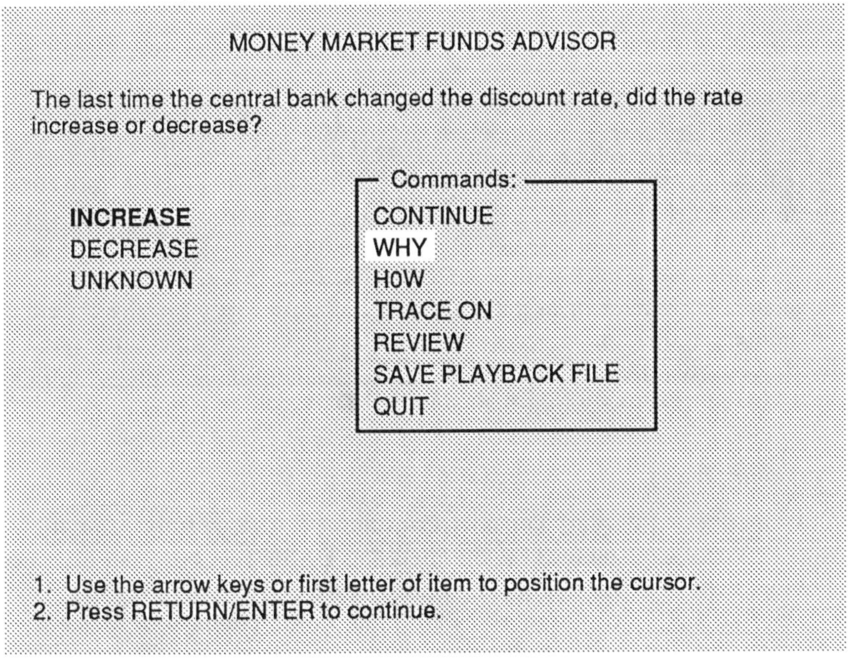

Figure 4.4. EASY "HOW" and "WHY" menu. (Courtesy of Texas Instruments, Inc.).

consultation. This way users can trace how their responses invoked certain rules in order to reach a defined goal.

4. Integration Capability with Existing Programs and Databases

Method of Integration

EASY supports integration with other programs and data through the use of "External Access Functions," which fall into three categories:

— Calls to DOS programs ("DOS-CALL" command)
— Read access of ASCII data from files ("READ-FROM-FILE" command)
— Complete dBASE integration (through 11 dBase commands)

According to the EASY manual, the primary purpose of DOS calls is simply to execute external programs, such as when extensive math calculations or statistical analysis must be performed. The READ-FROM-FILE command is useful when the developer wants to use external data files and read in values to be associated with a defined parameter with a certainty value of 100 percent.

Compatibility with Other Programs

Because EASY can be used with dBASE files, the tool offers the expert system builder the opportunity to create intelligent front ends or back ends to standard dBASE applications. For example, as a front end to dBASE, EASY can help gather, structure, and validate data that will go into a dBASE file. As a back end, EASY can use data in a dBASE format as input to a parameter or as part of the information carried in the system's recommendation. Direct access of Lotus files is not possible with EASY, but once Lotus files are saved in an ASCII format on disk, they can then be accessed or retrieved through standard DOS calls.

Portability Issues

As mentioned earlier, Personal Consultant EASY is fully compatible with Personal Consultant Plus. In effect, an EASY rule base can become a component of a larger, more structured expert system in PC Plus. This means that EASY can be used as an initial development tool that is appropriate for inexperienced builders and still not leave out the possibility for developing highly complex expert system applications later with PC Plus.

5. Run-Time Licensing for Delivered Systems

EASY comes with a run-time diskette, which is needed to perform a consultation without the development tool present. Additional run-time diskettes can be purchased through TI's Data Systems Group, so distributing knowledge bases widely will have an additional cost.

Both the run-time and development diskettes are not copy protected, and they may be reproduced only in accordance with TI's licensing agreement. Also, run-time knowledge bases can be saved in a PROTECTED format, after which they cannot be modified without the development tool.

VP-EXPERT
Paperback Software, Inc.

1. Fit of the Tool to the Problem

Paperback Software's VP-EXPERT is primarily a rule-based expert system building tool, but it offers several additional features and costs less than $100. Its dominant control mechanism is backward-chaining; however, the program can do limited forward-chaining through the use of a special command. VP-EXPERT offers a standard IF . . . THEN rule structure and can handle situations involving uncertainty very effectively.

Moreover, VP-EXPERT also supports a limited induction feature that can generate rules from data. But, unlike true induction tools, even when this feature is used in VP-EXPERT, the end result is that the program still performs its reasoning from a standard IF . . . THEN rule set. According to the manual, VP-EXPERT's induction feature is more of a "translation" or transforming activity, rather than a process that "generalizes" rules from data. That is, once a matrix or table of data is set up (as shown in chapter 2), the program simply goes down line-by-line and generates a corresponding IF . . . THEN rule. At most, the induction feature will eliminate duplicate rules. It does not, therefore, "optimize" the rule set into the most efficient form. Still the feature provides an excellent shortcut in the rule building process. Because VP-EXPERT's induction capability is limited and ultimately IF . . . THEN rules are used in the system's inference mechanism, we have categorized the tool as "rule-based."

With its combined features, VP-EXPERT fits many standard rule-based applications, such as those where procedural knowledge is used, and is also appropriate in instances where data in tabular form will be converted directly into IF . . . THEN rules.

2. Effectiveness of the Developer Interface

Documentation, On-Line Help, Tutorials

VP-EXPERT comes with one manual which serves as introduction, tutorial, and reference guide. It has an effective layout, incorporates plenty of graphics, and is well written overall. Important screens have been captured and put into the manual, and critical information is often boxed in or set off from the rest of the text. VP-EXPERT uses a knowledge base on cheese selection for revealing its primary features and has provided it on disk as well. Other sample knowledge bases are included, and most are referenced in the manual.

Because VP-EXPERT is targeted at an inexperienced audience, the manual justifiably offers a sort of "primer" on key concepts and the expert system building process in Section 1, which is labeled the "Beginner's Guide." Here basic commands, system actions, and other important concepts are covered. VP-EXPERT's inference mechanism or "engine" is also covered in detail in this section, and key terms such as "variable" (VP-EXPERT's word for factor), confidence factor, backward-chaining, and so on are defined here. Section 1 of the manual also shows how the induction feature works and offers a step-by-step overview of how to build a working expert system. Subsequent portions of the manual offer reference materials and include sections on using VP-EXPERT with external spreadsheets or databases files. In all, the manual is comprehensive and quite impressive given the low cost of the tool.

Knowledge Entry and Command Functions

VP-EXPERT takes a straightforward "editor" approach to knowledge entry. That is, rules can be typed in directly, and, even when induction is used, the editor is still the primary means for finishing or refining the expert system. This means that, in many ways, VP-EXPERT will look somewhat like a programming language to many first-time developers, as shown in Figure 4.5.

Also, with 67 key words and some rigid syntactical constraints, some degree of learning must go on before a developer becomes proficient with the tool. This is perhaps why Paperback Software seems to place emphasis on the simple induction method as a way of generating a working knowledge base quickly. In addition, when the induction feature is used, several key words will automatically be placed in the working expert system file.

The editor in VP-EXPERT is also integrated with the run-time environment. This means that when the program encounters an error, the editor will be invoked at the exact spot where the error occurred. Also,

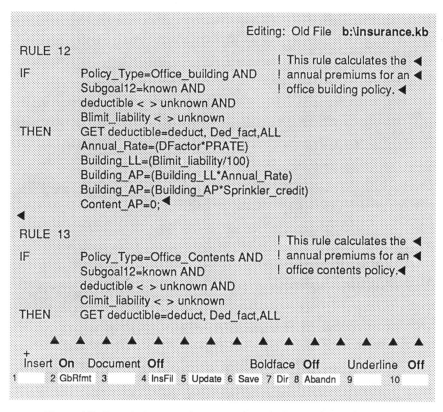

```
                                        Editing: Old File  b:\insurance.kb
RULE 12
                                        ! This rule calculates the  ◄
IF        Policy_Type=Office_building AND   ! annual premiums for an ◄
          Subgoal12=known AND               ! office building policy. ◄
          deductible < > unknown AND
          Blimit_liability < > unknown
THEN      GET deductible=deduct, Ded_fact,ALL
          Annual_Rate=(DFactor*PRATE)
          Building_LL=(Blimit_liability/100)
          Building_AP=(Building_LL*Annual_Rate)
          Building_AP=(Building_AP*Sprinkler_credit)
          Content_AP=0;◄
◄

RULE 13
                                        ! This rule calculates the  ◄
IF        Policy_Type=Office_Contents AND   ! annual premiums for an ◄
          Subgoal12=known AND               ! office contents policy.◄
          deductible < > unknown AND
          Climit_liability < > unknown
THEN      GET deductible=deduct, Ded_fact,ALL

          ▲  ▲  ▲  ▲  ▲  ▲  ▲  ▲  ▲  ▲  ▲  ▲  ▲  ▲
+
Insert On   Document Off                  Boldface Off      Underline Off
1       2 GbRfmt  3       4 InsFil 5 Update 6 Save 7 Dir 8 Abandn 9      10
```

Figure 4.5. Sample knowledge base script in VP-EXPERT (Courtesy of Paperback Software, Inc.).

because VP-EXPERT does take a direct editing approach to entering rules, the developer can, over time, create very sophisticated knowledge bases. In addition to the basic IF . . . THEN structure, the package also offers high- level math, complex confidence calculations, and an ELSE clause for constructing more complex rule structures. These functions, however, are entered in a program-like form, which may initially put off some PC users and area experts who have no programming experience. Still, this kind of advanced capability is welcomed by developers who become more familiar with the tool and start to tax its overall capabilities.

VP-EXPERT uses a three-window screen for development and system-testing with a command line on the last line of the screen, as shown in Figure 4.6.

During a consultation, the two bottom windows are called the "rules" and "results" windows, while the top window is what the user would

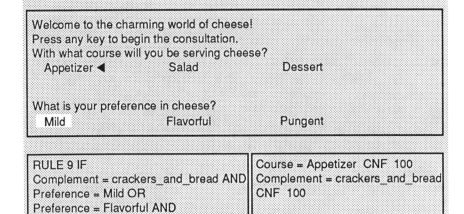

Figure 4.6. Three-window development screen in VP-EXPERT
(Courtesy of Paperback Software, Inc.).

normally see during a consultation. These windows in effect reveal the inner workings of the expert system's reasoning. As each rule is fired, the rule window will scroll through the rule set and the results window will show the values for all variables, including the result variable. Since this visual review process can occur very rapidly during a consultation, there is a software switch to slow down the execution speed in order to actually see how the system is reasoning. The three-window format can be turned off in the delivered system by putting the RUNTIME statement in the first line of the knowledge base.

VP-EXPERT also allows the developer to chain knowledge bases together by using the SAVEFACTS statement, which stores all of the variables and their values that were used during a consultation. Then, when the CHAIN and LOADFACTS statements are incorporated into the expert system, it will read this saved information into a "live" or running consultation. This way, the developer can link together many smaller knowledge bases, which, if combined in one big knowledge base, might exceed memory capability.

Visualization of Knowledge Structure and Tracing

In addition to its three-window feature for viewing the system's logic, VP-EXPERT also supports two other methods for visualization of the reasoning process. A TRACE feature, when invoked, will save the search pattern that led to a particular result during a consultation. This "TRACE" can then be shown as a decision tree, either graphically or in text format. To use the graphics form, the PC used for development must have at least a CGA-compatible graphics card. An entire tree can be viewed, or the developer can "zoom in" on a portion of the captured trace. As an alternative to the graphics display, VP-EXPERT will reveal the system's reasoning in a text mode. These two visualization methods are shown in Figures 4.7 and 4.8, respectively.

Uncertainty-handling

VP-EXPERT handles certainty or "confidence factors" in a variety of ways. First, both rule and response confidence values can be entered into

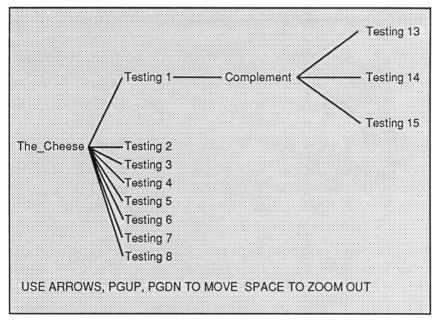

Figure 4.7. Graphics display of system reasoning (Courtesy of Paperback Software, Inc.).

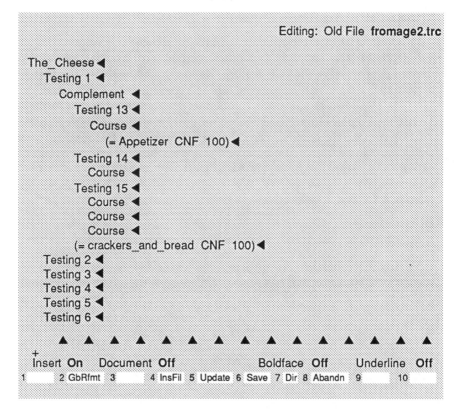

Figure 4.8. Text display of system reasoning (Courtesy of Paperback
Software, Inc.).

the system. That is, a certainty or confidence factor can be attached to the
THEN or ELSE part of a rule, or the user can indicate the level of certainty
associated with a response. The program then calculates the certainty of
a result using predefined formulas. VP-EXPERT establishes its certainty
values by using a "truth threshold," meaning that, on a scale of 0 to 100,
the program assigns the level of truth or falsity to a variable or result,
where any value less than 50 indicates a false condition. Because several
parts of the system can be involved in this type of certainty calculation,
VP-EXPERT can handle complex situations requiring uncertainty.

Graphics-handling and Integration

Though VP-EXPERT offers a high-level graphics feature for tracing
system logic, it does not provide any general capability for graphics in-

tegration beyond some visual icons that are included in a new version of the tool. That is, no utilities for capturing, presenting, compressing, or cropping visual images are provided. However, since VP-EXPERT will conveniently make DOS calls, the developer can use external programs for graphic presentation. We suspect that the reason that no graphics-handling has been added is to keep the price of the product down. Also, Paperback Software sells another product, DRAW IT, for $29.95, which allows the developer to either generate or capture charts, illustrations, or other kinds of graphics and then bring these into a developed expert system through an external DOS call.

3. Effectiveness and Friendliness of the User Interface

User Response Format

In many ways, it is difficult to distinguish the user interface from the developer interface in VP-EXPERT beyond removal of the three-window feature used for development. In this sense, VP-EXPERT is much like Lotus 1-2-3 in that the developer and user see the same menu system and command structure, as shown in Figure 4.9.

This can be both an advantage and disadvantage. On the positive side, the user has the same access to the knowledge base and can therefore modify it accordingly, using many of the tool's advanced features. But in order to do so, the user, as when working with Lotus, must know what the commands mean. So the developer has to ask in advance if this kind of interface is appropriate for the user of the system.

VP-EXPERT offers an effective but somewhat cumbersome way to respond to questions. To enter a response, the user must make a selection by first moving among choices with the cursor keys, then locking the desired choice by pressing the ENTER key, and finally pressing the END key to accept the response. When users wish to assign a certainty value to a response, a different format is used. First the HOME key must be pressed, and then the user must enter a number from 0 to 100, indicating the level of certainty in the response. All of this is to say that VP-EXPERT seems to be designed with more attention to the developer interface than to providing the user with a polished delivery system. This is, however, consistent with Paperback Software's goal of making the VP-EXPERT the best low-cost tool for learning about expert systems technology without compromising on system performance.

VP-EXPERT is also in many ways quite primitive in its communication with the end user in that there are no special features specifically implemented to help retrieve or display textual information to the end user,

Welcome to the charming world of cheese!
Press any key to begin the consultation.
With what course will you be serving cheese?
  Appetizer ◄   Salad   Dessert

What is your preference in cheese?
  Mild ◄   Flavorful   Pungent

What consistency of cheese would you prefer?
  Soft ◄   Firm

The most appropriate cheese for this course is Montrachet served with crackers and bread.

1Help   2 Go   3WhatIf 4Variable 5Rule 6Set   7Edit   8Quit
1Help 2How? 3Why?   4Slow 5Fast 6Quit

Figure 4.9. Typical user response screen in VP-EXPERT (Courtesy of Paperback Software, Inc.).

beyond using the BECAUSE clause to bring textual information associated with rules to the screen. Again, we believe that this is due in part to the fact that VP-EXPERT uses really one interface, which is targeted more at the developer than the user. So, if looked at from the developer point of view, the interface uses windows to effectively display important and relevant information needed for system construction. But once the RUN-TIME statement is added to the top of the knowledge base, all of these developer-oriented features are removed and the user is left with simple text screens and limited windowing capability for HOW and WHY functions. VP-EXPERT does, however, allow for the use of color, blinking, and inverse video by adding special key words to the knowledge base.

Replay Capability

VP-EXPERT supports one method of replaying a consultation for the purpose of changing a particular response. For an immediate replay when only one response is to be changed, the "WHAT-IF" command can be used to ask the user for the variable name to be changed. Then, once a valid variable name is entered, the system will set that variable to the value UNKNOWN and then rerun the knowledge base, asking only that question which has been changed. Only one variable name can be changed with the WHAT-IF feature, as shown in Figure 4.10.

Because WHAT-IF works directly from the variable name, this feature is perhaps most appropriate for the system developer, since the variable names may be meaningless to the end user. The WHAT-IF command is especially useful when we consider that the normal response requires as many as three separate keystrokes.

Explanation of Reasoning

VP-EXPERT offers basic support for explaining system reasoning through standard HOW and WHY questions. To use these questions within a knowledge base, the developer must associate textual information with a particular rule or variable by using the BECAUSE statement. WHY text

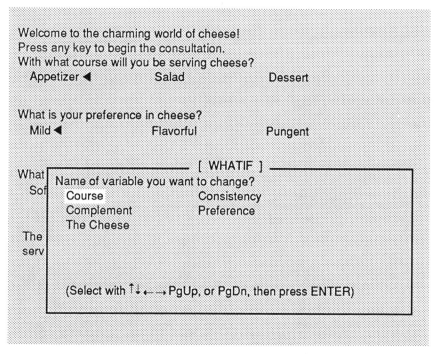

Figure 4.10. VP-EXPERT's "WHAT-IF" feature (Courtesy of Paperback Software, Inc.).

essentially tells the user why a question is being asked, which means it displays the text associated with the BECAUSE clause of the rule that is fired, as shown in Figure 4.11.

The HOW command, in contrast, shows the user how the variable associated with a question gets its value. If the user inputs the value to the variable in the form of a response to a query, then the system simply echoes this action. If the variable got its value from a rule, then that rule is displayed. This means that VP-EXPERT's HOW feature is more useful to the developer than the user because it reveals system rules. This is consistent with the fact that, as indicated earlier, VP-EXPERT really does not distinguish much between the user and developer in terms of its interface.

4. Integration Capability with Existing Programs and Databases

Method of Integration

One of VP-EXPERT's many strong points is its ease of integration with external spreadsheet and database programs. Earlier, we mentioned that the tool can import data directly from Lotus, dBASE, or ASCII files by its induction feature. In this fashion, the data held in spreadsheet or da-

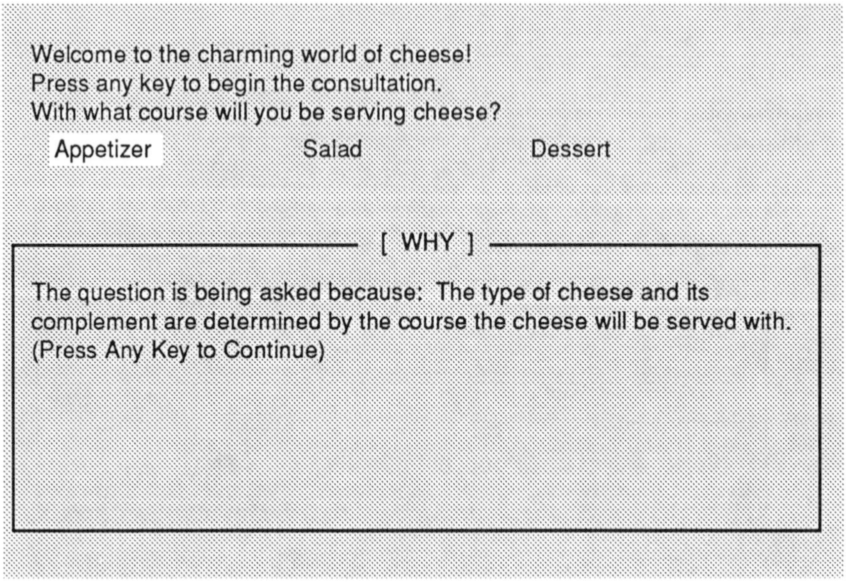

Welcome to the charming world of cheese!
Press any key to begin the consultation.
With what course will you be serving cheese?
  Appetizer   Salad   Dessert

──────────────── [WHY] ────────────────

The question is being asked because: The type of cheese and its complement are determined by the course the cheese will be served with. (Press Any Key to Continue)

Figure 4.11. BECAUSE Text with Rules in VP-EXPERT (Courtesy of Paperback Software, Inc.).

tabase form can become system knowledge as it is expressed in rules. But VP-EXPERT's integration features go well beyond this induction capability.

VP-EXPERT also supports three other kinds of integration:

— DOS execution calls
— Spreadsheet/worksheet access
— Database manipulation

VP-EXPERT allows for three different kinds of DOS calls, which are to be used in conjunction with *.BAT, *.EXE, and *.COM files. The tool is also designed to work with Paperback Software's family of products, such as VP-Planner and VP-Info; this implies that the program is compatible with both Lotus and dBASE products as well. For use with VP-Planner (a Lotus 1-2-3 look-alike), VP-EXPERT even has a WORKON command which invokes the spreadsheet package in real time to perform calculations. Then, when the external program is exited, the program returns the user to the point at which VP-EXPERT branched out. This feature is particularly important if the data in the program is to be used as knowledge later. Thus, when the spreadsheet is called and data changed, this modification can also be reflected in the knowledge as well. This action reflects a fairly sophisticated use of VP-EXPERT and will require the developer to test the expert system thoroughly under conditions in which the data used to create rules can be altered "on the fly."

Compatibility with Other Programs

When used with Lotus or dBASE products, VP-EXPERT allows the developer to both READ and WRITE information to specially formatted files with various commands. The "WKS" and "PWKS" commands read and write data to Lotus data files but do not alter these files in terms of the size of the cells or the type of information they contain (alphabetic or numeric). In the case of dBASE files, the "GET" and "MENU" commands retrieve data, and the "PUT" and "APPEND" commands allow the transfer of new or updated data to the dBASE file. Because of these special commands, VP-EXPERT can become a very powerful tool for building either front ends or back ends for spreadsheet and database programs, as illustrated in EXAMPLE 5 in chapter 5.

Portability issues

VP-EXPERT is portable only in the sense that it uses a common rule-based format to contain and structure its knowledge. This means that once the rules are created or induced in VP-EXPERT, they can, in some cases, with minimal modification be imported into any one of a number of expert system shells or tools on the market.

5. Run-Time Licensing for Delivered Systems

VP-EXPERT offers a run-time version of the program at additional cost for distributing large numbers of knowledge bases most cost-effectively. For example, Paperback Software publishes the "Anthony Dias Blue Wines on DISK" program (which was created with VP-EXPERT) for $39.95. But we suspect that, with a total package price of $99, the company probably does not sell many run-time versions of VP-EXPERT. It is simply easier to ask the user to buy the complete package and thus have the .capability to alter the expert system knowledge base at a later time. VP-EXPERT also comes in a non-copy protected format for an additional $15.

INDUCTION TOOLS

The two tools discussed in this section, SuperExpert and 1st-Class/FUSION, are similar in concept in that both use the same type of induction method and incorporate menu-oriented interfaces. But the respective capabilities and advanced features of the tools vary greatly.

These distinctions can be important when one considers that there is over a $1,000 difference in price between the tools when the advanced version of 1st-Class/FUSION is used in the comparison. Even when SuperExpert is compared to 1st-Class without FUSION, there is still a $300 difference. Understanding these price differences requires a careful look at the tools themselves. We believe that both vendors have picked appropriate pricing strategies for their markets and the respective capabilities of their tools.

SUPEREXPERT
Softsync, Inc.

1. Fit of the Tool to the Problem

SuperExpert by Softsync is exclusively an induction-based expert system development tool, which makes it appropriate for situations in which knowledge can be expressed in a set of examples. SuperExpert is an early version of this type of tool, was developed in England using the FORTH programming language, and does not distinguish between the developer and user interface. Additionally, the concepts behind SuperExpert were actually at one time part of a much larger mainframe-oriented expert system development tool that was scaled down to run on the PC. But, according to Softsync, the company that is now marketing SuperExpert in the United States, many enhancements will be added as the product gains a wider share of the market.

The largest knowledge bases that SuperExpert can handle are those with:

— 31 attributes (factors) per knowledge base
— 8 values per attribute
— 8 results (recommendations)
— 200 examples
— 4 subproblems per knowledge base

Subproblems in SuperExpert are actually links to other knowledge bases in the form of backward- or forward-chaining. This means that, although the size of individual knowledge bases may seem limited, by linking many "problems" or knowledge bases together, the developer can build a large, complex system on a PC. One interesting knowledge base example that SuperExpert provides on disk involves NASA's Space Shuttle, in which an expert system actually helps to make a decision as to whether the orbiter should be automatically or manually landed. This application, which is actually a subset of a much larger expert system developed on a mainframe, demonstrates nicely the overall capabilities of the tool.

2. Effectiveness of the Developer Interface

Documentation, On-line Help, Tutorials

SuperExpert is accompanied by a manual which is written from the perspective of the lay user/developer and covers the basics of the system. Also included is a detailed section describing how the induction process works, which suggests that the tool was written in part to educate developers about this kind of tool. A valuable addition would be a command reference section that describes the key words used in the system.

Knowledge Entry and Command Functions

SuperExpert uses a basic spreadsheet-like interface, whereby users input various kinds of information through successive screens. In all, five screens are used:

— *filer* (for saving and retrieving files)
— *attribute* (for defining attributes or factors)
— *example* (for inputing examples)
— *query* (for running consultations)
— *options* (for changing system options)

The F1 function key invokes the main system menu, and the F2 key offers options for the current screen, as shown in Figures 4.12 and 4.13, respectively. Only one keystroke is required for selections.

With SuperExpert, the developer must tell the system what kind or type of attribute is being defined. Four types of attributes are possible:

— *logical* (for text type attributes)
— *integer* (for integer type attributes)
— *problem* (for linked or chained attributes)
— *class* (for result or recommendation attributes)

```
┌─────────┬──────────────────────────────┬───────────────────────┬──────────────────────┬───────┐
│ Num     │ SuperExpert   F1 for menu    │ bytes used:    12071  │ time:  05:04:58      │ Caps  │
│ Lock    │ FILER                        │ file:  SHUTTLE        │ date:  01-01-80      │ Lock  │
├─────────┴──────────────────────────────┴───────────────────────┴──────────────────────┴───────┤
│                         20 PROBLEM FILES ON DISK IN DRIVE A:                                    │
│   APPENDIX    AVGH                                                                              │
│   BUBBLY      BUY-    ┌─────────────────────────────────────────────────────┐                  │
│   CARPART1    CARP    │ General Menu  :                                      │                  │
│   DIET        DISK    │     A   —   A ttribute screen                        │                  │
│   EXPHOUSE    FAUL    │     E   —   E xample screen                          │                  │
│   FE1         FE2     │     O   —   O ptions screen                          │                  │
│   FE3         KIDN    │     R   —   R ule screen                             │                  │
│   MA1         MA2     │     Q   —   Q uery screen                            │                  │
│   SHUTTLE     SUND    │     X   —   eXit SuperExpert                         │                  │
│   UMBRELLA    USST    │     !   —   Induce a rule                           │                  │
│                       │     ?   —   Display current problem                 │                  │
│                       │     F1  —   General menu                            │                  │
│                       │     F2       CURRENT SCREEN COMMANDS                 │                  │
│                       │     F3  —   Display Statistics                      │                  │
│                       │     F4  —   Edit Problem Description                 │                  │
│                       │     Alt-N —  New problem                            │                  │
│                       │     Alt-S —  Go to Sub-problem                      │                  │
│                       │     Alt-T —  Go to Top level                        │                  │
│                       └─────────────────────────────────────────────────────┘                  │
└────────────────────────────────────────────────────────────────────────────────────────────────┘
```

Figure 4.12. Main system menu in SuperExpert (Courtesy of Softsync, Inc.).

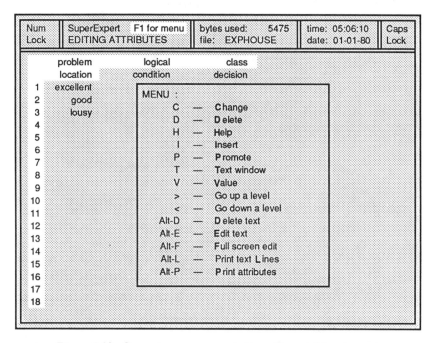

Figure 4.13. Current screen menu in SuperExpert (Courtesy of Softsync, Inc.).

This typing or classifying of attributes means that the developer must know in advance the type of data that the system will be working with, and mismatching of attribute types is not allowed.

The basic development process with SuperExpert has six steps:

1. Open a new file.
2. Assign attributes by type and include potential values.
3. Give the system some examples.
4. Induce a decision tree.
5. Query and test the system (i.e., run a consultation)
6. Decorate the system by adding text to attributes and classes (i.e., factors and results).

The addition of text to attributes and classes is done through a menu-driven text editor that allows the developer to set screen attributes, such as color and blinking. The editor allows the "chain" command to be inserted into the system. A typical text screen that includes a forward chain associated with a class or decision is shown in Figure 4.14.

```
The house you are considering is in

the expensive range.

%chain EXPHOUSE
```

Figure 4.14. Text screen showing chaining in SupertExpert
(Courtesy of Softsync, Inc.).

Note that the "%" sign is used before the key word "chain" and that
the command stands on a line by itself. These are some of the conventions
that must be observed when using command statements in SuperExpert.
To induce a rule in the program, a "!" character can be entered from any
screen.

Visualization of Knowledge Structure and Tracing

SuperExpert allows the developer to visualize a particular knowledge
base by providing a decision tree as shown in Figure 4.15.

This decision tree is made up of "nodes," including "terminal nodes"
or leaves which contain the class or decision of any given branch. Also, a
NULL node can exist when a branch is created for which there exists no
example in the knowledge base, and a CLASH node can result from having
two identical examples with two different classes or decisions. In this case,
the CLASH nodes (and examples) are removed from the knowledge base
and put on a virtual "shelf" so that they can be retrieved later. Longer
decision trees of more than 20 lines should probably be printed out for
reviewing.

SuperExpert does, however, offer a BACKTRACE feature that offers
the user a "roadmap" of the query session, as shown in Figure 4.16.

According to the manual, the BACKTRACE feature is "useful for
testing each branch of the design structure," whereby the developer can
determine if the system is actually doing what it is designed to do.

Uncertainty-Handling

SuperExpert does not provide any defaults for handling uncertainty or
entering confidence factors within a knowledge base. However, the manual

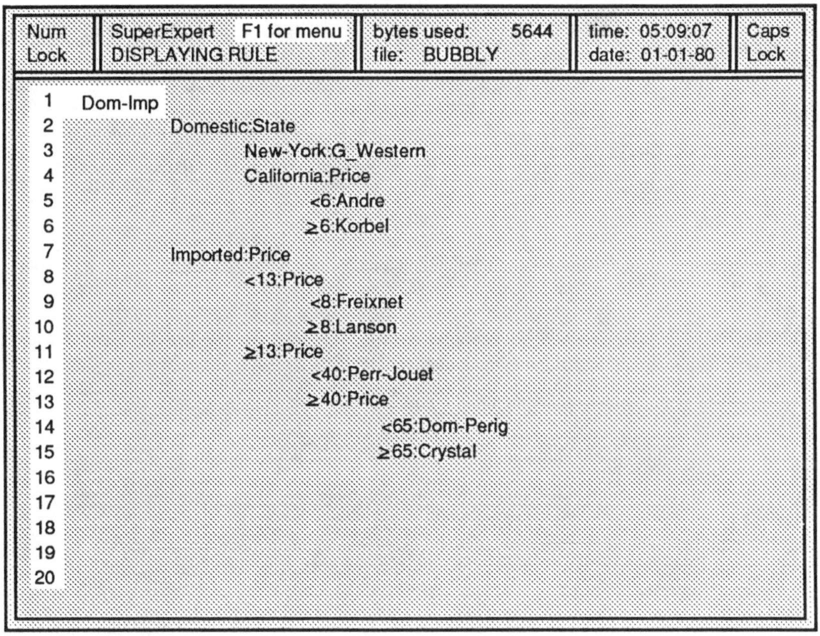

Num Lock	SuperExpert F1 for menu DISPLAYING RULE	bytes used: 5644 file: BUBBLY	time: 05:09:07 date: 01-01-80	Caps Lock

```
 1   Dom-Imp
 2              Domestic:State
 3                     New-York:G_Western
 4                     California:Price
 5                            <6:Andre
 6                            ≥6:Korbel
 7              Imported:Price
 8                     <13:Price
 9                            <8:Freixnet
10                            ≥8:Lanson
11                     ≥13:Price
12                            <40:Perr-Jouet
13                            ≥40:Price
14                                   <65:Dom-Perig
15                                   ≥65:Crystal
16
17
18
19
20
```

Figure 4.15. SuperExpert decision tree (Courtesy of Softsync, Inc.).

does suggest two ways that the developer can introduce uncertainty into a knowledge base—

1. by questions that go beyond a "yes" or "no" type of response to include answers such as "Always, Frequently, Sometimes, Never"
2. by adding an additional attribute and using it exclusively for entering in confidence factors. (The values for these confidence factors would then be added within a defined minimum and maximum range as examples in the global knowledge base and, therefore, would affect the decision process.)

These methods can be valuable when certainty factors will be combined to determine an absolute confidence factor associated with a particular decision or "class."

Graphics-handling and Integration

SuperExpert offers no graphics handling in its current version, and we suspect that the vendor may be waiting for more market acceptance before

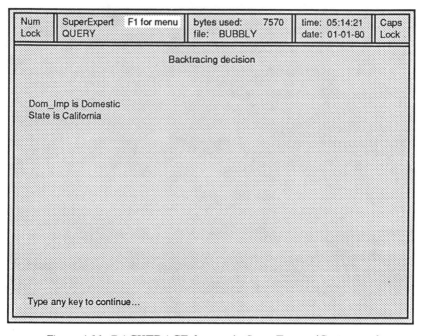

Figure 4.16. BACKTRACE feature in SuperExpert (Courtesy of
Softsync, Inc.).

committing to full-featured graphics support, which would enhance the
product greatly. SuperExpert does, however, offer support for color, reverse video, and other screen attributes.

3. Effectiveness and Friendliness of the User Interface

User Response Format

SuperExpert's user interface is the same as the developer interface; that
is, the developer/user simply presses "Q" twice from the title screen to
run the Query or consultation part of the system, as shown in Figure 4.17.

This suggests that the user and developer are thought to be the same
person, and thus not many run-time enhancements or user-oriented features have been implemented in the package. So responses must be typed
in by the user even if the screen contains effective prompts.

The package does, however, allow the developer to improve the user
interface by setting screen attributes. For example, system attribute names
can be embedded in screen text, and the "CLEARSCREEN" and "CON-
TINUE" commands offer a "paging-like" interface. Color, reverse video,

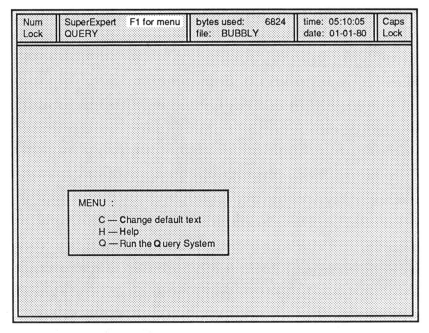

| Num Lock | SuperExpert F1 for menu QUERY | bytes used: 6824 file: BUBBLY | time: 05:10:05 date: 01-01-80 | Caps Lock |

```
MENU :
     C — Change default text
     H — Help
     Q — Run the Query System
```

Figure 4.17. Query screen menu in SuperExpert (Courtesy of Softsync, Inc.).

and blinking are also possible, and TITLE and EXIT screens can be added to the knowledge base as well.

Replay Capability

SuperExpert currently offers no capability for replaying a consultation. The package does, however, allow the user to enter a "?" to repeat a particular question.

Explanation of Reasoning

SuperExpert provides no default way for the user to directly ask HOW a particular decision was reached or WHY a question is being asked. This may be in part due to the perspective from which the tool was developed. Why, for example, offer HOW and WHY questions in a tool that can reveal the decision tree with a single keystroke? This strategy not only presumes a knowledgeable user but also indicates that SuperExpert applications are not intended to be distributed without the development package. In fact, currently no separate run-time version of the tool exists.

4. Integration Capability with Existing Programs and Databases

Method of Integration

SuperExpert supports integration of data in one type of format: ASCII CSV (comma-separated variable), as shown in the sample database line below.

name,address,city,state,zip

That means that if the database or spreadsheet program does not offer this type of data format, then the data will have to be run through an external conversion process (see "Compatibility with other programs" section below).

Once the data has been converted to an ASCII CSV format, the developer must define a set of attributes that match the data exactly. That is, "logical" and "integer" attribute types must match the data elements that are imported from a file. After the proper attributes are defined, the data is then imported into the Examples screen using the "LOAD" command. The developer must keep in mind that only integers which are less than 32,768 can be imported into the example base.

Compatibility with other Programs

To aid in the data conversion process to ASCII CSV format, Softsync offers two packages, PC Converter Plus and Report Plus, which are very low in cost. Either of these conversion programs will offer compatibility not only with Lotus and dBASE but also with over 30 other packages. No predetermined commands for reading or writing data to specially formatted files are provided with SuperExpert.

Portability Issues

Knowledge bases developed with SuperExpert are expected to be run only with the development tool. Therefore, portability is not a SuperExpert feature.

5. Run-Time Licensing for Delivered Systems

SuperExpert is not copy-protected and does not offer a separate run-time version. Though the user is expected to buy the entire development package to run a particular knowledge base, in cases when wide distribution of knowledge bases is expected, Softsync will issue a one-time distribution license for the software for an additional fee.

1st-CLASS/FUSION
1st-Class Expert Systems, Inc.

1. Fit of the Tool to the Problem

The 1st-Class/FUSION product line offered by 1st-Class Expert Systems is induction-based and therefore perfectly suited to situations where knowledge can be expressed in examples or derived from data in a tabular form. This means that both 1st-Class and the more capable FUSION package are alike fundamentally; but significant differences exist in the two products in terms of their overall capabilities, advanced features, and utility programs.

Both 1st-Class and FUSION are general purpose expert system shells with Lotus 1-2-3 look-alike interfaces, and both offer considerable flexibility in designing knowledge bases that use special kinds of forward- and backward-chaining techniques. That is, by using a chaining technique, several knowledge bases can be linked together to create a very large expert system application whose size is limited only by the amount of available disk space. The type of chaining is implemented by marking either factors or results within a knowledge base with a "#" sign. For example, the factor labeled #QUESTION1 would indicate a backward chain and the result named #RECOMMEND1 would result in a forward chain to knowledge bases of the specified name. Thus, 1st-Class and FUSION use the terms forward- and backward-chaining in a unique way that should not be confused with how these terms were defined in chapter 2.

Both 1st-Class and FUSION offer four different methods for creating a decision tree:

1. Simple match method (which matches examples to results one-by-one, as in a database design)
2. Left-to-right method (which asks questions in the order that they were entered into the system)
3. Optimized method (for creating a generalized rule that asks the least number of questions to reach a given result)
4. Customization method (for making tailored decision trees)

Once a decision tree or rule has been induced, the examples used during the induction process can then be deleted to conserve file and memory space and to speed up the program during run-time; this is especially useful when chaining is involved since many knowledge bases might be loaded and unloaded from memory during a single consultation.

Both 1st-Class and FUSION can import data directly from spreadsheets, assign weights to particular examples, and provide statistics about the examples contained in a knowledge base. Each tool comes with a separate development and run-time program.

While 1st-Class is limited to 32 results per knowledge base, FUSION can handle 128 results. Also, FUSION has better mathematical and graphics-handling capabilities and is bundled with several useful utility programs. In fact, FUSION's utility programs are so useful and extensive that they can, for some applications, place FUSION into a higher category of tool than 1st- Class. While some of FUSION's utilities deal with screen functions such as windowing and graphics, the most impressive external programs include automatic code generators, which take the decision trees generated by FUSION's induction system and translate them into IF . . . THEN rules, "C" source code, or Pascal programs. This means that any application developed with FUSION can be ported to a mainframe or minicomputer environment (more on this translation feature later in the section "Portability Issues"). It should be pointed out, however, that only the logic and text portions of the expert system are converted to rule sets or program source listings, and not the screen capabilities or attributes that are designed for the IBM PC environment. These attributes must still be added, along with basic input/output statements, by an experienced programmer.

FUSION is, however, more than double 1st-Class in price, so we have primarily focused in this book on the basic version of the package (which is less than $500), while still covering FUSION's major capabilities or additions. Our intent is not necessarily to try to compare 1st-Class to its "bigger brother," nor to compare either product to other tools. Rather, we hope that through our investigation of the various features and differences of the programs, our readers will not only learn more about the induction tools on the market but will gain a better insight into the features that have been sought after in tools of this kind. As you will read later, 1st-Class was the tool selected for the Zenith Data Systems expert system project that appears in the case materials appended to chapters 3 through 6.

2. Effectiveness of the Developer Interface

Because both 1st-Class and FUSION use Lotus 1-2-3 look-alike developer interfaces the tools are not only familiar to many PC users and area experts, especially in a business setting, but they are among the easiest products to master in a relatively short period of time. In this sense, if you know Lotus, then you will know how to "get around" in 1st-Class/ FUSION. So we offer below less detail on how the interface actually works and focus on the features and capabilities of the tools themselves.

Documentation, On-line Help, Tutorials

The 1st-Class/FUSION documentation is very thorough and profession-ally done. The package also comes with numerous exemplary knowledge bases on disk and includes an extensive tutorial/demo program that is keyed to the manual. Background reading on induction is also included in the manual, as is a glossary of terms and a selected bibliography.

Knowledge Entry and Command Functions

Basically, there are six major screens in 1st-Class/FUSION as defined below:

Files (which shows filenames and allows for disk functions)
Definitions (which allows for factor and result definitions)
Examples (which holds examples in the knowledge base)
Methods (which allows the user to select one of four methods for creating a rule)
Rule (which shows the rule graphically and allows the user to customize it)
Advisor (which allows the developer to execute the run-time version of the program)

In each of these screens, the user is offered a number of options in a Lotus-like menu form, that is, with key words that can be invoked by entering a highlighted letter, as shown in Figure 4.18.

One of the most efficient development features is that once a factor, result, or example value has been entered, it never has to be keyed in again. That is, the program will prompt the developer with menus that contain all of the typed-in information in a highly structured and efficient way. Entire lines in the example table can even be replicated when only minor changes are needed to create an example similar to one already previously entered. Another efficiency feature of 1st-Class/FUSION is the developer's ability to add new factors or results "on the fly" while either putting in examples or customizing a rule. This means that the developer

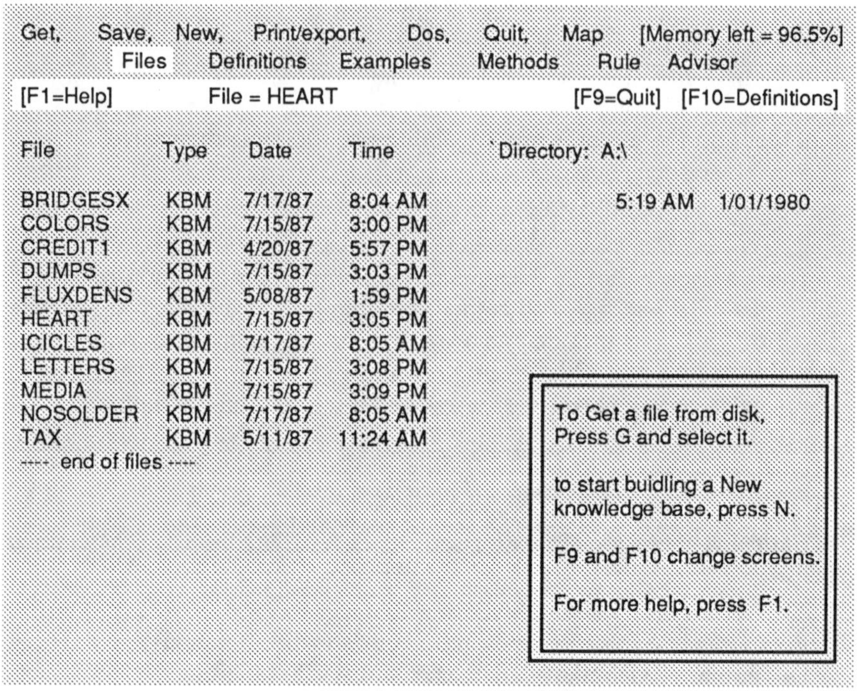

Get,	Save,	New,	Print/export,	Dos,	Quit,	Map	[Memory left = 96.5%]
	Files	Definitions	Examples		Methods	Rule	Advisor
[F1=Help]		File = HEART				[F9=Quit] [F10=Definitions]	

File	Type	Date	Time	Directory: A:\
BRIDGESX	KBM	7/17/87	8:04 AM	5:19 AM 1/01/1980
COLORS	KBM	7/15/87	3:00 PM	
CREDIT1	KBM	4/20/87	5:57 PM	
DUMPS	KBM	7/15/87	3:03 PM	
FLUXDENS	KBM	5/08/87	1:59 PM	
HEART	KBM	7/15/87	3:05 PM	
ICICLES	KBM	7/17/87	8:05 AM	
LETTERS	KBM	7/15/87	3:08 PM	
MEDIA	KBM	7/15/87	3:09 PM	
NOSOLDER	KBM	7/17/87	8:05 AM	
TAX	KBM	5/11/87	11:24 AM	
---- end of files ----				

To Get a file from disk,
Press G and select it.

to start buidling a New
knowledge base, press N.

F9 and F10 change screens.

For more help, press F1.

Figure 4.18. Lotus-like menu in 1st-Class/FUSION (Courtesy of 1st-Class Expert Systems, Inc.).

can sometimes avoid going back and forth between the major program screens to make substantive program changes.

A text editor is included for generating text screens and setting screen attributes. For example, as shown in Figure 4.19, line drawing with IBM graphics characters is possible, as is inverse video, blinking, and color attributes, which must be established with codes embedded in the text part of the program (shown as '12' and '31' in the boxed-in area).

The editor will also import ASCII text files and display text with automatic paging controlled by the PgDn key. The text windows that are created with the editor are a very important feature of 1st-Class/FUSION since they are directly attached to factors and results. That is, the factor or result values can carry with them any type of command, text, or graphic as defined through the editor window. This means that, in one situation, the developer might associate some text with a factor or result (such as the phrasing of a question or the explanation of a result), but, in another case, execute an external program call or DOS command through the text window. However, external program calls, which can be invoked through

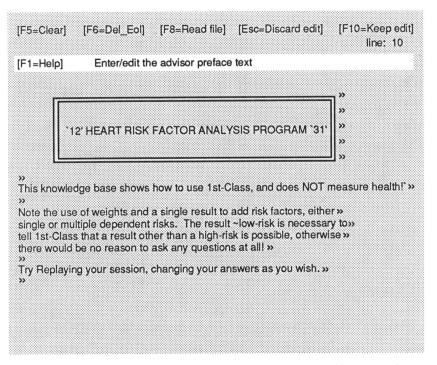

Figure 4.19. Custom screen features in 1st-Class/FUSION (Courtesy of 1st-Class Expert Systems, Inc.).

the function keys, do require the use of key words that must be contained within curly brackets.

Visualization of Knowledge Structure and Tracing

Perhaps 1st-Class/FUSION's greatest strength is its ability to show graphically the structure of the knowledge base. This feature is critical in an induction-based system because the program itself is often determining the actual shape of the decision tree. That is, the developer enters in examples to be used as knowledge and then uses an induction method in 1st-Class/FUSION to generate a rule. Since this rule was not predetermined, the only way to tell if it is useful or valid is to look at it graphically in the form of a decision tree. If the tree looks good, then the system logic should work. One useful feature of the rule screen in 1st-Class/FUSION is that it includes lines for each of the tree or decision branches, which can be printed out on any IBM graphics-compatible printer. Figure 4.20 shows a typical decision tree in 1st-Class or FUSION.

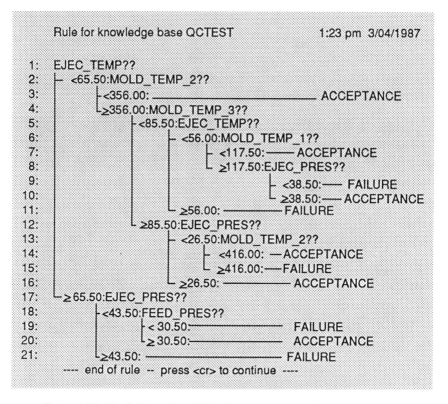

```
Rule for knowledge base QCTEST                    1:23 pm  3/04/1987

 1:  EJEC_TEMP??
 2:  ├─ <65.50:MOLD_TEMP_2??
 3:  │        ├<356.00: _____ ACCEPTANCE
 4:  │        └>356.00:MOLD_TEMP_3??
 5:  │                 ├<85.50:EJEC_TEMP??
 6:  │                 │       ├─ <56.00:MOLD_TEMP_1??
 7:  │                 │       │       ├ <117.50:────ACCEPTANCE
 8:  │                 │       │       └ >117.50:EJEC_PRES??
 9:  │                 │       │                ├ <38.50:──── FAILURE
10:  │                 │       │                └ >38.50:──── ACCEPTANCE
11:  │                 │       └ >56.00: ─────────FAILURE
12:  │                 └ >85.50:EJEC_PRES??
13:  │                         ├ <26.50:MOLD_TEMP_2??
14:  │                         │       ├ <416.00: ─ACCEPTANCE
15:  │                         │       └ >416.00:──FAILURE
16:  │                         └ >26.50: ─────────ACCEPTANCE
17:  └─>65.50:EJEC_PRES??
18:         ├<43.50:FEED_PRES??
19:         │       ├< 30.50:─────────── FAILURE
20:         │       └>30.50:─────────── ACCEPTANCE
21:         └>43.50: ─────────────── FAILURE
 ---- end of rule -- press <cr> to continue ----
```

Figure 4.20. Typical 1st-Class/FUSION decision tree (Courtesy of 1st-Class Expert Systems, Inc.).

Tracing in 1st-Class/FUSION is usually accomplished by simply looking at the rule to see the decision path. If a problem path is noted in the rule, then the developer can MARK the rule in the trouble spot; 1st-Class/FUSION marks the corresponding example in the Examples screen, and the developer can then edit the example base accordingly and generate a new rule which will correct the problem. Another way to correct a problem in a rule is to simply edit it right on the screen using the "CUSTOMIZE" option. When edited this way, however, customized rules may no longer be consistent with the example base since there may be no example that corresponds to the edited change in the rule.

FUSION has, in addition, a "DEBUG" feature, which will write to a file a running trace of a particular consultation that includes the factors that were used to reach a result. Using report generation as a system trace is also possible with 1st-Class/FUSION. Reports can include a detailed summary of a consultation session (questions and responses) or a simple listing of the factors used along with their associated values.

To trace the flow of logic between a collection of knowledge bases, FUSION (but not 1st-Class) offers a special MAP utility which reveals how subcomponents or modules of a system are linked through either forward or backward chains. A sample MAP is shown in Figure 4.21.

The only option that would improve the MAP function would be the ability to show all of the links or chains at one time, with the intent that the developer could see the entire system mapped out at a glance.

Uncertainty-handling

1st-Class/FUSION handles certainty factors by assigning weights to particular examples in the knowledge base. This weighting feature allows the developer to have several identical examples in the knowledge base, each with a different weight. Then, when a rule is induced from this type of knowledge base, the program will automatically rank the results according to the weighting scheme. Weights do not, however, carry over from one

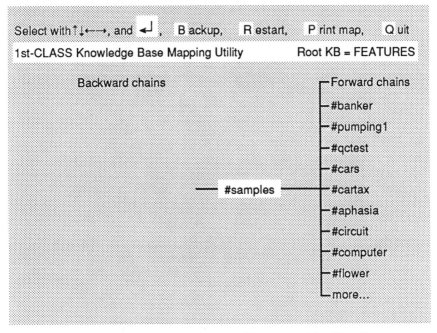

Figure 4.21. MAP utility in FUSION (Courtesy of 1st-Class Expert Systems, Inc.).

knowledge base to another when chaining is involved. Both 1st-Class and FUSION offer basic statistics describing the knowledge base in terms of the number of examples, the frequency of results, the relative result weights across the knowledge base, and so on.

Graphics-handling and Integration

Both 1st-Class and FUSION offer extensive graphics-handling and windowing capabilities, with FUSION offering additional utility programs for capturing and displaying a variety of graphics images. The standard way to implement text windows in 1st-Class/FUSION is to use a function key and place a command line in the text screen associated with either a factor or result. For example, an embedded FUSION command in the text screen that looks as follows

{2:CALL HELPW TEXT 1 1 1 80 10}

would open a help window on screen when the F2 key is depressed. This window would also have the following pre-defined dimensions (Line 1,Column 1) to (Line 10,Column 80), or the top ten lines of a normal screen. The information in this window would come from the file TEXT. An example of a text window that is invoked with the embedded command

{2:CALL HELPW QCTEXT 1 40 6 76 24}

is shown in Figure 4.22.

Omitting the symbol 2: in the command line would automatically execute the "HELPW" command when the factor or result associated with it is used in the program.

If a graphic image is to be retrieved, then the command line in FUSION might look like this

{CALL PIC IMAGE1}

where it is expected that no function key will be used to invoke the graphic image and that the entire screen will be used for display. The "PIC" command works with the "CAPTURE" utility, which can capture screens in IBM CGA, EGA, or MDA formats. A special utility program called "SLIDE1" is used to display graphic images created with Microsoft's PC Paint program, as shown in Figure 4.23.

Overall, then, FUSION offers a wealth of support for displaying full-

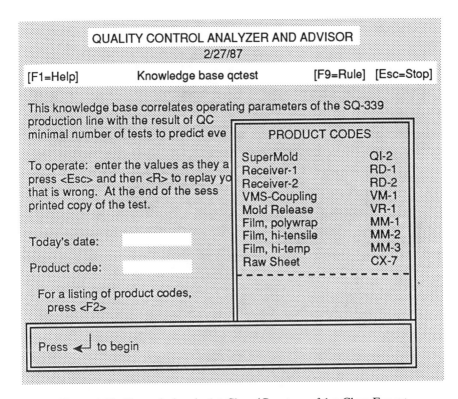

Figure 4.22. Text window in 1st-Class (Courtesy of 1st-Class Expert
Systems, Inc.).

screen graphics on most standard IBM PCs or clones that have a CGA
graphics adapter installed.

3. Effectiveness and Friendliness of the User Interface

User Response Format

The user interface in 1st-Class/FUSION is quite flexible. The standard
input format for users is to use a cursor-controlled light bar to select a
response and then press the RETURN key to accept this choice, as shown
in Figure 4.24.

Another alternative for user input is to invoke a fill-in-the-blank screen
that has been custom-designed by the developer, as demonstrated in Figure
4.25.

1st-Class/FUSION can also accept input either from files or other pro-

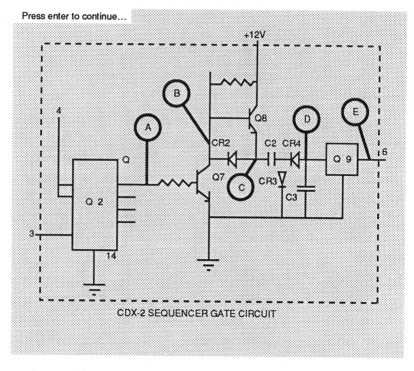

Figure 4.23. PC Paint graphic screen in 1st-Class/FUSION (Courtesy of 1st-Class Expert Systems, Inc.).

grams running under DOS and the user can back up to the last response during a consultation.

As mentioned earlier, 1st-Class/FUSION also offers the opportunity for the user to receive additional information through windowing and graphical techniques, which can be invoked through the function keys. This information can be on-line help, a complete explanation of reasoning (discussed later), or simply an extensive explanation of a result or recommendation. Also mentioned earlier was the product's ability to generate tailored reports, which can communicate to the end user critical information on how the system reached its result.

Replay Capability

Replay capability in 1st-Class/FUSION can be accomplished in one of two ways: (1) through the instant replay command "R" that is offered at the end of each consultation session; or (2) by reading in the answers to

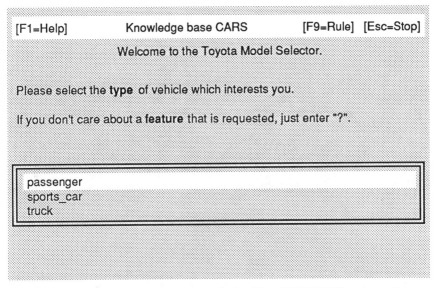

Figure 4.24. User response screen in 1st-Class/FUSION (Courtesy of 1st-Class Expert Systems, Inc.).

the system's factors or questions from an external file. 1st-Class does not, however, create this file during a normal consultation; it must be created by an editor before the consultation is run or by using FUSION's "READ" and "WRITE" commands. Using answer files, then, is equivalent to running 1st-Class or FUSION in batch mode, which is important when the expert system application is to be embedded into another program. Both programs also offer the option of resuming a session that has been abruptly terminated. When either program is restarted after an abrupt termination, users are prompted to discern if they wish to continue with the earlier consultation.

Explanation of Reasoning

1st-Class/FUSION offers no default mechanism for asking HOW or WHY questions, but instead offers the developer the flexibility of using either the windowing or reporting features to get this type of information to the end user. For example, while the user may initially see a typical question appear on the screen during a consultation, a function key might be depressed to open an on-screen window that provides a lengthy explanation as to why the question is being asked. This equivalent of WHY information can be stored in a file on disk, and HOW questions can be

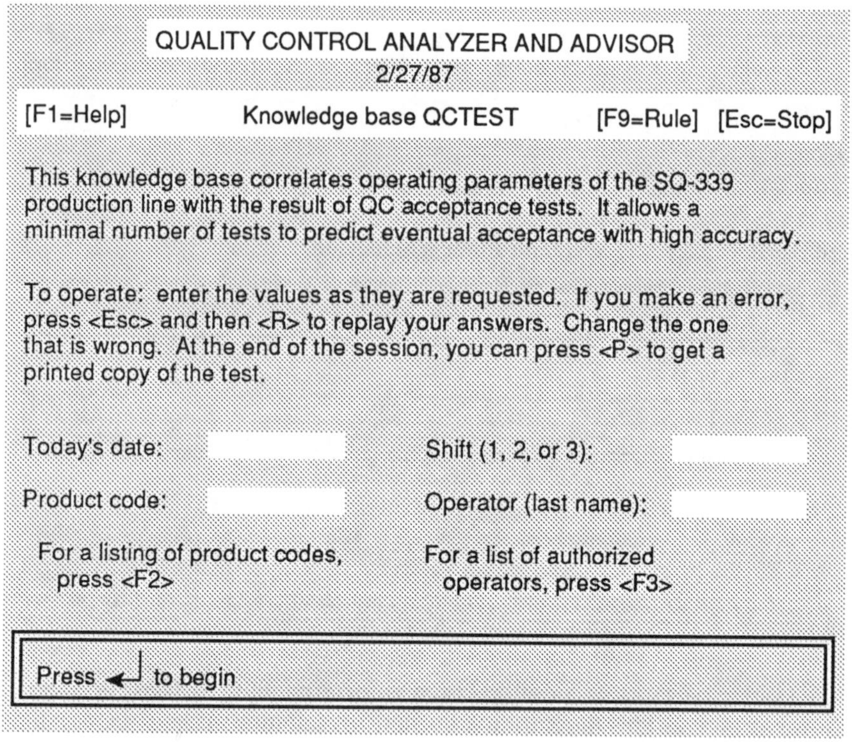

```
┌─────────────────────────────────────────────────────────────────┐
│              QUALITY CONTROL ANALYZER AND ADVISOR                 │
│                           2/27/87                                 │
│  [F1=Help]            Knowledge base QCTEST        [F9=Rule] [Esc=Stop] │
│                                                                   │
│  This knowledge base correlates operating parameters of the SQ-339│
│  production line with the result of QC acceptance tests. It allows a │
│  minimal number of tests to predict eventual acceptance with high accuracy. │
│                                                                   │
│  To operate: enter the values as they are requested. If you make an error, │
│  press <Esc> and then <R> to replay your answers. Change the one  │
│  that is wrong. At the end of the session, you can press <P> to get a │
│  printed copy of the test.                                        │
│                                                                   │
│  Today's date:     [      ]        Shift (1, 2, or 3):    [      ] │
│                                                                   │
│  Product code:     [      ]        Operator (last name): [      ] │
│                                                                   │
│     For a listing of product codes,    For a list of authorized   │
│          press <F2>                        operators, press <F3>  │
│                                                                   │
│  ┌──────────────────────────────────────────────────────────────┐ │
│  │ Press ◄┘ to begin                                            │ │
│  └──────────────────────────────────────────────────────────────┘ │
└─────────────────────────────────────────────────────────────────┘
```

Figure 4.25. Fill-in-the-blank screen in 1st-Class/FUSION (Courtesy of 1st-Class Expert Systems, Inc.).

handled in a similar fashion. Figure 4.26 shows a typical WHY explanation in a window while a question is being asked.

4. Integration Capability with Existing Programs and Databases

Method of Integration

1st-Class/FUSION has extensive integration capability with other programs and databases. First, the program will import external data to be used as examples within a knowledge base. The program can also directly read and write data files that were created with Lotus 1-2-3 or dBASE once they have been written into an ASCII report form. In addition, the products take advantage of DOS ERRORLEVEL numbers, which indicates that 1st-Class/FUSION has good communication ability with the MS DOS operating system. In fact, the programs can make DOS calls and read standard files. This is the primary means for opening windows, calling up graphics, and so on.

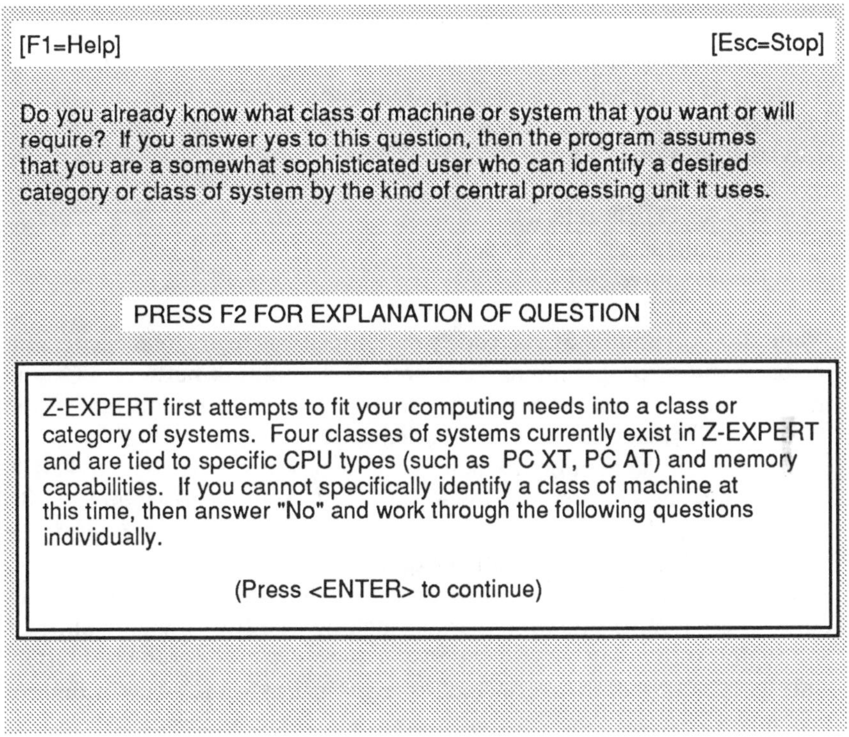

[F1=Help]   [Esc=Stop]

Do you already know what class of machine or system that you want or will require? If you answer yes to this question, then the program assumes that you are a somewhat sophisticated user who can identify a desired category or class of system by the kind of central processing unit it uses.

PRESS F2 FOR EXPLANATION OF QUESTION

Z-EXPERT first attempts to fit your computing needs into a class or category of systems. Four classes of systems currently exist in Z-EXPERT and are tied to specific CPU types (such as PC XT, PC AT) and memory capabilities. If you cannot specifically identify a class of machine at this time, then answer "No" and work through the following questions individually.

(Press <ENTER> to continue)

Figure 4.26. WHY Explanation in 1st-Class window (Courtesy of 1st-Class Expert Systems, Inc.).

Compatibility with Other Programs

As mentioned earlier specially formatted data files can be used with the 1st-Class and FUSION packages. For example, Lotus spreadsheet files can be directly imported into 1st-Class/FUSION as long as they are saved in an ASCII (*.PRN) version. For dBASE file access, four commands are provided in FUSION only, which have the following functions:

— SEEK (which will find a desired RECORD)
— GET (which will read a field value from a RECORD)
— PUT (which will update a field value)
— APPEND (which will add a new record to the file)

1st-Class/FUSION will not, however, invoke Lotus or dBASE in real time and pass values back and forth from cells or records.

Portability Issues

Of all the tools covered in this book, FUSION (but not 1st-Class) offers the greatest portability as a result of its unique code generators. In essence, FUSION can take the graphical decision tree of any knowledge base and convert it into one of three forms:

— IF . . . THEN rule sets
— "C" language source code
— Pascal source code

While the "C" and PASCAL code generators may create great excitement in the world of programming, and provide a vital link between PCs and minicomputers and mainframes, we think that the most important of the "translation" features for the experienced expert system builder is the production rule generator. By being able to create a set of IF . . . THEN rules from a decision tree, the developer is able not only to get an English-like (pseudocode) listing of the system's logic, but also to import the converted rule set into many other expert system tools with minimal work. This means that the logic created with FUSION is many portable to all other rule-based tools on the market, making FUSION a highly efficient and rapid prototyping tool for the PC. A simple decision tree in FUSION with its corresponding "translated" rule set in English is given in Figures 4.27 and 4.28.

5. Run-Time Licensing for Delivered Systems

1st-Class/FUSION has a royalty-free distribution policy on the run-time version of its packages. That means that any knowledge bases that are created with either package can be distributed freely or sold without additional payment to 1st-Class Expert Systems, Inc. There are, however, restrictions on how the product must be distributed. For example, the program's copyright screen cannot be removed, and the distribution disks must have a copyright notice on them. The development program cannot under any circumstances be distributed according to the licensing agreement. Neither the run-time nor development programs are copy-protected. Also, if security is an issue, 1st-Class Expert Systems will work with customers to help encrypt a knowledge base.

Hybrid Tools

The tools discussed in this section, from Knowledge Garden and IntelligenceWare, are categorized as "hybrid" in that they draw on a

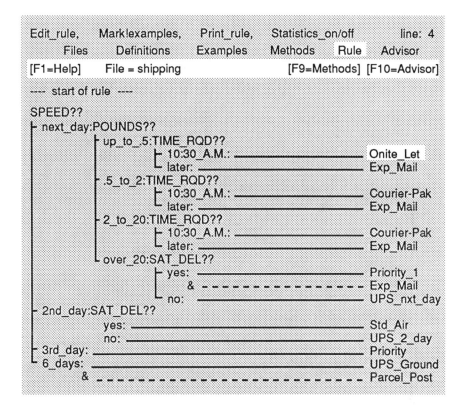

```
Edit_rule,    Mark examples,    Print_rule,    Statistics_on/off        line: 4
       Files      Definitions    Examples    Methods    Rule    Advisor
[F1=Help]      File = shipping                    [F9=Methods] [F10=Advisor]

---- start of rule ----

SPEED??
├ next_day:POUNDS??
│         ├ up_to_.5:TIME_RQD??
│         │          ├ 10:30_A.M.: _____ Onite_Let
│         │          └ later: _____ Exp_Mail
│         ├ .5_to_2:TIME_RQD??
│         │          ├ 10:30_A.M.: _____ Courier-Pak
│         │          └ later: _____ Exp_Mail
│         ├ 2_to_20:TIME_RQD??
│         │          ├ 10:30_A.M.: _____ Courier-Pak
│         │          └ later: _____ Exp_Mail
│         └ over_20:SAT_DEL??
│                    ├ yes: _____ Priority_1
│                    │   & - - - - - - - - - - - - - - Exp_Mail
│                    └ no: _____ UPS_nxt_day
├ 2nd_day:SAT_DEL??
│         yes: _____ Std_Air
│         no: _____ UPS_2_day
├ 3rd_day: _____ Priority
└ 6_days: _____ UPS_Ground
      & - - - - - - - - - - - - - - - - - - - - - - Parcel_Post
```

Figure 4.27. Typical FUSION decision tree before translation
(Courtesy of 1st-Class Expert Systems, Inc.).

variety of approaches and methods to offer the expert system developer greater flexibility. In addition, both tools combine rule-based and induction techniques and have additional features. As mentioned in chapter 2, however, with this flexibility comes greater tool complexity. This means that, if hybrid tools are to be used to their full potential, they will require more expertise on the part of the developer. But the benefit of hybrid tools is that sophisticated expert system applications can be achieved, even at the PC level.

The tools covered in this hybrid category are unique in many ways and indicate what the future of PC-based expert systems might look like. In particular, they draw on concepts such as statistical inference, inexact reasoning, topic structures, and hypertext. Since tools in the hybrid category are idiosyncratic, we cannot provide a general discussion of their

```
RULES FOR shipping;


RULE    Ship_By1
IF      SPEED       IS next_day
AND     POUNDS      IS up_to_.5
AND     TIME_RQD    IS 10:30_A.M.
THEN    Ship_By IS Onite_Let


RULE    Ship_By2
IF      SPEED       IS next_day
AND     POUNDS      IS up_to_.5
AND     TIME_RQD    IS later
THEN    Ship_By IS Exp_Mail


RULE    Ship_By3
IF      SPEED       IS next_day
AND     POUNDS      IS .5_to_2
AND     TIME_RQD    IS 10:30_A.M.
THEN    Ship_By IS Pak


RULE    Ship_By4
-- More --
```

Figure 4.28. Translated program source code from figure 4.27
(Courtesy of 1st-Class Expert Systems, Inc.).

approaches and techniques. Rather, we explore these dimensions in discussing the various tools themselves. At some point, the inexperienced
developer may discover that a particular hybrid tool is too complex to be
of immediate use. But, as with other software applications, once they are
learned to a certain point, they may quickly become either too slow or
too inflexible for the sophisticated developer. We have selected tools that
not only are low in cost (under $500) but are sold with the assurance that
they are approachable at an introductory level, that is, suitable for the
experienced PC user or area expert. In fact, if one wishes only to use
rules, then the hybrid tools covered in this section offer no more difficulty
than those discussed earlier. So what should be kept in mind when going
through this section is how the tool's advanced features might help to
create a more effective or efficient expert system application.

Knowledgepro and Knowledgemaker
Knowledge Garden, Inc.

1. Fit of the Tool to the Problem

Knowledge Garden offers expert system building tools that are targeted at the experienced PC user or area expert and sell for under $500. Two of these tools, KnowledgePro and KnowledgeMaker, are discussed in detail here, for together they make up a unique hybrid working environment for expert systems development.

KnowledgeMaker is an inductive "front end" used for generating a set of IF . . . THEN rules from data. Once generated, these rules can then be formatted for input into a variety of rule-based expert system tools on the market, including KnowledgePro. Since KnowledgeMaker is actually written in KnowledgePro, we can consider the programs to be a single development package; keep in mind, however, that the rules created through KnowledgeMaker's induction feature can be ported to a number of other expert system tools on the market.

KnowledgePro, in contrast, is a highly structured expert system development tool that offers a full range of features and strategies for developing sophisticated knowledge based systems. In particular, KnowledgePro works quite well for situations requiring standard rule-based logic, but the tool also offers the ability to use "topics" for system organization, and offers "hypertext" as a program control mechanism. Each of these concepts is defined below.

KnowledgePro TOPICS

In most PC-based expert systems that use rules, usually no structure exists by which the knowledge can be organized into a hierarchy within a single knowledge base. That is, the rules themselves form one global knowledge base, regardless of their number. Even induction-based tools contain a global knowledge base that is made up of all the examples in the system. However, when a forward or backward chain to a knowledge subproblem or module is implemented with an inductive tool, the developer can then begin to "structure" the overall problem into related units or modules. Since these individual components are part of the total system, communication must necessarily occur between them. The technical term for this communication between modules is "parameter passing."

In KnowledgePro, a "topic" is another way of structuring knowledge and achieving communication between its various parts, either within a single knowledge base or among several knowledge bases. According to the KnowledgePro manual, "a topic is a subject or theme, a 'piece of knowledge,' that can behave in a number of ways within the system." Topics are basically used for structural organization as well as places for information storage. Thus they can be arranged hierarchically, use inheritance, be assigned certain properties such as the types of values they can hold, store system commands, procedures, or variable values, and, most importantly, achieve communication with the end user in a highly interactive way (discussed below in the "Hypertext" section). Since all topics within a knowledge base are "descendants" of the main topic, the system automatically takes on a hierarchical structure that is important for keeping information compartmentalized or modular within the system. One of the immediate benefits of the topic approach is that it fits the knowledge acquisition process in a natural, intuitive way. Rather than asking PC users or area experts to express their knowledge in IF . . . THEN rules, KnowledgePro allows them to simply enter information in free form into a set of topics.

The way the KnowledgePro topic system works is simple in principle, but can be quite complex in some implementations. First, think of a hierarchy of topics as shown in Figure 4.29, where the topic animal has three nested subtopics: dog, bird, cat.

Next, a topic must be called or referenced, which means that its value must now be determined. So the system will search from the bottom of the hierarchy of topics toward the top to find a particular topic value. In the example above, if the main topic "animal" is called or referenced, the system will tell us the following information:

A dog has 4 legs.
A cat has 4 legs.
A bird has 2 legs.

This simple example indicates two features of topic organization: (1) topics are arranged and searched hierarchically from the bottom up and (2) topics can "inherit" properties from their "parent" topics. Note again in the example above that the topic "animal" has three descendants or nested

```
topic animal.
    :Legs = 4.    (*  The default number of Legs for an animal  *)
    dog( ).
    cat( ).
    bird( ).
    say('
            A dog has ',?dog:Legs,' Legs.
            A cat has ',?cat:Legs,' Legs.
            A bird has ',?bird:Legs,' Legs.').

    topic dog.
    end.  (*  dog  *)

    topic bird.
            :Legs = 2.  (*  Override the default  *)
    end.  (*  bird  *)


    topic cat.
    end.  (*  cat  *)


end.  (*  animal  *)
```

Figure 4.29. TOPIC hierarchy in KnowledgePro.

sub-topics, named dog, bird, and cat. So when the topics "dog" and "cat" are referenced within "animal" they take on the default value for ":legs" as defined in line 2 of the program. But when the TOPIC "bird" is called, the default value for :legs is overridden by the statement ":legs = 2". In other words, the search pattern goes from bottom to top in the TOPIC hierarchy. This feature is valuable for developing a complex structure for knowledge representation within a single knowledge base. That is, a large problem expressed in a global topic can be broken down into a hierarchical arrangement of discrete, nested topics. This means that the overall problem is now put into manageable units.

The topics themselves can contain questions for user input or can store a set of rules for making decisions. These rules, which can be expressed in IF . . . THEN form, may even have been generated by the induction utility program, KnowledgeMaker. Thus, KnowledgePro achieves a hybrid development environment by combining two key expert system strategies along with the topic structure into one coherent system. An excerpted example of a set of rules within a set of topics is shown in Figure 4.30.

```
topic 'patient covered'.

if ?relation is self
then 'patient covered' is yes.

if ?relation is spouse
and ?policy is family
then 'patient covered' is yes.

if ?relation is spouse
and ?policy is individual
then 'patient covered' is no.

If ?relation is 'natural child'
and ?'age group' is 'under 19'
then 'patient covered' is yes.

if ?relation is 'natural child'
and ?'age group' is '19 or over'
and ?unfit is Yes
and ?certified is Yes
then 'patient covered' is yes.

topic relation.
ask ('How is the patient related to the policyholder ?',relation,
      [self,spouse,'natural child','other child']) .
end. (* relation *)

topic policy.
ask ('Is this a family or an individual policy ?',policy,
      [family,individual] ) .
end. (* policy *)
```

Figure 4.30. Rules within topics in KnowledgePro (Courtesy of Knowledge Garden, Inc.).

Hypertext

Though the topics within a KnowledgePro expert system can be called or referenced in any order that the developer has established, the user can also greatly affect program control by means of a technology called "hypertext." Hypertext is a generic term for a type of application in which "live" or "sensitive" areas of a screen (called buttons) can be used to control direction or "branching" within a program. Figure 4.31 shows a typical hypertext screen where the "buttoned" information is in inverse video.

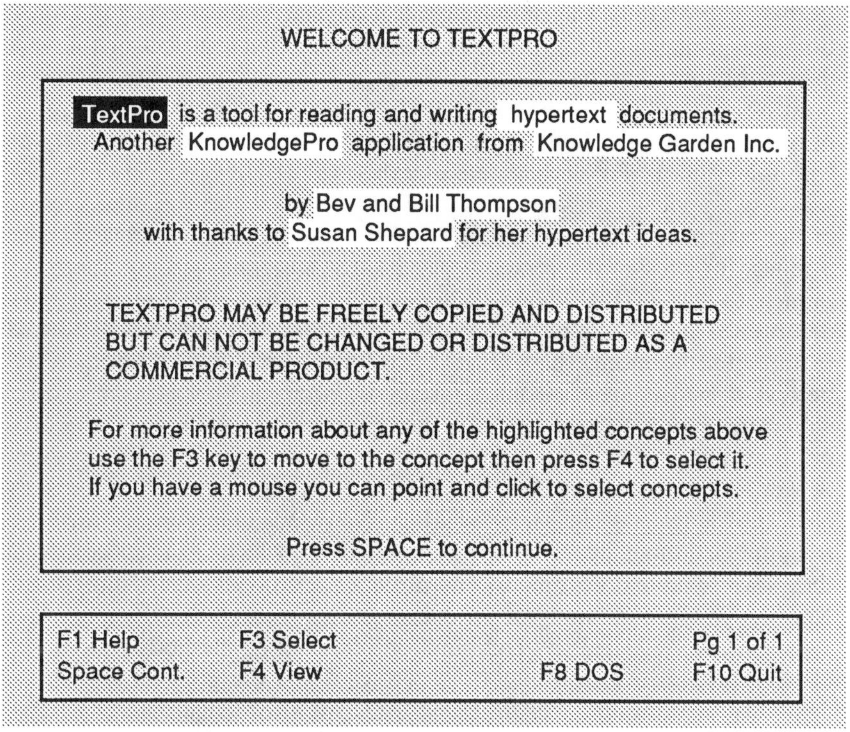

```
                    WELCOME TO TEXTPRO

 ┌─────────────────────────────────────────────────────┐
 │  TextPro  is a tool for reading and writing  hypertext  documents. │
 │  Another  KnowledgePro  application  from  Knowledge Garden Inc.   │
 │                                                       │
 │              by Bev and Bill Thompson                 │
 │    with thanks to Susan Shepard for her hypertext ideas. │
 │                                                       │
 │                                                       │
 │  TEXTPRO MAY BE FREELY COPIED AND DISTRIBUTED         │
 │  BUT CAN NOT BE CHANGED OR DISTRIBUTED AS A           │
 │  COMMERCIAL PRODUCT.                                  │
 │                                                       │
 │  For more information about any of the highlighted concepts above │
 │  use the F3 key to move to the concept then press F4 to select it. │
 │  If you have a mouse you can point and click to select concepts.   │
 │                                                       │
 │              Press SPACE to continue.                 │
 └─────────────────────────────────────────────────────┘

 F1 Help          F3 Select                      Pg 1 of 1
 Space Cont.      F4 View            F8 DOS       F10 Quit
```

Figure 4.31. Hypertext marked information in KnowledgePro
(Courtesy of Knowledge Garden, Inc.).

In this fashion, a screen may contain one or more buttons which can be activated by a cursor or mouse to branch to another part of the program. When integrated with the topic approach discussed above, hypertext offers the end user the opportunity to control the execution of the program by means other than simply responding to questions that lead to predetermined pathways. Consider the example below:

```
ask ('Is this a #m526 form#m ?', form, [Yes,No]).


topic '526 form'.
window ().
say ('The 526 forms say Application for Permit').
close_window ().
end. (* 526 form *)
```

In this circumstance, the primary control mechanism is the Yes/No question concerning the "526 form," defined in the first line. But if the user does not know what the "526 form" is, then a different part of the program must be invoked to either provide this information or offer a different set of questions entirely. So the words "526 form" are marked in the first line with the symbol "#m" to indicate that this is a hypertext concept or topic, which will appear in inverse video on the screen in the run-time version of the program. If the user either "clicks" onto the highlighted word with a mouse or presses the function key F4, the program will automatically branch to the TOPIC called "526 form." In effect, the user will have determined a new pathway through the system by using this hypertext feature. Furthermore, the TOPIC "526 form" could have additional hypertext sensitive areas within its screens, offering further user control within the system. The developer, therefore, sets up the hypertext words but does not predetermine the user's pathway through the expert system. A word or phrase defined as a hypertext topic can even call an entirely new knowledge base in KnowledgePro. Knowledge Garden also offers a free, public domain hypertext program, TextPro, which lets users construct their own hypertext documents and provides additional advertising for the Knowledge Garden family of products.

In sum, KnowledgePro's combination of induction methods, rule-based logic, topic schema, and hypertext control offers the greatest amount of flexibility in using the tool to create effective knowledge-based systems. KnowledgePro, with its inductive front-end KnowledgeMaker, will therefore be appropriate for either rule- or example-based systems. KnowledgePro also offers the ability to incorporate higher level structures for knowledge representation through topics and provides a high degree of user control with its hypertext feature.

Initially, the time it might take to implement this kind of complexity within an expert system may seem too great for the inexperienced developer. Indeed, with 115 key words to be used at various times during development and rigid syntactical constraints to be observed, KnowledgePro may begin to look like a programming language to some. But there is a difference. KnowledgePro does not build on a programming paradigm that would require extensive knowledge of, say, variable typing or data structures. Rather, the tool allows the experienced PC user or area expert to represent in an intuitive, natural way the kind of complexities that are often found in useful knowledge based systems. Because of this feature alone, the makers of KnowledgePro can rightly claim that they are in the "communications" business as much as they are in the expert systems camp.

2. Effectiveness of the Developer Interface

Documentation, On-line Help, Tutorials

Both KnowledgeMaker and KnowledgePro come with on-line and printed documentation. However, since KnowledgePro draws on hypertext for communication with the user, a key feature of both tools is their ability to offer a high degree of context-sensitive, on-line help. In fact, the on-line documentation with its topic control structure is distributed in source code version, so it can be further modified if desired. Contained in each printed manual are tutorials and examples which not only show the tools' features but also provide background information and comparisons to standard types of expert systems implementations. Particularly effective is a section that compares the efficiency of rules vs. topics to achieve the same result.

The KnowledgeMaker manual is also effective in providing background information on how the inductive process works. Both KnowledgeMaker and KnowledgePro were written by Bev and Bill Thompson, who are noted authorities on induction methods and other types of expert systems; their writings have appeared in BYTE magazine and elsewhere. So it is not surprising that their documentation on induction is of especially high quality.

Knowledge Entry and Command Functions

Both KnowledgeMaker and KnowledgePro use an efficient Wordstar-like editor for entering rules and topic statements. A system command menu is provided on screen, and the hypertext feature is used for on-line help that is context sensitive. During development, KnowledgePro can also read information from files, such as those containing rules created by KnowledgeMaker or some other program. During run-time, KnowledgePro has several methods for accepting terminal input or importing data into the system from external files.

Visualization of Knowledge Structure and Tracing

KnowledgePro offers the capability for viewing the organization of a knowledge base. By pressing the F6 key, the developer can see the structure of an entire knowledge base in hierarchical form, as shown in Figure 4.32.

By placing the cursor on any one of the topics in the tree-like diagram and pressing the RETURN key, the developer can identify the values,

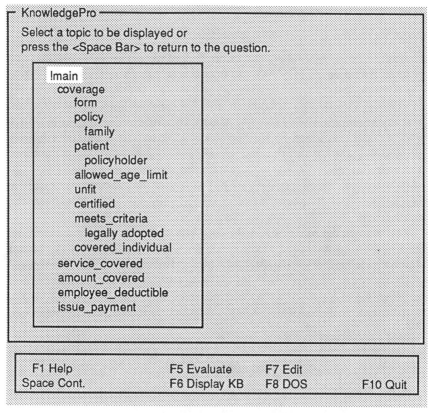

Figure 4.32. TOPIC structure in KnowledgePro (Courtesy of
Knowledge Garden, Inc.).

procedures, and inheritance properties associated with the selected topic,
as indicated in Figure 4.33.

This is the general way that knowledge bases are debugged in
KnowledgePro. When a problem or error is encountered, the program
allows the developer to enter the editor by pressing F7.

A TRACE feature is also included with KnowledgePro, which essentially
allows the developer to see each command as it is executed within the
system. TRACEs can be either sent to the screen or printer. The developer
can also run the EVALUATE option by pressing F5. This allows for direct
input of KnowledgePro commands while a knowledge base is running. In
this way, the developer can interrupt the system logic to insert program
changes and achieve rapid prototyping. These features, though they may

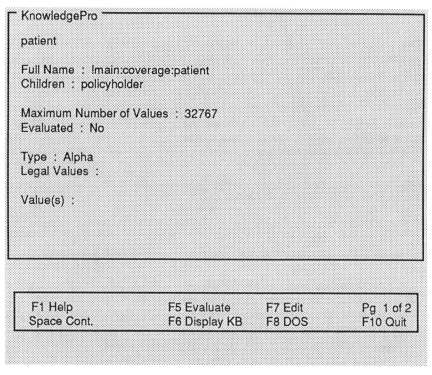

Figure 4.33. TOPICS defined in KnowledgePro (Courtesy of
Knowledge Garden, Inc.).

seem initially foreign to the inexperienced developer, quickly become invaluable for creating a finished system in the shortest amount of time.

Uncertainty-handling

KnowledgePro deliberately does not incorporate uncertainty-handling or confidence factors. Since the tool is based on a philosophy of "communication" rather than complex inference techniques, it makes sense that it would force the developer to ask the user more specific questions than hedge the system's advice by associating confidence factors with its recommendations. For example, in a typical expert system using uncertainty, a hypothetical question might be, "Is the turbo charger noisy?" And the user would typically respond Yes or No and then indicate the degree of confidence associated with the response. In contrast, KnowledgePro, by not providing default representations or values for uncertainty, might ask the user to indicate a more accurate level of noise from a menu. Or, using the hypertext feature, the user might click on a highlighted button for "noisy" to reference a topic by the same name, which would then explain exactly how to determine what "noisy" really means. In other words, the developers of KnowledgePro simply believe that if the developer is explicit enough in the information conveyed to the user and in the questions asked, then the incorporation of certainty or confidence factors may be unnecessary. However, because KnowledgePro is a language, uncertainty systems could be explicitly programmed in, though this would be a rigorous task for most non-technical developers.

Graphics-handling and Integration

KnowledgePro provides excellent graphics and windowing capabilities, as one would expect of a tool that uses hypertext. Most impressive is KnowledgePro's use of multiple, overlapping on-screen windows, which can incorporate many features such as color, frames, blinking, half-intensity, and titles. Custom-designed windows that will be used often can be set up as a topic and then referenced throughout the program. The developer can even set up a master "parameter file" that contains all of the system defaults for screen color and sizing, windows, and so on.

KnowledgePro does not provide a utility for capturing graphic images, but it can display graphics created with PC Paint. In time, Knowledge Garden hopes to have hypertext-like access to graphical information as well.

3. Effectiveness and Friendliness of the User Interface

User Response Format

KnowledgePro offers the most flexibility of any tool that we have tested for user input and control of the system. User input can be handled a number of ways. Direct user response consisting of a single character, multiple characters, a single line, or multiple lines are all possible. Menu-type responses, however, are the most common type of input format, as shown in Figure 4.34.

Direct file-accessing for input is also possible. KnowledgePro even lets the user open a window to the editor during a consultation to input paragraph responses.

Another method of input or response can be achieved through KnowledgePro's hypertext feature. As mentioned earlier, hypertext will actually allow the user to control the direction of the program as well as

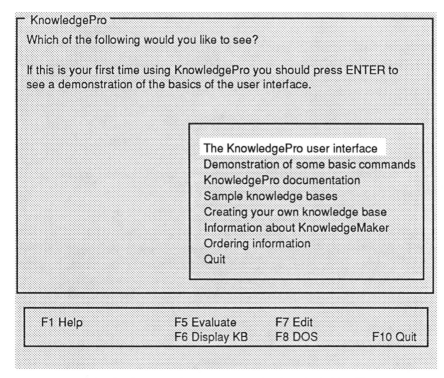

```
┌─ KnowledgePro ──────────────────────────────────────────┐
│ Which of the following would you like to see?           │
│                                                         │
│ If this is your first time using KnowledgePro you should press ENTER to │
│ see a demonstration of the basics of the user interface.│
│                                                         │
│              ┌──────────────────────────────────┐       │
│              │ The KnowledgePro user interface   │       │
│              │ Demonstration of some basic commands│     │
│              │ KnowledgePro documentation        │       │
│              │ Sample knowledge bases            │       │
│              │ Creating your own knowledge base  │       │
│              │ Information about KnowledgeMaker   │       │
│              │ Ordering information              │       │
│              │ Quit                              │       │
│              └──────────────────────────────────┘       │
└─────────────────────────────────────────────────────────┘
┌─────────────────────────────────────────────────────────┐
│ F1 Help              F5 Evaluate      F7 Edit            │
│                      F6 Display KB    F8 DOS      F10 Quit│
└─────────────────────────────────────────────────────────┘
```

Figure 4.34. Typical user response screen in KnowledgePro (Courtesy of Knowledge Garden, Inc.).

bring to the screen critical information needed to make a valid or useful response. The hypertext marked words can be activated by either pressing F4 or by clicking on them with a mouse. When more than a screen or window full of information is presented, KnowledgePro will handle paging automatically, taking advantage of the PgUp and PgDn keys.

Replay Capability

KnowledgePro offers no defined replay capability. However, because of the tool's power and flexibility, the sophisticated developer can implement this feature through a program "looping" structure.

Explanation of Reasoning

KnowledgePro does not contain the standard HOW and WHY explanation functions for two reasons. First, Knowledge Garden believes that these commands are really only useful to the developer. As a knowledge base becomes more complex, so its logic becomes less neatly structured and, therefore, an explanation of the reasoning process is less useful to the end user. Second, since hypertext can be used to give more information about a particular question or topic, and the DISPLAY KB command (F6) will provide a hierarchical view of the knowledge base (as shown in Figure 4.32), it becomes unnecessary to have any additional explanation facilities. The idea, again, is to be as explicit as possible in conveying information rather than to rely on lengthy explanations of the reasoning process.

4. Integration Capability with Existing Programs and Databases

Method of Integration

KnowledgePro offers the ability to communicate with other programs, read and write DOS files, and execute standard DOS commands. This kind of communication can occur through direct statements within a knowledge base or can be invoked through function keys. When calling external programs or DOS functions, KnowledgePro will provide the option of pausing until the external task is completed before resuming execution of the knowledge base.

Compatibility with other Programs

Integration with other popular applications programs, databases, and standard programming languages is achieved in KnowledgePro through a special "external library" of utility programs. The result is that the developer can write a topic in almost any language supported by the DOS environment and integrate this external function transparently into a working knowledge base with minimal effort. The current KnowledgePro external library supports Lotus 1-2-3, dBASE, PC Paint, and Turbo Pascal.

Portability Issues

Because of KnowledgePro's unique Topic structure, the program will "import" rules and program subroutines from a great many packages and environments, but, once complete, working knowledge bases created in KnowledgePro are generally not portable to other systems. This is not the case, however, with KnowledgeMaker, which generates from examples a rule set that can be directly used with five specified expert system shells.

5. Run-Time Licensing Delivered Systems

KnowledgePro comes with a run-time version that can be distributed without royalty for the purpose of publishing knowledge bases. The

KnowledgePro development tool, however, comes with a single-user license and is not copy-protected. Knowledge Garden will also publish selected knowledge bases and pay authors a royalty. The company's intent is to develop over time a limited library of KnowledgePro applications in diverse areas and thus move away from being solely a generic tool vendor. To date, the company has published Stock Expert, which allows users to analyze the stock market with the help of an on-line expert system.

AUTO INTELLIGENCE
IXL
INTELLIGENCE/COMPILER
IntelligenceWare, Inc.

1. Fit of the Tool to the Problem

IntelligenceWare, Inc. offers a family of expert system development products that clearly distinguishes the company as the "knowledge acquisition people" within the expert systems industry. In addition, its highest level tool, Intelligence/Compiler, rivals some of the most sophisticated expert system development tools on the market and compares with mainframe tools in terms of power. Since there exists such a wide range among its product offerings, IntelligenceWare can justly claim that its tools are not only appropriate to the experienced PC user or area expert but, at the highest end, suitable for programmers as well. According to Dr. K. Parsaye, IntelligenceWare president, "The area expert may indeed begin small with a rule-based system, but in time will learn enough about a particular package to use its more sophisticated and complex features, which will sometimes include logic-based programming as well." While we agree with Dr. Parsaye in cases where an area expert is very dedicated to the task of building an expert system, we find that the Intelligence/Compiler may tax the talents and expertise of the typical PC user. In contrast, IntelligenceWare's tools for knowledge acquisition, Auto Intelligence and IXL, are highly developed and are targeted squarely at the experienced PC user and area expert. In this section, we focus not only on the acquisition tools, but have also included the entire family of products in order to give our readers a better understanding of what is possible with IntelligenceWare products. Each product discussed here sells for less than $500.

Auto Intelligence

Auto Intelligence, as its name implies, is a knowledge acquisition tool that carries on a lengthy dialogue with an area expert and then provides at the end of a query session a complete IF . . . THEN rule set that "captures" the expert's knowledge. Since we provide in chapter 5 a sample session with Auto Intelligence, we will not discuss the discrete steps in the knowledge acquisition process here. Rather, we focus on why we think that Auto Intelligence can become an important tool for building PC-based expert systems.

In building almost any expert system, the most difficult task is acquiring the system's knowledge and representing it in some form, most commonly in rules. This difficulty has even led to the notion of the "knowledge acquisition bottleneck," which suggests that this is where most of the time and money will be spent during the expert system development process. Even when a rule-based or induction tool is used, the developer must still be able to identify the system's factors as well as its recommendations in a manual way. Sometimes, these knowledge base elements might only be known in some intuitive sense, yet they must be represented concretely within the expert system. So what Auto Intelligence promises is the automation of the tedious and costly process of identifying expert system components, such as the factors or results along with their related values. It does so by drawing on what we know about how humans make decisions.

In effect, Auto Intelligence helps the expert system developer identify the criteria used for decision-making in a given circumstance and then analyzes examples in order to induce a generalized set of rules. Thus, Auto Intelligence is said to be a "structure discovery system" as well as an "expert system generator." The tool has five basic parts:

— The *interview manager*, which interacts with the area expert
— The *structure discovery system*, which captures the components used in the decision-making process
— The *example manager*, which keeps track of data in the form of examples
— The *induction system*, which classifies and generalizes the data within the examples to produce IF . . . THEN rules
— The *expert system generator*, which generates a working expert system by bringing together the various knowledge components generated by other program modules

This basic program architecture is shown graphically in the diagram in Figure 4.35.

One should keep in mind that expert systems generated with Auto Intelligence do not have to be run on the Intelligence/Compiler offered by IntelligenceWare, nor do you need this particular inference engine or development tool to use the automated knowledge acquisition package.

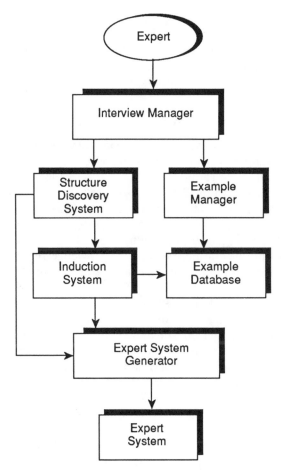

Figure 4.35. Auto Intelligence architecture (Courtesy of
IntelligenceWare, Inc.).

Although Auto Intelligence does include an inference mechanism, it does
not include basic features to perform input/output functions or screen/
keyboard addressing. It simply generates the logic portion of the expert
system in the form of IF . . . THEN rules, which can then be imported
into the Intelligence/Compiler, TI's PC Plus, GURU, LISP, and
PROLOG.

Auto Intelligence also allows an expert to express the level or degree
of confidence associated with a particular response. Thus, the rules that
are generated can have confidence factors automatically attached to them.
In IntelligenceWare terminology, this means that rules can be either "ex-

act" or "inexact," or a combination of both, and extensive calculations are performed internally to generate the absolute confidence factor that may be attached to any given rule. The ability to deal with situations involving inexact reasoning is a strength not only of Auto Intelligence but of the other IntelligenceWare products as well.

IXL: The Machine Learning System

IntelligenceWare bills IXL: The Machine Learning System as the "first step" in the evolution of intelligent database tools. Drawing on principles of induction and statistical inference, IXL analyzes large databases, such as those constructed with dBASE, to generate from data a set of rules that may have been largely unknown to the database user. Thus, the package, like induction-based tools, promises to generate rules from data. Its strength is that is goes beyond induction tools and draws on statistical procedures to produce a more elaborate knowledge representation than could be attained from induction techniques alone. Since IXL uses processes which are resource intensive and quite time-consuming, the tool is meant to be run overnight on a PC and can therefore deal with very large databases. In the company's words, IXL uses "free CPU cycles." The output from IXL is, again, a set of standard IF . . . THEN rules. Like Auto Intelligence, IXL can deal with both exact and inexact reasoning to generate confidence factors that are associated with rules. Though the tool works nicely with the Intelligence/Compiler, it does not require this inference engine for operation.

Like Auto Intelligence, IXL has five distinct components:

— The *user interface*, which uses windowing techniques to set up database access and view or edit the generated rules
— The *data dictionary*, which records and manages database concepts such as records, fields, and data types
— The *discovery module*, which searches for patterns and relationships among the data elements
— The *induction engine*, which generates rules from the information provided from the discovery module
— The *database interface*, which reads records from a variety of databases whose data are kept in specially formatted files

The architecture of IXL is shown in diagram form in Figure 4.36.

The importance of IXL to the expert system building community is that it provides a unique opportunity to gain a maximum leveraging effect on existing data. If it is true (as *Megatrends* author John Naisbitt claims), that

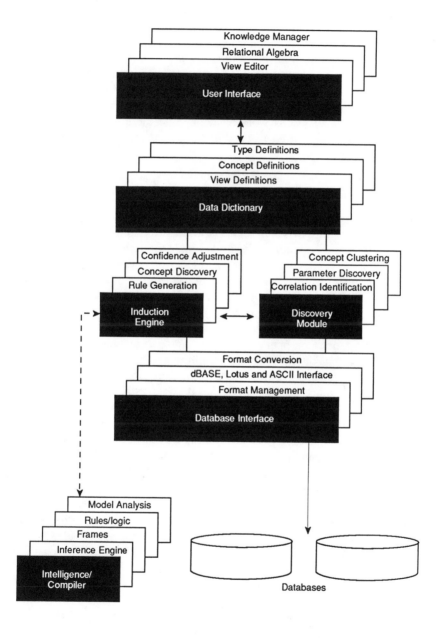

Figure 4.36. IXL Architecture (Courtesy of IntelligenceWare, Inc.).

"we are drowning in information but starved for knowledge," then tools like IXL will provide at least a partial answer to this dilemma. We say "partial" here because it is up to the area expert and system builder to determine if the many rules generated through IXL are of any value. We think that this type of discovery tool along with others provided by major manufacturers of database technologies will help to define better over the years the true value and potential for the integration of PC-based expert systems with current database designs. In sum, IXL is worthy of consideration if the developer is working with large databases that could be profitably analyzed in order to produce an expert system that would help decision-making.

Intelligence/Compiler

The Intelligence/Compiler is a general purpose expert system development tool that supports a variety of approaches and techniques. To gain a better sense of its overall power and complexity, we must keep in mind the fact that both Auto Intelligence and IXL were written with the Intelligence/Compiler. In effect, by looking at the three tools together we find within the IntelligenceWare products a hybrid working environment that blends the basic approaches of rules and induction and includes other techniques and methods as well.

The Intelligence/Compiler was, according to IntelligenceWare, developed as an "extension" of the programming paradigm and therefore tends to be quite complex. By combining several approaches into a comprehensive tool, IntelligenceWare believes that it achieves a "uniform approach to knowledge representation and inference methods." In order to understand the full meaning of this claim, one needs to know the tool in more detail than can be gained here in a multipurpose book. The basic architecture of the Intelligence/Compiler is shown in Figure 4.37.

Though it is a sophisticated tool, we have included the Intelligence/Compiler as part of the IntelligenceWare product line for three reasons:

1. The tool works well as the inference engine for Auto Intelligence and IXL and thereby shows another type of hybrid approach to expert system building.
2. The tool provides greater flexibility in handling situations that call for inexact or semi-exact reasoning (defined later).
3. The tool costs less than $500.

NOTE: Method of presentation for IntelligenceWare products
    Though we will be referring at times to the three tools collectively in

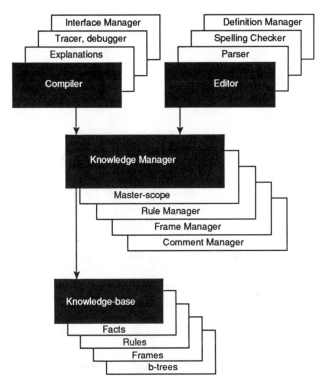

Figure 4.37. Intelligence/Compiler architecture (Courtesy of
IntelligenceWare, Inc.).

the sections below, we will primarily focus on the user and developer
interfaces, the handling of uncertainty and graphics, and integration and
run-time issues. Thus, we will address the features of the three tools
generally and call out in detail only those tool-specific items that are
significantly different.

2. Effectiveness of the Developer Interface

Documentation, On-line Help, Tutorials

The IntelligenceWare products come with highly technical documentation in both printed and on-line form. We find this documentation adequate
as reference material but think it could be improved through the addition
of "how-to" sections targeted at the inexperienced developer. Particularly
effective are the tutorial and technical reports that go "behind the scenes"
to show how the tools work and how expert systems can be created with

them. The tutorial on expert systems technology is done so well that it is now offered as a separate product, Experteach-III, and is included with the Intelligence/Compiler package. All of the tutorial disks incorporate extensive graphics and are professionally done. Clearly, IntelligenceWare sees its role as teaching developers how its products help to define certain areas of the expert systems market.

Knowledge Entry and Command Functions

The basic developer interface for the IntelligenceWare products is an elaborate menu system. Because of their uniqueness, Auto Intelligence and IXL have their own custom interfaces, which are described in detail in the product documentation. Intelligence/Compiler, in contrast, provides a highly intelligent editor which actually interprets statements as they are entered and helps to head off any errors. We believe that IntelligenceWare took an "editor-oriented" approach with Intelligence/Compiler package because it is the most direct and efficient way to enter information into a knowledge base and would be a familiar method to programmers. When used in conjunction with Auto Intelligence and IXL, the Intelligence/Compiler editor allows the developer to finish or modify knowledge bases that were automatically generated with the other tools. The next version of IntelligenceWare products will offer a Dialogue Manager, which will run under Microsoft Windows and offer an improved graphics-oriented developer interface.

Visualization of Knowledge Structure and Tracing

The rules generated with Auto Intelligence and IXL can be read into the Intelligence/Compiler directly, as well as into other common rule-based expert system building tools. Thus, there is no facility provided for viewing the rules graphically within the inductive tools themselves. Rather, reasoning patterns can be revealed or "traced" with the Intelligence/Compiler in an interactive way once the rule base has been transferred to this system.

One method provided for viewing the reasoning process at work is windowing, whereby the developer can slow down the system to "creep" speed and watch the execution of each rule within a window. Another way to "look" at system logic or reasoning is to invoke the "TRACE" command, which will allow the developer to view the steps taken by the inference engine to reach a particular goal. Also, since IntelligenceWare plans to offer in the next version of its products a graphical knowledge representation function under Microsoft Windows, a visual tracing of the reasoning process will be possible.

Uncertainty-Handling

Of all the tools covered in this text, the IntelligenceWare products offer the best handling of uncertainty, which is not only accomplished in Auto Intelligence and IXL but is also carried to a further extent in the Intelligence/Compiler. In the latter tool, three kinds of uncertainty handling or confidence factors are incorporated:

— Exact reasoning (100 percent certainty in rules or responses)
— Inexact reasoning (where confidence factors are associated with knowledge elements)
— Semi-exact reasoning (where exact reasoning and in-exact reasoning are combined to produce an overall confidence level in a recommendation)

The interesting thing to note here is that IntelligenceWare has placed great stock in dealing with "fuzziness" or uncertainty, while other vendors, such as Knowledge Garden, have deliberately excluded this dimension in their tools entirely. Expert systems tools obviously differ greatly; it is the problem to be solved that should define the type of tool selected. Thus, the Intelligence/Compiler is well suited to situations involving complex uncertainties.

Graphics-handling and Integration

All of the IntelligenceWare products use graphics and windows extensively for both the developer and user interfaces. Currently, built-in functions (or "predicates," as they are called by the vendor) are used to open and close windows and control screen attributes. In the next release of the products, Microsoft Windows will offer improved graphics-handling. Also, DOS calls to external graphics programs can be incorporated.

3. Effectiveness and Friendliness of the User Interface

User Response Format

The primary means of user input with all of the IntelligenceWare products is through menus, as shown in Figure 4.38.

Limited flexibility is currently offered in screen design through built-in functions, which may result from the fact that all three tools primarily have the developer in mind. With the Intelligence/Compiler, even the reference manual devotes most of its attention to the development envi-

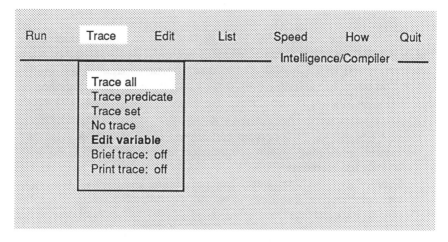

Figure 4.38. Sample User Response in Intelligence/Compiler (Courtesy of IntelligenceWare, Inc.).

ronment. However, the user interface should be much improved when IntelligenceWare implements its Dialogue Manager in Microsoft Windows.

Replay Capability

Standard replay capability is deliberately not offered within the Intelligence/Compiler. The reason for this is that the tool uses a "pattern-matching" technique for working with the system logic, as opposed to a straight-forward, decision tree type of searching technique. This means that when one answer is changed in an Intelligence/Compiler consultation, the search path may become totally changed. Being able to change one response, but leave the rest of the system intact, is not always possible, so there is less of a need for a replay function.

Explanation of Reasoning

The Intelligence/Compiler supports the standard HOW and WHY reasoning explanation options, but these questions must be set before execution of the knowledge base so that an explanation log file will be created. Explanation features in the Intelligence/Compiler are more thorough and complex than in most systems.

HOW explanations are shown through an *explanation tree*, which not only reveals the rules or "clauses" used during execution, but tells the user how certain goals were reached. For example, in a case where inexact reasoning was used, several rules may have been fired to reach a valid GOAL. Thus, the HOW explanation retraces how the system arrived at its conclusion, which means showing all of the rules associated with a GOAL or recommendation.

Similarly, when WHY questions are asked, more precise information concerning the reasoning process is provided. This means that the user will actually get the rules in the form of a "hypothesis" that the system is trying to test, as shown in the example in Figure 4.39.

This kind of WHY explanation is not only more thorough, but uses more of the system's power to reveal the reasoning process at work. For example, most expert system tools handle WHY questions by simply allowing the developer to attach a predetermined text to a given question in a *static* environment. In other words, the expert system is presumed to ask a question each time for the same reason. But with Intelligence/Compiler, a WHY query reconstructs the execution pattern in order to determine why the system is asking the question at that point in time. IntelligenceWare refers to this kind of explanation as *dynamic*.

This kind of HOW and WHY explanation facility may, however, appear

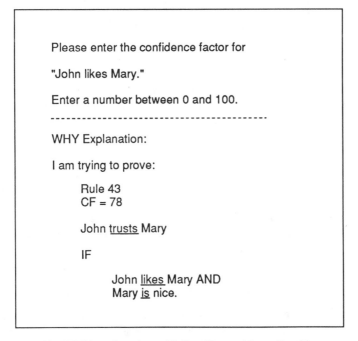

Figure 4.39. WHY explanation with Intelligence/Compiler (Courtesy of IntelligenceWare, Inc.).

cryptic to the user. For example, the user may be unable to directly interpret the rules when they are displayed, and an explanation tree may provide too much detail to be read by anyone other than the developer. Again, flexibility and complexity has its price. Therefore, these features should be implemented only when the developer is sure that the user will understand the reasoning process. Such may be the case in diagnosis situations, where presumably a technical person might want to interpret the detailed answers given to a WHY question.

4. Integration Capability with Existing Programs and Databases

Method of Integration

The Intelligence/Compiler and IXL offer full integration capability with a number of application programs and database files. Additionally, the Intelligence/Compiler will interface directly with Microsoft "C" in order to allow developers to write their own portions of an expert system in a conventional language.

Compatibility with other Programs

When integrated with other software packages, both the Intelligence/Compiler and IXL offer the ability to access dBASE and Lotus files directly. dBASE files can be converted into "b-trees," which are then used for database searching within the Intelligence/Compiler or they can be read in dynamically during program execution. Data in Lotus files can be read in directly by specifying spreadsheet cells by their rows and columns.

Portability Issues

Because of the unique reasoning process and overall complexity involved in the Intelligence/Compiler, portability of knowledge bases created with this tool is not possible. However, the rules that are generated with Auto Intelligence or IXL can be directly ported to a number of systems on the market that use a rule-based approach to knowledge representation.

5. Run-time Licensing for Delivered Systems

All IntelligenceWare products come with a single-user license and are not copy-protected. Also, no royalty or fee is associated with the rule bases generated with Auto Intelligence or IXL, and the Intelligence/Compiler comes with a "stand-alone" compile feature for publishing knowledge bases with no royalty to IntelligenceWare. When the stand-alone compile feature is invoked, all of the knowledge bases used for an application will be pulled together into one knowledge base with a .CMP file extension. Then this master file along with a copy of the ICX.EXE program can be distributed with no additional payment to IntelligenceWare. The .CMP file is encrypted to offer security to those wishing to publish or sell their knowledge bases.

Z-EXPERT CASE STUDY — PART TWO
TOOL SELECTION

1. Fit of the Tool to the Problem

With a clear sense of the Z-EXPERT concept in mind, the developers began to search for an appropriate tool that would meet the developmental needs of the project and satisfy potential users. From the outset, it was thought that a rule-based system might handle this task. For example, the basic knowledge in Z-EXPERT could be expressed as follows:

IF a user wishes to do a lot of programming,
AND IF the user intends to use graphics,
AND IF the user will be using applications that use many large files,
THEN the best machine is an advanced PC with VGA video and a hard disk.

But what was not immediately apparent was how the necessary knowledge would be identified and then put into the expert system in IF . . . THEN form. One admittedly brute-force approach would have been to simply think up all the possible user configurations and then express this knowledge in a lengthy series of IF . . . THEN statements or rules. A more expeditious, though incomplete, way to handle the problem would be to pick only a handful of isolated rules for entry into the system, with the intention that a limited number of rules could describe a majority of potential users. This approach is similar to the Ford Motor Company expert system for diagnosing robots that was profiled in chapter 1, where the rules covered only a subset of the entire problem. But neither of these solutions really fit the bill.

A better strategy was to simply look at a large number of case studies of past purchases to see if some generalized "rules" could be "induced" and then put into an expert system that could recommend Zenith system configurations with the same degree of success as a trained Zenith representative. Convinced of this strategy, the developers searched for an inductive tool that could transform a set of examples into a universal decision tree that could be applied to new situations. Consequently, the field of tool selection became quite narrow, as only induction tools were considered, and ultimately 1st-Class by Expert Systems, Inc. was selected as the development tool.

2. Effectiveness of the Developer Interface

1st-Class was considered initially not only because of its inductive capability but also because the developer interface resembled Lotus 1-2-3 and was therefore familiar and easy to use. Also, from the outset the developers knew that, at some point, the Zenith staff could potentially take over the on-going maintenance of the system, which would require not only updating product information in external files but also changing system logic often as new Zenith systems became available.

This meant that a modular approach would be desirable so that each piece of the expert system could be worked on independently. For example, Zenith might change monitor or video options often, so the knowledge affecting this area should be kept separate from, say, disk storage information. Thus a modular system approach among system modules would be useful, and 1st-Class offered this feature as well.

Another area that had to be considered was how the knowledge could be visualized. Since the developers were using case studies of past purchases, the rules or decision tree that would be induced had to be validated. Additionally, if Zenith staff members were to follow up and maintain the system, they may be unfamiliar with reading and interpreting production rules in IF . . . THEN form. So a graphical decision tree would perhaps be more immediately understandable. 1st-Class again provided this capability. A sample decision tree from an early version of Z-EXPERT is shown in Figure 4.40.

3. Effectiveness and Friendliness of the User Interface.

Although Z-EXPERT was built by developers with a good understanding of expert systems technology, the product was still an expert system that would be used by the most nontechnical of users, i.e., those who had not yet purchased a PC. This meant that users of the system would not understand any technical jargon of the computer trade, nor would they know anything about expert systems technology. Additionally, the system, if it were to be used at all in busy college bookstores, would have to be easier to use than, say, a Zenith catalog or product list. Consequently, the fewer keystrokes for user input the better, preferably with the user hitting

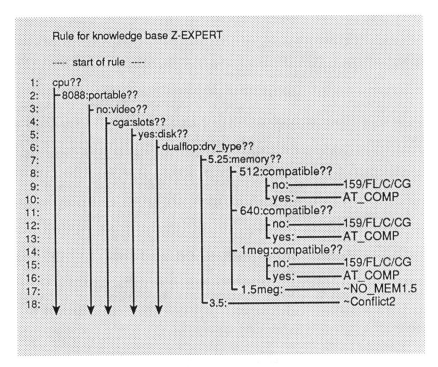

Rule for knowledge base Z-EXPERT

---- start of rule ----

```
1:   cpu??
2:   ├8088:portable??
3:              ├no:video??
4:                  ├cga:slots??
5:                     ├yes:disk??
6:                        ├dualflop:drv_type??
7:                                  ├5.25:memory??
8:                                   ├512:compatible??
9:                                      ├no:────────159/FL/C/CG
10:                                     └yes:────────AT_COMP
11:                                   ├640:compatible??
12:                                      ├no:────────159/FL/C/CG
13:                                     └yes:────────AT_COMP
14:                                   ├1meg:compatible??
15:                                      ├no:────────159/FL/C/CG
16:                                     └yes:────────AT_COMP
17:                                   └1.5meg:──────── ~NO_MEM1.5
18:                                 └3.5:──────── ~Conflict2
```

Figure 4.40. Decision tree from Z-EXPERT.

one or at most two keys. Also, since users might want to play WHAT-IF with the system (and not just accept the first system Zenith recommendation), some capability for replaying would be desirable. 1st-Class, with its light bar option for user input and its replay capability, fit here as well.

Another critical factor affecting Z-EXPERT's potential success was its ability to communicate to the user how a particular system recommendation was generated and why certain questions were being asked. Therefore, minimal HOW and WHY explanation capabilities were required, and here 1st- Class was more than adequate. However, an added bonus would be if the tool selected could provide this information in a user-friendly, graphical way. For example, it would do little good to offer the naive user a set of rules to ponder or a decision tree to explore. Rather, text windows would be more appropriate to display this kind of information, and here 1st-Class offered an excellent vehicle for this task. Not only could HOW and WHY windows be called from the keyboard, but a single text file could be established for all of the explanation information, and then a 1st-Class utility named HELPW could selectively retrieve the text as needed.

4. Integration Capability with External Programs and Databases

Because Z-EXPERT would perhaps one day be maintained by someone other than the developers, the ability to read external information from disk files became a necessity. The actual Zenith systems that would be recommended would change often, so embedding them as text into the various knowledge bases would not be a good idea. The person updating this routine information would not only have to know how to modify the knowledge bases themselves, but would have to enter the 1st-Class development environment in order to accomplish this task. A better idea was to use ASCII files in DOS and read them in with a window utility program, as in the case with the explanation of the system's reasoning.

Since Z-EXPERT would only be run on Zenith PCs, portability was not an issue and was, therefore, not considered in the tools investigated.

5. Run-Time Licensing for Delivered Systems

Because Z-EXPERT was intended to be a give-away product (that is, it was not meant to be sold), it would not have been desirable to have to purchase a run-time license for each copy that would be distributed. So a tool with a royalty-free run-time distribution policy was essential. Also, since Zenith would encourage its sales reps to duplicate Z-EXPERT widely in order to further its goal of offering better pre-sales support, a non-copy-protected version of the program would greatly facilitate the distribution process. Fortunately, 1st-Class satisfied all of these run-time considerations as well.

NOTE:

We wish to point out that other tools on the market could have been used for the Z-EXPERT project. In fact, most of the tools in this book could have been used if some of the criteria for selection were less critical. For example, if windowing could have been omitted, Super-Expert could have been used for Z-EXPERT. Or, if users would have been satisfied with VP-EXPERT's general purpose interface, rule-oriented explanation capabilities, and run-time policy, then this tool might have worked for the Z-EXPERT project as well. Our point is that not every tool will fit the application as neatly as 1st-Class did for Z-EXPERT, and in most cases compromises will have to be made. What is important, however, is that the developer identify those criteria that are the most important for tool selection in a particular situation.

5
System Prototyping and Building

In chapters 3 and 4, we suggested that the first steps in expert system development included making sure that an appropriate and worthwhile problem has been identified, that resources have been assessed to be adequate, and that a suitable development tool has been chosen. The next phase in building an expert system involves developing a working knowledge base and an effective interface. As mentioned earlier, a system with some complexity is best approached incrementally; that is, the developer will not, at this stage of the building process, attempt to transfer to the system the *entire* body of knowledge that will ultimately be represented, but only a representative sample. This process is known as *prototyping*.

PROTOTYPING

Prototyping a system has at least the following four advantages:

1. A prototype enables the developer to judge whether the system is feasible. Being unable to get the system to perform well on a subset of the intended problem suggests that the system will not be capable of handling the entire problem. A prototype thus provides the opportunity to "prove the concept," or test the validity of an expert systems solution to the problem. The developer may discover after running the prototype that the problem at hand may really be ill-suited for an expert systems approach.

2. A prototype allows the developer to test the suitability of the development tool that has been selected. Testing even an incomplete system may reveal that the knowledge representation scheme, the control or inference mechanisms of the tool, or its user-interface capabilities may be inadequate for the problem at hand. The prototype will also suggest the speed with which the completed system will run; a small system whose run-time is unacceptable indicates that the completed version will be even slower and that a different tool, or at least a different organization of the knowledge, may be required.

3. A prototype will suggest the amount of time required to build the whole system, an estimate that is essential for determining a cost/benefit ratio. As a result of the prototyping experience, developers may discover that their initial time estimate was either too optimistic or too pessimistic.

4. If developers need to gain the support of a supervisor before building an expert system, one means of doing so is to present the supervisor with a working prototype of the system. To suggest the potential of a fully developed system, a prototype often makes a more convincing argument than even a cogent and well-prepared verbal or written presentation of the concept.

As an example, the National Agricultural Library (Greenbelt, Maryland) has the grand goal of developing an expert system to help users of the library locate suitable reference materials. Because of the tremendous breadth of the collection at the National Agricultural Library, not everyone was convinced that the project was feasible. To test the concept, the expert system developers produced a system named TILAPIA, which addresses only a small portion of the collection relating to aquaculture. Because this prototype was successful, the expert system development team was encouraged to build on TILAPIA and work toward the goal of a complete agricultural reference advisor.

Building a Prototype

There are at least two different approaches for selecting a subset of a problem to build a prototype:

1. *Restrict the number of recommendations.* If the system will contain, say, 60 possible recommendations, build the prototype as if there were only 10 or so results. For example, an expert system to advise a customer on a suitable choice of a wine should contain a dealer's entire wine collection, perhaps several hundred varieties. However, a developer of a prototype may wish to assume that the dealer's wine collection is much smaller, say 10 select wines, and try to get the system working correctly for this subset of the problem.

2. *Restrict the number of factors.* Ordinarily, an expert system will consider several factors when offering its advice. In the wine example above, appropriate factors might be the meal with which the wine is to be served, or the body, color, age, and cost of the wine. By initially considering only a *few* of the factors, the developer reduces the complexity of the problem and builds a system which, though incomplete, will suggest what modifications the original development plan may require.

The Value of a Prototype

A prototype, then, is a scaled-down version of the entire expert system. It contains some, but not all, of the knowledge of the full system, and its user interface is, if not fully refined, at least developed enough to impress those in a position to approve the project. Its purpose is to test the feasibility of the concept, suggest the amount of time that the project may involve, indicate the suitability of the development tool, and, under certain circumstances, "sell" the project to a supervisor. Assuming a prototype suggests that the project is on the right course, it often serves as a base upon which the developer builds the full version by continuing to incorporate new knowledge into the system (adding factors or recommendations to the prototype) and refining the user interface. Another possibility, of course, is that the prototype will be trashed; this, too, could be a valuable experience in that it would save the time and money involved in developing a complete system that was destined to fail.

KNOWLEDGE ACQUISITION

The process of transferring knowledge is ageless. Parents routinely engage in this activity with children; teachers and authors practice this skill professionally; newspaper journalists transfer knowledge to their readers. Transferring knowledge from one person to another seems very natural. Yet when it comes time to transfer knowledge from an expert to a computer, the naturalness of the activity disappears. Without a doubt, this phenomenon results from a computer's limited ability to understand and its requirement of a rigorous structure for the information it is to hold. When a parent teaches his or her child to add, for instance, the parent knows the background and experiences of the child and can often relate the concept of addition to these experiences. Newspaper columnists make assumptions about their readers and can often get their point across without even explicitly stating it. The computer, in contrast, has *no* background and needs to have its data spelled out: no anecdotes, no analogies, no ambiguities. The computer wants precise and specific data and rigid control.

A second major problem in transferring knowledge to a computer is acquiring the knowledge in the first place. Very frequently, experts know the correct advice to offer but have great difficulty in explaining the process they went through to reach a conclusion. Getting experts to articulate their knowledge is arguably the most difficult aspect of building an expert system. In years past, "knowledge engineering" was largely an ad hoc activity; there was no systematic method of extracting the knowledge of an expert. Now, with years of experience, some generic knowledge engineering techniques have been documented in articles and books, and are even incorporated in some development tools (as chapter 4 has indicated). Some universities actually offer graduate study in knowledge engineering.

While making no claims of offering a definitive approach to knowledge engineering, we feel that, after reading this chapter, you will at least be able to begin this process. Our experience has been the same as that of the early practitioners: the more you practice the art of knowledge engineering, the better you become. One advantage we all have over the early developers is the use of software tools that facilitate the knowledge acquisition and representation processes.

The expertise or knowledge that a developer intends to capture in an expert system may exist in many forms. It may be the developer's *own* expertise which will be put into machine form (as in the case of the TI-LAPIA expert system mentioned above). It could be that the developer wants to put in machine form the knowledge which already exists in *printed* form (for example the information contained in the troubleshooting section of a computer owner's manual). Or perhaps the developer has in mind cloning the expertise of *someone else* (say, a bank loan officer). Although knowledge engineering techniques will necessarily vary somewhat depending on the source of the knowledge, a standard procedure will work in most instances.

The Stages of Knowledge Engineering

First, the developer must discover or decide what the *results* or recommendations of the expert system are to be. In the case of an expert system to diagnose malfunctions of an automobile's electrical system, for example, the results would be recommendations concerning tests or actions to take to remedy a particular problem. A system to identify vehicles would have as its result a classification scheme for all the vehicles which are to be considered (helicopters, planes, trucks, etc.).

Once the results of the expert system are recognized, the developer must identify the *factors* that distinguish the results from each other. Whether a car sputters or backfires may be a significant question in diagnosing ignition problems, and so this could become a factor in an expert system. Similarly, a critical factor in classifying a vehicle is whether its medium is air, land or water.

Next, a first attempt is made at establishing the relationship among the identified factors and the results of the system.

Rules

During the rules stage, the developer may actually write out a collection of IF . . . THEN rules which captures this relationship. Returning to the vehicle classification example introduced in chapter 2, the rules describing the collection of vehicles might look like this:

1. IF the vehicle travels through air THEN the vehicle is an aircraft.
2. IF the vehicle travels on land THEN the vehicle is a motor vehicle.
3. IF the vehicle travels on water THEN the vehicle is a boat.
4. IF the vehicle is an aircraft and the vehicle has rotors THEN the vehicle is a helicopter.
5. IF the vehicle is an aircraft and the vehicle has wings THEN the vehicle is an airplane.
6. IF the vehicle is an airplane and the vehicle has no propellers THEN the vehicle is a jet.
7. IF the vehicle is a motor vehicle and the vehicle has two wheels THEN the vehicle is a motorcycle.
8. IF the vehicle is a motor vehicle and the vehicle has four wheels and the vehicle is used for commercial purposes THEN the vehicle is a truck.
9. IF the vehicle is a motor vehicle and the vehicle has four wheels and the vehicle is used for transportation purposes THEN the vehicle is a car.

These rules relate the nine results (aircraft, motor vehicle, boat, helicopter, airplane, jet, motorcycle, truck, and car) to the factors (medium, rotors, wings, propellers, wheels, and purpose).

Decision Trees

An alternative means of classifying vehicles would be to sketch a tree diagram such as that in Figure 5.1 to pictorially represent the correlation among factors and results. Such diagrams are called decision trees.

Examples

Another developer may find it more natural to link the factors and results by means of examples such as those in Figure 5.2.

Pre-Existing Data

Other situations might suggest considering a spreadsheet of data which already exists to be a set of examples. In any event, depending at least in part on the type of development tool selected, the developer, working

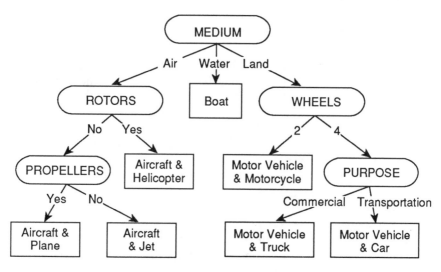

Figure 5.1. Tree diagram for vehicle classification.

MEDIUM	ROTORS	PROPELLERS	WHEELS	PURPOSE	RESULT
Air	No	No	*	*	Aircraft & Jet
Air	No	Yes	*	*	Aircraft & Plane
Air	Yes	*	*	*	Aircraft & Helicopter
Water	*	*	*	*	Boat
Land	*	*	2	*	Motor vehicle & Motorcycle
Land	*	*	4	Commercial	Motor vehicle & Truck
Land	*	*	4	Transportation	Motor vehicle & Car

(* indicates that the factor does not apply to this result)

Figure 5.2. Examples for vehicle classification.

with the tool's knowledge acquisition facilities, must now attempt to translate the knowledge from one form to another.

Weights and Uncertainties

At the same time, the nature of the problem may suggest the necessity to assign weights or certainty factors to the rules, examples, or branches of the tree that the developer has produced. The range of permissible values for certainty factors depends on the shell (some allow any number between 0 and 100, others range from 1 to 10 or from − 100 to 100; still others allow the developer to graphically select a point on a number line corresponding to the degree of confidence in the knowledge entered into the system). As mentioned in chapters 2 and 4, certainty factors are not so much mathematical probabilities as they are rules of thumb or estimates of the confidence in a rule or example; they may be based on historical data, or they may represent nothing more than the intuition of the expert or developer.

Refining the System

Next, the expert needs to critique the work up to this point, and to indicate any required changes in the knowledge base to the developer, who then edits the system accordingly. The process repeats until no further changes are necessary. This procedure, called validation, is fully described in chapter 6.

The knowledge acquisition cycle as described above is summarized pictorially in Figure 5.3.

The following six examples illustrate the knowledge acquisition cycle at work and exemplify how various development tools can facilitate this process.

This example illustrates a situation where an area expert enters his own knowledge into Texas Instrument's PC EASY, a rule-based expert system development tool.

EXAMPLE 1: PC EASY (courtesy of Texas Instruments, Inc.).

The manager of a small firm finds that he is frequently asked for advice by his employees concerning their travel arrangements. Specifically, they want to know whether they should fly or drive to their destinations and, if they fly, what type of local transportation he would recommend. After giving some thought to the manner in which he makes these decisions, the manager realizes, first of all, that his decision to approve air travel depends entirely on the distance the employee is to travel. Secondly he concludes that if an employee does fly, then whether he recommends a rental car or taxi for local transportation depends on (a) whether the employee is entitled to a rental car discount, (b) whether the employee is familiar with the area, and (c) whether the employee is an independent person who likes to explore new places.

The manager has a copy of Texas Instruments' PC EASY development shell, and so he decides to build an expert system to advise his employees on their travel arrangements. Because this tool requires that rules be entered in IF . . . THEN form, the manager sits down and writes out six rules which appear to be those he uses most when personally consulting with the employees on travel matters:

1. IF the distance to be traveled is greater than 400 (miles) THEN it is definite that the primary mode of transportation is to fly.

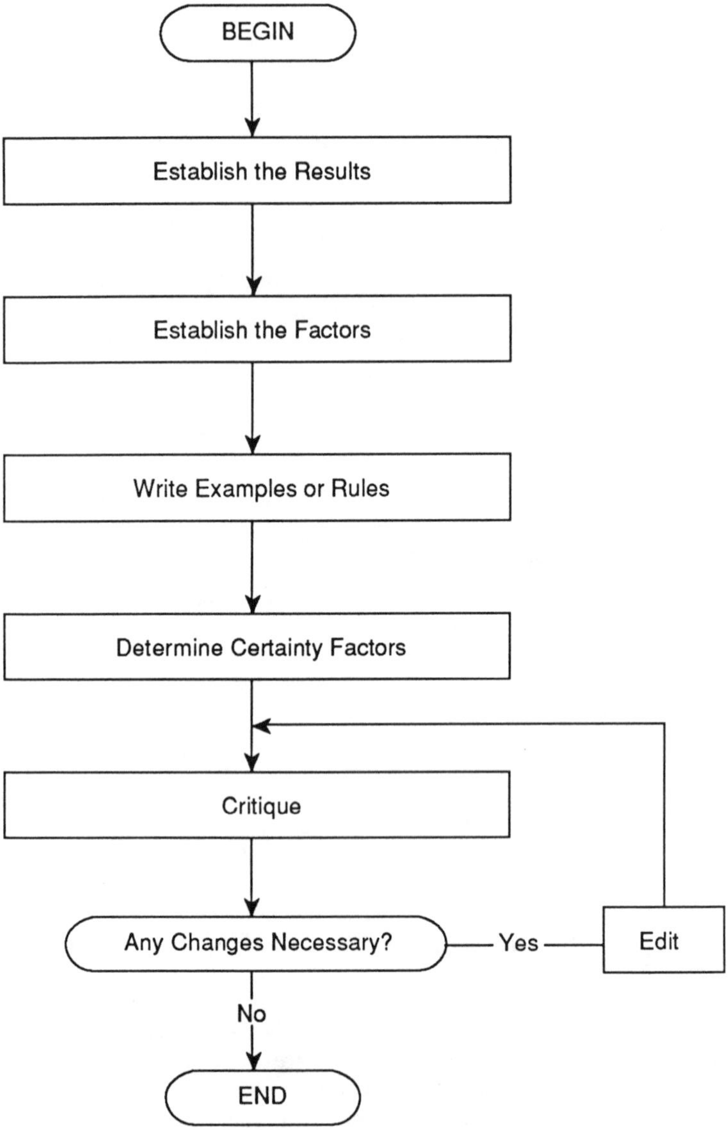

Figure 5.3. The knowledge aquisition cycle.

2. IF the distance to be traveled is not greater than 400 (miles) THEN it is definite that the primary mode of transportation is to drive.

3. IF the primary mode of transportation is to drive THEN it is definite that the mode of local transportation is to drive.

4. IF the primary mode of transportation is to fly THEN the mode of local transportation is car rental (CF = 0.5) or taxi (CF = 0.5).
5. IF the primary mode of transportation is to fly and IF the employee is either entitled to a rental car discount or else is an independent person who likes to explore new areas THEN it is definite that the mode of local transportation is car rental.
6. IF the primary mode of transportation is to fly and IF the employee is not familiar with the city or surrounding area THEN the mode of local transportation is taxi (CF = 0.4).

Satisfied that these rules represent his decision-making process, the manager enters the development environment of PC EASY, specifies the name of the knowledge base he is about to create, and is then prompted for the *goals* of the knowledge base. Two goals exist: primary transportation and local transportation. The manager therefore enters the two words: PRIMARY and LOCAL.

Because this is the first time PC EASY has come across these two words, it asks the manager to "translate" them so that the system will be able to make its recommendations in good English. The manager tells the system that by PRIMARY he means "the primary mode of transportation," and that LOCAL should be interpreted as "the mode of local transportation."

The next step is to enter the six rules. When the system prompts for the IF clause of the first rule, the manager types

DISTANCE > 400.

The system then prompts for the THEN clause to which the manager responds by typing

PRIMARY = FLY.

The word DISTANCE is new to the system and so, as above, PC EASY asks for an English translation. The manager responds that DISTANCE is to be translated as "the distance to be traveled."

The second rule is added in the same fashion. In response to the prompt for the IF clause, the manager types

DISTANCE < = 400,

and he then responds to the prompt for the THEN clause by entering

PRIMARY = DRIVE.

Rules (3) through (6) are then added in reply to prompts and would take this form:

Rule	IF Clause	THEN Clause
(3)	PRIMARY = DRIVE	LOCAL = DRIVE
(4)	PRIMARY = FLY	LOCAL = RENTAL CF 50 AND
		LOCAL = TAXI CF 50
(5)	PRIMARY = FLY	LOCAL = RENTAL
	AND DISCOUNT OR	
	INDEPENDENT	
(6)	PRIMARY = FLY	LOCAL = TAXI CF 40
	AND ! FAMILIAR	

The exclamation point in Rule (6) is PC EASY's expression for the word "not." As usual, whenever an unknown word appears in an IF clause (e.g., DISCOUNT, INDEPENDENT, FAMILIAR), PC EASY asks for an English translation.

Once he enters these six rules, the manager asks PC EASY to list the six rules both in English and in Abbreviated Rule Language (ARL) so that he can verify their correctness. PC EASY responds:

RULE001 [KB-RULES]
If the distance to be travelled is greater than 400,
Then it is definite (100%) that the primary mode of transportation is FLY.

IF: DISTANCE > 400
THEN: PRIMARY = FLY

RULE002 [KB-RULES]
If the distance to be travelled is less than or equal to 400,
Then it is definite (100%) that the primary mode of transportation is DRIVE.

IF: DISTANCE <= 400
THEN: PRIMARY = DRIVE

RULE003 [KB-RULES]
If the primary mode of transportation is DRIVE,
Then it is definite (100%) that the mode of local transportation is DRIVE.

IF: PRIMARY = DRIVE
THEN: LOCAL = DRIVE

RULE004 [KB-RULES]
If the primary mode of transportation is FLY,
Then 1) there is suggestive evidence (50%) that the mode of local transportation is RENTAL, and
     2) there is suggestive evidence (50%) that the mode of local transportation is TAXI.

IF: PRIMARY = FLY
THEN: LOCAL = RENTAL CF 50 AND LOCAL = TAXI CF 50

RULE005 [KB-RULES]
If 1) the primary mode of transportation is FLY, and
   2) 1) the employee is entitled to a rental car discount, or
      2) the employee is an independent person who likes to explore new areas,
Then it is definite (100%) that the mode of local transportation is RENTAL.

IF: PRIMARY = FLY AND DISCOUNT OR INDEPENDENT
THEN: LOCAL = RENTAL

RULE006 [KB-RULES]
If 1) the primary mode of transportation is FLY, and
   2) the employee is not familiar with the city or surrounding area,
Then there is weakly suggestive evidence (40%) that the mode of local transportation is TAXI.

IF: PRIMARY = FLY AND ! FAMILIAR
THEN: LOCAL = TAXI CF 40

Satisfied that PC EASY has correctly understood his input, the manager finally tests the system by performing trial runs for each possible scenario. Here is one such run:

| PC EASY: | What is the distance to be travelled? |
| MANAGER: | 619 |

| PC EASY: | Is the employee entitled to a rental car discount? |
| MANAGER: | No |

| PC EASY: | Is the employee an independent person who likes to explore new areas? |
| MANAGER: | Yes |

| PC EASY: | The primary mode of transportation is as follows: FLY
The mode of local transportation is as follows: RENTAL |

This being precisely the advice that he himself would have offered, the manager is satisfied that the system works correctly, at least for this situation. He then continues testing the system using other scenarios to convince himself that the system's advice would be the same as his under all circumstances. (See chapter 6 for a discussion of validation.) The manager saves the system, and it is now available for the use of his entire organization.

If the developer of an expert system is also the area expert, the knowledge acquisition process is considerably simplified. Being able to express expertise as a collection of IF . . . THEN rules allows the developer to build a knowledge base in a straightforward manner using a tool like PC EASY.

In this example, a manager wants to build an expert system to recommend the selection of a computer system. Unlike the case of Example 1, however, this manager does not know how to formulate her knowledge as a collection of IF . . . THEN rules. She opts, therefore, for IntelligenceWare's Auto Intelligence software which leads her through the knowledge discovery process by carrying on a dialogue.

EXAMPLE 2: Auto Intelligence (courtesy of IntelligenceWare, Inc.).

When she runs the Auto Intelligence program, the manager is asked for the topic of the proposed system (Computer System Selection) and a list of sub-selections or results, to which she might respond:

> Time shared Mainframe
> Network of Minis
> Large network of PCs
> Mixed network of PCs and Minis.

Auto Intelligence then attempts to acquire the traits that characterize these by displaying some of the subselections and asking the manager to choose one and to indicate a trait that distinguishes it from the others:

AUTO INTELLIGENCE: Please think of:
> Time shared Mainframe
> Mixed network of PCs and Minis
> What is a trait that distinguishes one from the other?

MANAGER: Scattered information

AUTO INTELLIGENCE: What is the opposite of scattered information?

MANAGER: Centralized information base

AUTO INTELLIGENCE: Please think of:
> Network of Minis
> Large network of PCs
> Mixed network of PCs and Minis
> What is a trait that distinguishes one from the others?

MANAGER: File transfer problems

AUTO INTELLIGENCE: What is the opposite of file transfer problems?

MANAGER: Single file system

Continuing in this fashion, Auto Intelligence conducts an interview with the manager and essentially plays the role of the knowledge engineer in that it extracts from the manager the list of factors which discriminate one computer configuration from another. After collecting these factors, Auto Intelligence needs to solicit some examples.

AUTO INTELLIGENCE: Please enter the names of some examples (of computer applications)

MANAGER: Industrial process control
Insurance company
Manufacturing automation
Scientific research
University
Government offices
Military contractor
Computer manufacturer
VLSI manufacturer

Auto Intelligence now sets out to capture the traits that discriminate among these by again choosing some of the applications and asking the manager to distinguish their characteristics. For example,

AUTO INTELLIGENCE: Please think of:
Industrial process control
Insurance company
Manufacturing automation
What is a trait that distinguishes Insurance company from the others?

MANAGER: Large amount of data

AUTO INTELLIGENCE: What is the opposite of large amount of data?

MANAGER: Small amount of data

When Auto Intelligence has a list of all its recommendations as well as the factors that discriminate among them, it asks the manager to match the traits with each of the selections. This is done by the manager's shading a portion of a line segment (using an arrow key on the keyboard) to indicate the degree of the match. (See Figure 5.4.)

The manager responds by depressing the arrow key, thereby shading the line from left to right, until she suggests graphically the suitability of a time-shared mainframe for problems involving large amounts or small amounts of data. With this information, Auto Intelligence calculates and displays the similarities of the example and the selections as in Figure 5.5.

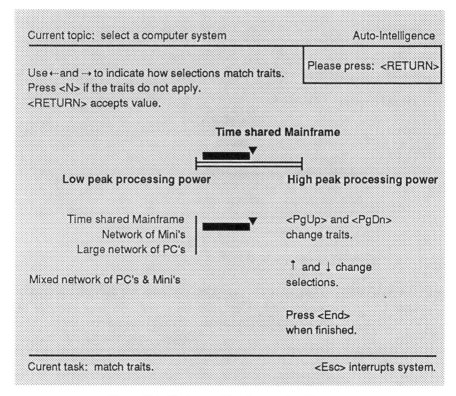

Figure 5.4. Trait-matching in auto intelligence.

Based on trait similarity, Auto Intelligence calculates that the example Insurance Company matches the selections as in Figure 5.6.

After refining its knowledge by further interviewing the manager, Auto Intelligence generates a set of IF . . . THEN rules and saves them in two versions: Text (so that the manager can review the rules for accuracy) and Code (so that the rules can be interpreted by Intelligence/Compiler, the inference mechanism which is the companion of Auto Intelligence). The manager studies the rules, editing them as necessary, and then runs Intelligence/Compiler on this rule set to see the expert system in action. The system is now ready for validation testing.

Using a tool like Auto Intelligence can be unnecessarily cumbersome if the knowledge that is to go into the expert system is easily obtained. But if an expert has only a vague idea of how the knowledge is organized, Auto Intelligence is an invaluable tool for discovering the structure of the knowledge and formulating it into rules.

Suppose now that the expert system is to clone the knowledge of a

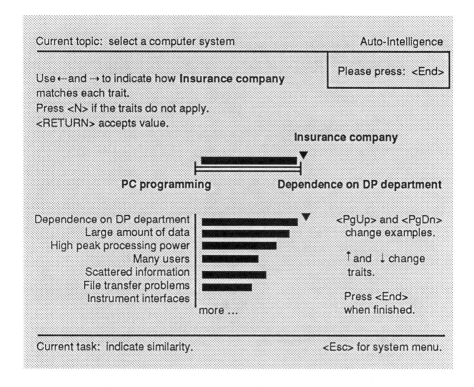

Figure 5.5. Insurance company computer system requirements.

human expert other than the developer of the system. A common knowledge engineering technique is simple observation. The developer follows the expert around, notes the decisions that the expert makes as well as the circumstances surrounding that decision, and, from this, attempts to extract the expert's knowledge. Another technique is to interview the expert (perhaps with a tape recorder or even a video cassette recorder) with the intention of gradually refining the expert's knowledge into a collection of rules or examples.

The following example illustrates how a developer using the SuperExpert inductive expert system shell might go about the process of cloning a human expert's knowledge.

EXAMPLE 3: SuperExpert.

Recognizing that the activity of its mortgage loan officers is highly cognitive, a bank decides to contract the services of an expert system developer to build

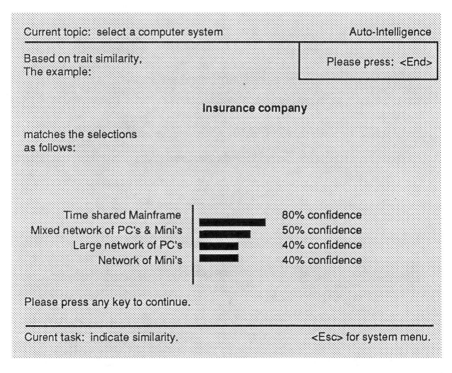

Figure 5.6. Match of insurance company requirements and computer systems.

a system which evaluates mortgage loan applications. Such a system would not only allow less-trained individuals to act as arbiters, it would also ensure consistency from one applicant to another and could also be used as an educational device for trainees in the bank's mortgage department. The developer has asked to interview the most experienced arbiter on the staff.

Developer: What can you tell me about how you reach your decision on whether or not to approve an application for a mortgage loan? Do you have a system?

Arbiter: Well, yes and no. I suppose I do have a system, but there are so many factors that go into my decision that it's really hard to describe. It depends on the size of the loan for one thing; and, of course, I have to assess the risk to the bank in granting the loan to a specific individual.

Developer: Suppose I came into your office and asked for a $65,000 loan. Let's suppose that there are exactly two outcomes: you either approve the loan or deny it. What would be the first thing you would need to know about me in considering my application?

Arbiter:	The first factor I consider is your income.
Developer:	Can you be more specific?
Arbiter:	Well, for a $65,000 loan we like to see an annual income of at least $25,000.
Developer:	Are you saying that if I make $25,000 the loan is mine?
Arbiter:	No! What I mean is I would have to deny the loan if your income were below $25,000; but if you made at least $25,000, other factors would have to be considered before I could approve.

(At this point the developer has narrowed the possible results or outcomes of the system to two: *Approve* and *Deny*. He has also identified *amount of the loan* and *annual salary* as factors considered by the arbiter in considering an application. For the purpose of building a prototype, he has elected to build a system that considers only loan applications in the amount of $65,000. He has already ascertained that if an applicant's income is below $25,000, the expert system should deny the loan; otherwise, the applicant *may* receive approval. The choice is to ask the arbiter to assign a weight to the likelihood of the loan being approved under these circumstances, or else to probe more deeply until a set of conditions is discovered which will not require the use of certainty factors. The developer opts for the second approach.)

Developer:	For example?
Arbiter:	Credit rating, for one. There are three different credit classifications: excellent, good, and poor. If your rating were poor, I couldn't make the loan.
Developer:	Even if my income were above $25,000?
Arbiter:	That's right. Regardless of your income, a poor credit rating means no loan; we can't risk it.

(The developer understands this response to mean that denying a loan to a poor credit risk is an absolute; no certainty factor is required here.)

Developer:	This is how I interpret what you've told me so far. How does it look?

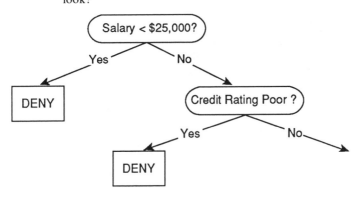

Arbiter: It looks good for a start.

Developer: What if my credit rating were excellent? Would you approve?

Arbiter: Absolutely. An excellent credit rating together with an annual income in excess of $25,000 would convince me to extend the loan.

(Hearing the word "absolutely" indicates to the developer that he need not be concerned about a certainty factor in this case, either. If the income exceeds $25,000 and the credit rating is excellent, the system should definitely approve the loan.)

Developer: Okay. That leaves the case where my credit rating is good. What happens now?

Arbiter: Then things get a little more complicated. I would have to assess your financial stability a little more carefully.

Developer: How?

Arbiter: By considering how long you've been at your current job.

Developer: Could you be more specific?

Arbiter: With an income in excess of $25,000 and only a good credit rating, I would like to see that you've held your current job for a couple of years, anyway.

Developer: Two years?

Arbiter: Three. If you have been on the job for less than 36 months, I would deny the loan.

Developer: And if I have been working that long on this job?

Arbiter: Approve.

(Because the developer intends to use SuperExpert, an inductive shell, he now attempts to frame the facts obtained during this interview in an example format.)

Developer: Let's summarize up to this point. Based on this interview I think I understand what goes into your decision-making process. Here are several hypothetical examples of $65,000 loan applications from individuals with various incomes, credit ratings, and years on the job. Tell me if you would have reached the same conclusions as I.

Case	Credit Rating	Years on Job	Income	Decision
1	Excellent	1	$30,000	Approve
2	Poor	6	$40,000	Deny
3	Excellent	1	$20,000	Approve
4	Poor	4	$30,000	Deny
5	Good	3	$40,000	Approve
6	Good	3	$20,000	Deny
7	Good	2	$30,000	Deny.

Arbiter: Almost. Only Case 3 is incorrect. Remember I said that, if the income is below $25,000, then I would not approve the loan under any circumstances. Even an excellent credit rating. Change the decision in Case 3 to "Deny" and all your examples would be correct.

Developer: Right. Let me ask you this. How certain are you of the decisions in the above set of examples?

(Here the developer is attempting to assess the confidence of the arbiter in the example set.)

Arbiter: These cases are rather straightforward; I am certain that these decisions are the ones I would have made.

(The developer interprets this last statement as meaning that there is no necessity for distinguishing one example from another by introducing certainty factors. The expert is fully convinced that these examples reflect his knowledge.)

Because he is using SuperExpert, the developer next enters the following information into the "attribute" screen of the shell that appears in Figure 5.7.

SuperExpert interprets this data to mean that there are two possible outcomes to its decision (Approve or Deny), and that there are three factors that go into the decision-making process: Credit (with possible values Excellent, Poor, and Good), Years (with integer values), and Income (again with integer values). The developer now switches to the Examples screen of SuperExpert and enters the data as in Figure 5.8.

Upon requesting that SuperExpert induce and display a decision tree corresponding to these examples, the diagram in Figure 5.9 appears on the screen.

At this point, the arbiter indicates that this tree does not exactly represent his decision methodology. Missing altogether is any reference to the amount of time the applicant has been on his present job, a factor which is critical in the case of an applicant with a credit rating of "Good." The developer addresses this problem by returning to the Examples screen of SuperExpert and adding three more examples so that the complete set of examples is as in Figure 5.10.

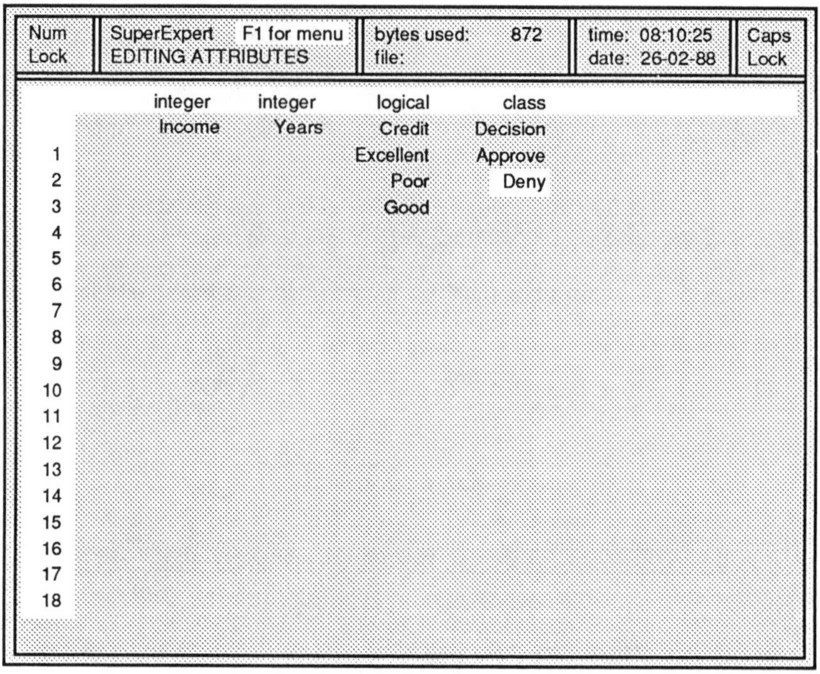

	integer	integer	logical	class
	Income	Years	Credit	Decision
1			Excellent	Approve
2			Poor	Deny
3			Good	
4				
5				
6				
7				
8				
9				
10				
11				
12				
13				
14				
15				
16				
17				
18				

Header bar: Num Lock | SuperExpert F1 for menu | EDITING ATTRIBUTES | bytes used: 872 | file: | time: 08:10:25 | date: 26-02-88 | Caps Lock

Figure 5.7. An attribute screen in SuperExpert.

At the developer's request, SuperExpert induces and displays a revised decision tree (see Figure 5.11).

Agreeing that this tree looks to be correct, the developer and arbiter run the system enough times to validate that it is correct. If the arbiter agrees that the system correctly describes his decision methodology, then the knowledge base for this simplified system is complete and the developer gets to work on the user interface and more general systems (loan amount not restricted to $65,000). More likely, however, the expert will discover at least slight discrepancies between the system's recommendations and his own. The arbiter may recognize, for example, that, under certain circumstances, he considers family size, family stability, and home ownership when reaching his decision. In this case, he works with the developer to identify the differences and modify the knowledge base accordingly by entering more examples. The question of validation of a knowledge base (testing for both accuracy and completeness) is the subject of chapter 6.

Induction provides an easy way to discover the structure of knowledge from a set of examples. If an expert is able to provide the developer with a complete and accurate set of examples, a tool such as SuperExpert can

Num Lock	SuperExpert F1 for menu	bytes used: 1675	time: 08:13:09	Caps Lock
	EXAMPLES SPECIFICATION PAGE	file:	date: 26-02-88	

	integer	integer	logical	class
	Income	Years	Credit	Decision
1	30	1	Excellent	Approve
2	40	6	Poor	Deny
3	20	1	Excellent	Deny
4	30	4	Poor	Deny
5	40	3	Good	Approve
6	20	3	Good	Deny
7	30	2	Good	Deny
8				
9				
10				
11				
12				
13				
14				
15				
16				
17				
18				

Figure 5.8. An examples screen in SuperExpert.

Num Lock	SuperExpert F1 for menu	bytes used: 2674	time: 08:14:06	Caps Lock
	DISPLAYING RULE	file:	date: 26-02-88	

1	Credit
2	Excellent:Income
3	<25:Deny
4	≥25:Approve
5	Poor:Deny
6	Good:Income
7	<35:Deny
8	≥35:Approve
9	
10	
11	
12	
13	
14	
15	
16	
17	
18	
19	
20	

Figure 5.9. A rule screen in SuperExpert.

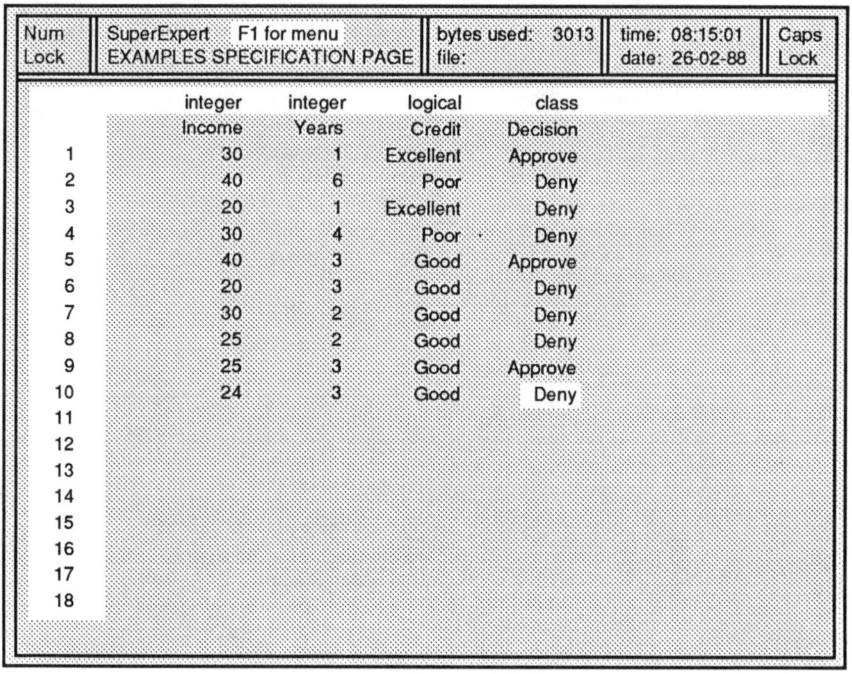

Num Lock	SuperExpert F1 for menu EXAMPLES SPECIFICATION PAGE	bytes used: 3013 file:	time: 08:15:01 date: 26-02-88	Caps Lock

	integer	integer	logical	class
	Income	Years	Credit	Decision
1	30	1	Excellent	Approve
2	40	6	Poor	Deny
3	20	1	Excellent	Deny
4	30	4	Poor	Deny
5	40	3	Good	Approve
6	20	3	Good	Deny
7	30	2	Good	Deny
8	25	2	Good	Deny
9	25	3	Good	Approve
10	24	3	Good	Deny
11				
12				
13				
14				
15				
16				
17				
18				

Figure 5.10. The revised examples screen.

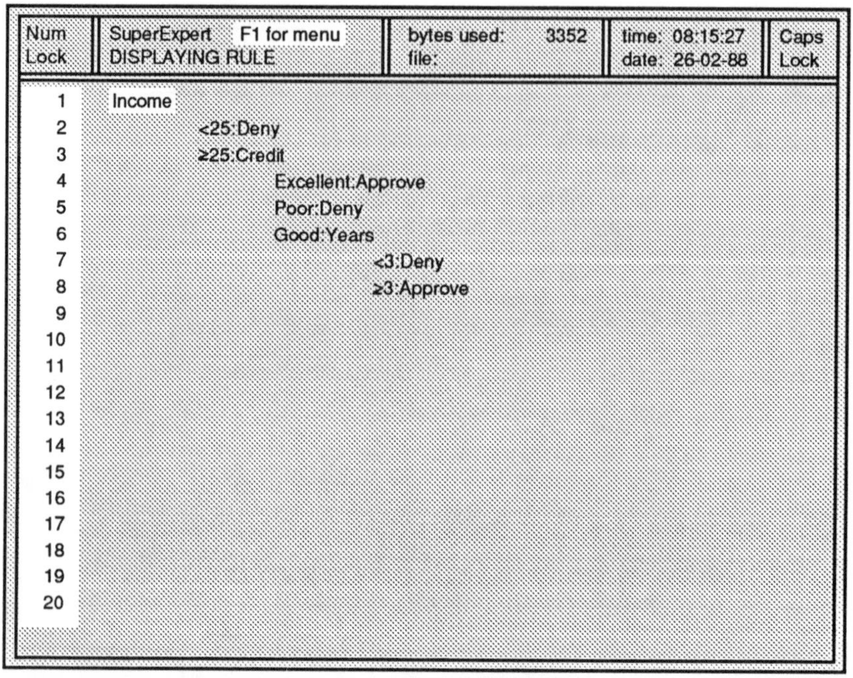

Num Lock	SuperExpert F1 for menu DISPLAYING RULE	bytes used: 3352 file:	time: 08:15:27 date: 26-02-88	Caps Lock

```
 1   Income
 2           <25:Deny
 3           ≥25:Credit
 4                   Excellent:Approve
 5                   Poor:Deny
 6                   Good:Years
 7                           <3:Deny
 8                           ≥3:Approve
 9
10
11
12
13
14
15
16
17
18
19
20
```

Figure 5.11. The revised rule screen.

quickly formulate a decision tree. Often, experts are astounded at how accurately the tree depicts their decision-making processes.

If the knowledge that is to go into an expert system can be expressed by the expert or developer as a set of rules, then nothing is to be gained by using an inductive tool. But if the knowledge resists formulation as rules, an inductive system can save a great deal of time in system development.

The next example illustrates the knowledge acquisition process when the knowledge to be captured already exists in spreadsheet form. Here, we assume that the developer has decided to use the 1st-Class development software from 1st-Class Expert Systems, Inc.

EXAMPLE 4: 1st-Class (courtesy of 1st-Class Expert Systems, Inc.).

A medical student studying kidney diseases has noticed that the factors which doctors consider when diagnosing a kidney disorder include (a) white cell blood count, (b) size of the kidney, (c) contour of the kidney, and (d) the kidney's density. Being a good record-keeper, he has recorded in a Lotus 1-2-3 spreadsheet twelve cases observed during a one week period (see Figure 5.12).

Here, BLOODCT represents the white cell blood count and the diagnosis codes have the following interpretations:

ischemia	—	ischemia
stone	—	kidney stones
maligtmr	—	malignant tumor
benign	—	benign tumor
normal	—	normal
venobstr	—	veinous obstruction
arterobs	—	arterial obstruction.

By convention, an * in the BLOODCT column indicates that the white cell blood count is not a factor in the example.

In an attempt to make sense out of this data collection, the student decides to use 1st-Class to induce a decision tree from this data. Because the data already exists in a Lotus 1-2-3 file, the student need not retype all the information; instead, he follows this procedure:

From within Lotus 1-2-3, the student prints this workfile to a file named, say, KIDNEYS. Lotus 1-2-3 automatically appends a PRN extension to the filename so that it appears in the directory as KIDNEY.PRN.

Leaving Lotus 1-2-3, the student executes the 1st-Class program, enters the Definitions screen, and declares the names and the possible values of the four factors as well as the diagnoses. The resulting screen looks like Figure 5.13.

Beneath the name of each factor is listed the possible values of that factor; the "#.#" in the first column indicates that BLOODCT is a numerical factor (as opposed to a literal factor) and that *any* number is a possible value.

	A	B	C	D	E	F
	A17: [W12]					READY
1						
2	BLOODCT	KIDSIZE	CONTOUR	DENSITY	DIAGNOSIS	
3						
4	*	small	smooth	increased	ischemia	
5	*	large	regular	increased	stone	
6	*	normal	irreg	decreased	maligtmr	
7	*	normal	regular	decreased	benign	
8	*	normal	smooth	normal	normal	
9	*	large	smooth	increased	venobstr	
10	*	large	irreg	drecreased	maligtmr	
11	*	small	regular	decreased	arterobs	
12	30	small	irreg	normal	infection	
13	130	small	irreg	normal	maligtmr	
14	*	large	irreg	increased	normal	
15	*	small	smooth	decreased	benign	
16						
17						
18						
19						
20						
26–Feb–88 08:26 AM						

Figure 5.12. Kidney data in Lotus 1-2-3.

The student switches from the Definitions screen to the File screen and asks 1st-Class to "Get" the file named KIDNEY.PRN. When the student then changes to the Examples screen of 1st-Class, he notices that the spreadsheet he created in Lotus 1-2-3 now forms the example set for his knowledge base in 1st-Class (see Figure 5.14).

With three keystrokes, 1st-Class induces a decision tree from this data and displays it as in Figure 5.15.

Two sections of the tree arouse the student's curiosity. First of all, line 5 contains a "no-data" result; this means that there is no example for the case when the contour of the kidney is smooth, its density is increased, and its size is normal. Tomorrow morning, he should ask his mentor about this scenario, enter a new example into the knowledge base, and rebuild the decision tree to tie up this loose end.

Secondly, because only two examples contained information about the BLOODCT, 1st-Class used the average of these two values ([30 + 130]/2 = 80) as the pivotal value distinguishing a kidney infection from a malignant tumor (see rule lines 17 and 18). This is another item that the student should check

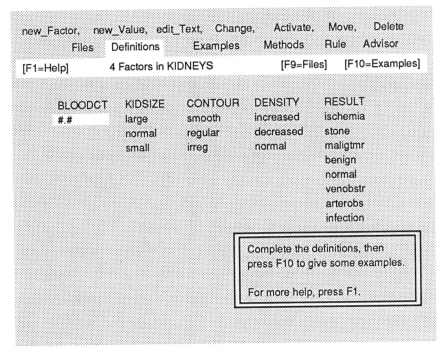

new_Factor, new_Value, edit_Text, Change, Activate, Move, Delete

| Files | Definitions | Examples | Methods | Rule | Advisor |

[F1=Help]　　　　4 Factors in KIDNEYS　　　　[F9=Files]　[F10=Examples]

BLOODCT	KIDSIZE	CONTOUR	DENSITY	RESULT
#.#	large	smooth	increased	ischemia
	normal	regular	decreased	stone
	small	irreg	normal	maligtmr
				benign
				normal
				venobstr
				arterobs
				infection

Complete the definitions, then
press F10 to give some examples.

For more help, press F1.

Figure 5.13. Definitions screen in 1st-Class.

new_Example, Replicate, Change, Activate, Move, Delete

| Files | Definitions | Examples | Methods | Rule | Advisor |

[F1=Help]　　　　12 Examples in KIDNEYS　　　　[F9=Definitions]　[F10=Methods]

	BLOODCT	KIDSIZE	CONTOUR	DENSITY	RESULT	WEIGHT
> 1:	*	small	smooth	increased	ischemia	[1.00]
2:	*	large	regular	increased	stone	[1.00]
3:	*	normal	irreg	decreased	maligtmr	[1.00]
4:	*	normal	regular	decreased	benign	[1.00]
5:	*	normal	smooth	normal	normal	[1.00]
6:	*	large	smooth	increased	venobstr	[1.00]
7:	*	large	irreg	decreased	maligtmr	[1.00]
8:	*	small	regular	decreased	arterobs	[1.00]
9:	30.	small	irreg	normal	infection	[1.00]
10:	130.	small	irreg	normal	maligtmr	[1.00]
11:	*	large	irreg	increased	normal	[1.00]
12:	*	small	smooth	decreased	benign	[1.00]

Figure 5.14. Examples screen in 1st-Class.

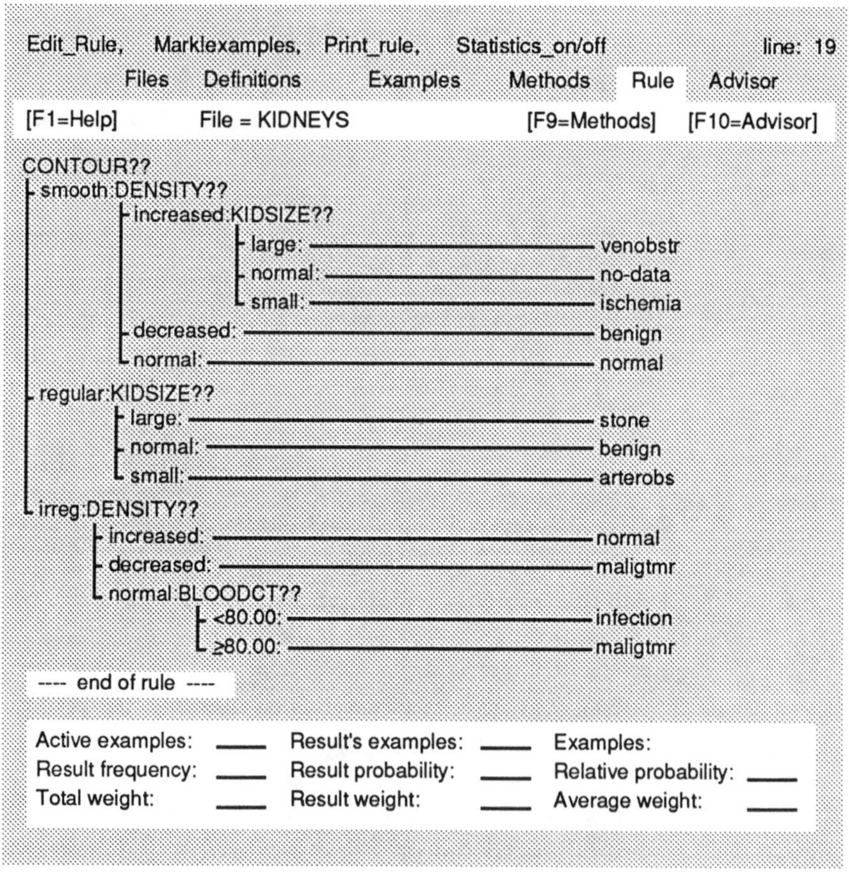

Edit_Rule,   Marklexamples,   Print_rule,   Statistics_on/off   line: 19

    Files   Definitions   Examples   Methods   Rule   Advisor

[F1=Help]   File = KIDNEYS   [F9=Methods]   [F10=Advisor]

```
CONTOUR??
├ smooth:DENSITY??
│        ├ increased:KIDSIZE??
│        │            ├ large: ─────────────────────── venobstr
│        │            ├ normal: ────────────────────── no-data
│        │            └ small: ─────────────────────── ischemia
│        ├ decreased: ──────────────────────────────── benign
│        └ normal: ─────────────────────────────────── normal
├ regular:KIDSIZE??
│        ├ large: ─────────────────────────────────── stone
│        ├ normal: ───────────────────────────────── benign
│        └ small: ──────────────────────────────────── arterobs
└ irreg:DENSITY??
         ├ increased: ─────────────────────────────── normal
         ├ decreased: ─────────────────────────────── maligtmr
         └ normal:BLOODCT??
                  ├ <80.00: ────────────────────────── infection
                  └ ≥80.00: ────────────────────────── maligtmr
---- end of rule ----
```

Active examples: ____   Result's examples: ____   Examples:

Result frequency: ____   Result probability: ____   Relative probability: ____

Total weight: ____   Result weight: ____   Average weight: ____

Figure 5.15. A decision tree in 1st-Class.

with his mentor. The mentor may approve this rule or else will suggest new examples to add to the knowledge base in order to refine the decision tree.

This ability of 1st-Class to utilize data that already exists in spreadsheet form is especially useful if the data collection is extensive, say more than a hundred rows. Not only does the data's importation save the developer the time of retyping, it also circumvents the possibility of transcription error. But perhaps its biggest advantage is that it facilitates the analysis of data that might otherwise have been too difficult to investigate. This is the "leveraging" effect: getting more information from a spreadsheet by transforming it into a decision-tree format.

This example, like Example 4, illustrates how an expert system shell can be integrated with other software. In Example 5, Paperback Software's VP EXPERT development shell is integrated with Lotus 1-2-3. But rather than using the data contained in a Lotus worksheet as a set of *examples* to induce a decision tree, Example 5 suggests how an expert system can be employed as an intelligent *front end* for an electronic spreadsheet.

EXAMPLE 5: VP EXPERT.

A demographer in Washington, D.C., is conducting a research project that involves collecting extensive census data in the form of birth, death, and migration records of the residents of a certain region of Bangladesh. She has twelve assistants out in the field who interview the residents and record their findings on forms which are, in turn, mailed to D.C. There, the data are transcribed into electronic spreadsheet form using Lotus 1-2-3 for the demographer's analysis.

Several sources of error may result in the data being incorrect (or "dirty") by the time the demographer sees it. First of all, the data collectors may occasionally enter some misinformation on their forms. Secondly, the respondents themselves may provide erroneous information. And finally, the staff that transcribes the data into Lotus 1-2-3 may inadvertently enter wrong data in a cell. As a result of this third error source, the SEX column of a worksheet, which is supposed to contain only the letters M (male) or F (female), may hold an occasional N or G instead. The demographer can use an expert system to clean up this type of error.

Suppose that the name of the Lotus 1-2-3 workfile which contains birth records is BIRTH.WKS and that its five columns are labelled:

ID SEX PLACE DOB MOTHER'S_ID

where ID is a 12-digit identification number associated with the subject, SEX contains the code M or F, PLACE is a 5-digit code corresponding to the place of birth, DOB is the date of birth, and MOTHER'S_ID is the 12-digit identification number of the subject's mother.

The demographer decides to "clean" the SEX column of BIRTH.WKS using Paperback Software's VP EXPERT development tool. After she specifies the name of her workfile using VP EXPERT's CCALL clause, she will need to use these five key words:

WKS	— reads information from a single cell, range, or specific row or column of a spreadsheet file
PWKS	— writes data into a single cell, range, or specific row or column of a spreadsheet file

FIND   — causes VP EXPERT's inference engine to look for a value of a variable. This may be accomplished, for example, by chaining to an ASK statement which queries the user for the value of a variable, or by finding a rule which assigns a value to the variable in its THEN or ELSE part

RESET   — removes any value assigned to a variable and returns it to UNKNOWN

WHILEKNOWN   — begins a loop that is repeated as long as the value of the variable in the WHILEKNOWN clause has a value.

Using these key words together with the Rule named SEXCHECK (see next page), the demographer writes the following ACTIONS block:

```
ACTIONS
   WKS Sexcheck.Column = SEX.BIRTH  ! This takes the SEX
                                    ! column of the
                                    ! spreadsheet named BIRTH
                                    ! and loads its values
                                    ! into an array in
                                    ! VP EXPERT named Sexcheck

   WHILEKNOWN Sexcheck[X]           ! Begin the loop and
                                    ! continue until the end
                                    ! of data

       FIND Check                   ! Get a value for the
                                    ! variable called "Check".
                                    ! In this case, the infer-
                                    ! ence engine chains to
                                    ! the rule named SEX_CHECK

       X = X + 1                    ! Move down to the next
                                    ! entry in the Sexcheck
                                    ! array

       RESET Check                  ! Change the value of
                                    ! Check from OKAY or
                                    ! OUT_OF_RANGE to
                                    ! UNKNOWN
   END                              ! This signals the end of
                                    ! the loop

   PWKS Sexcheck.Column = SEX.BIRTH; ! Now write the corrected
                                     ! records back to the
                                     ! spreadsheet
```

In order to enable this ACTIONS block to succeed in finding a value for the variable "Check," the demographer includes this rule in the knowledge base:

```
Rule SEX_CHECK
IF Sexcheck[X] = M OR Sexcheck[X] = F
THEN Check = OKAY
ELSE Check = OUT_OF_RANGE
        FIND NEW_SEX          ! Ask the user to correct
                              ! the sex code
    Sexcheck[X] = NEWSEX;     ! Insert the corrected
                              ! value into the Sexcheck
                              ! array
```

With slight modifications to the rule and ACTIONS block, the demographer can easily use VP EXPERT to check the rest of the data in BIRTH.WKS (ID, PLACE, DOB, MOTHER'S_ID) for out-of-range errors.

Example 5 suggests that the ability of an expert system tool to "hook" with other software, particularly spreadsheets, can be a great advantage in assuring accuracy of data.

The final example of this section demonstrates two hybrid tools at work, KnowledgeMaker and KnowledgePro. Here, examples are first converted to rules which are then combined with "topics" to create a modular, hierarchically organized knowledge base. Notice the leveraging effect as described in chapter 1: The inductive tool brings to life a seemingly amorphous collection of data.

EXAMPLE 6: KnowledgeMaker/KnowledgePro (courtesy of Knowledge Garden, Inc.).

A student advisor at a small college is concerned that several of her advisees have been withdrawing from college without graduating. She theorizes that whether a student graduates or withdraws is related to three factors: the student's rank in his high school class, his Scholastic Aptitude Test (SAT) scores, and whether the student is working at a job while attending school. In an attempt to confirm her theory, she organizes the data on her 15 most recent advisees as in Figure 5.16.

Here, the STATUS column has two possible entries: "drop" (meaning that the student has withdrawn before graduation) and "grad" (which means the student has graduated). The "top," "middle," and "bottom" entries in the RANK column indicate in which third of their high school classes her advisees graduated. The entries in the WORK column indicate whether a student had a part-time job while in college, while the SAT column describes whether the

STATUS	RANK	WORK	SAT
drop	bottom	yes	below
drop	middle	no	below
grad	middle	yes	above
drop	bottom	yes	above
grad	top	yes	above
grad	top	yes	below
grad	top	no	below
drop	middle	no	above
drop	bottom	no	below
grad	bottom	no	above
grad	top	yes	above
drop	top	yes	above
drop	top	yes	above
drop	top	yes	above
drop	top	yes	above

Figure 5.16. Records of the advisor's 15 students.

student's SAT scores were above or below the average of all students in the college.

Even after gathering this data, however, the advisor still is not certain that a correlation exists. The underlying organization of the information contained in this data is not evident. At this point, the advisor appeals to KnowledgeMaker, a tool which, like SuperExpert and 1st-Class, can induce the structure hidden in this data collection. After she enters the examples (in precisely the same fashion as above), she is asked by KnowledgeMaker to specify the format of the output.

KnowledgeMaker is capable of displaying the structure of the knowledge either as a decision tree or else as a collection of rules. Furthermore, should the advisor choose to have KnowledgeMaker output a rule collection, she will have the option of specifying whether she wants the rules to be tailored to any number of expert system shells (KnowledgePro, M1, Insight 2+, EXSYS) or whether she would prefer plain English. This feature demonstrates the versatility of KnowledgeMaker that was hinted at in chapter 2. Though it is not an expert system shell (it has no inference mechanism, and is, therefore, not capable of processing rules) it does have the ability to generate from examples a rule set which can be *directly* imported (with no editing) to a *number* of inference mechanisms.

Because the advisor has access to KnowledgePro, she opts for having KnowledgeMaker transform her examples into a rule set which she can then feed to KnowledgePro. KnowledgeMaker responds by displaying a screen similar to the one in Figure 5.17.

The screen in Figure 5.17 is a little different from others we have seen up to this point. The first difference is in nomenclature. What other development tools call "factors" or "attributes" or "variables," KnowledgePro refers to as "topics." The knowledge base above has four topics: "status," "work," "sat," and "rank." The last three of these topics, appearing at the bottom of the screen, are similar to each other:

— They each contain a "set_single_valued()" statement to indicate that each should receive precisely *one* value. In the case of "rank," for example, the value should be either "bottom," "middle," or "top."

— They each contain an "ask" statement whose effect is to display a question on the screen and to capture the user's answer as the value of the topic.

— The "ask" statements each contain a menu of legitimate responses to the question being asked. This menu is displayed at the time the question is asked.

The topic "status" contains all the rules that KnowledgeMaker induced from the examples. The question marks preceding the names of the topics in a rule (?rank, ?sat, ?work) indicate that the values of these topics need to be established before the rule can be processed. KnowledgePro accomplishes this by branching off to the topic in question and performing its actions (asking the user a question and capturing the answer). The decimal numbers appearing in the second rule of the "status" topic reflect the fact that there are six examples in which "rank" was "top," "sat" was "above," and "work" was "yes." In two of these three examples, the "status" was "grad"; in the other four, "status" was "drop."

Once the advisor's examples have been converted to KnowledgePro rules, she can use her system as a predictor of whether a student is going to graduate from college. With more experience, the advisor will have a larger collection of examples, and the rules may consequently be redefined. Alternatively, by using KnowledgePro, the advisor can add new topics directly to the knowledge base without going through KnowledgeMaker.

Example 6 indicated how KnowledgeMaker (an induction engine) and KnowledgePro (an inference engine within a knowledge processing environment) work together in developing an expert system. If developers can formulate the knowledge which the system is to contain as a collection of IF . . . THEN . . . ELSE rules without the assistance of an induction engine, then they need not use KnowledgeMaker; they can organize the relevant factors as a collection of "topics" and enter their rules directly into KnowledgePro. One advantage of the "topic" structure is that new topics can be added anywhere in the knowledge base without jeopardy;

```
goal is status  .  set_single_valued(?goal).

topic status  .
    If ?rank is top
    and ?sat is below
    then status is grad.

    If ?rank is top
    and ?sat is above
    and ?work is yes
    then status is [grad,'( .33)', drop,'( .67)'].

    If ?rank is middle
    and ?work is yes
    then status is grad.

    If ?rank is middle
    and ?work is no
    then status is drop.

    If ?rank is bottom
    and ?work is yes
    then status is drop.

    If ?rank is bottom
    and ?work is no
    and ?sat is above
    then status is grad.

    If ?rank is bottom
    and ?work is no
    and ?sat is below
    then status is drop.

    topic work  .
        set_single_valued().
        ask('What is the value of WORK ?', work, [yes,no]).
    end.  (*work*)

    topic sat  .
        set_single_valued().
        ask('What is the value of SAT ?', sat, [below,above]).
    end.  (*sat*)

    topic rank  .  set_single_valued().
        set_single_valued().
        ask('What is the value of RANK ?', rank,
            [bottom, middle, top]).
    end.  (*rank*)
end.  (*status*)
```

Figure 5.17. A KnowledgePro rule set.

by contrast, adding new *rules* may or may not alter the logic of the system depending upon where in the knowledge base the rule is inserted. Now that we have seen several examples of the knowledge acquisition process, we turn our attention to the second major stage in prototyping and building an expert system: developing a user interface.

THE USER INTERFACE

Chapter 2 suggested the importance of developing an appropriate and effective user interface as part of an expert system. If the system is difficult for the intended users to operate, chances are that they will fall back on their old ways of solving the problem and not use the system at all. They may simply not be willing to expend the intellectual effort required to use a new technology. Some clerical support groups, for example, continue to resist word processing software and refuse to part with their faithful, reliable typewriters. Most, however, have adapted to this technology, and we feel that this acceptance is in large measure due to the user friendliness of the more popular word processing packages. Just as their ease of use has endeared word processing software to this group, we expect that expert systems designed with the potential user in mind, that is with careful attention paid to the user interface, will be widely adopted by their potential users.

Besides ease of use, another aspect of an effective user interface is the facility for explanation of the system's reasoning as discussed in chapter 4. Although studies reveal that people tend to have a lot of faith in information generated by a computer, no serious user of an expert system will accept its recommendations if the system is unable to explain how it reached its conclusions. This is especially true if the advice of the system differs from what the user would have guessed. A necessary component of a user interface is the ability to answer the question "How did you reach this conclusion?"

Another request that a user may make of the system is for the system to explain *why* it is asking the user a certain question. The user may feel, for example, that a certain question is irrelevant to the problem at hand and may be curious as to why the expert system even raises it. A well-designed user interface can accommodate this type of request for additional information.

Below, we elaborate on the critical characteristics of an expert system's user interface as they are summarized in Figure 5.18.

Ease of Use/Communication with End User

What makes an expert system (or any other software, for that matter) easy to use? Is it an explicit set of instructions on each screen? A Help

---

1. Ease of use/Communication with end user

2. Explanation of system reasoning (How and Why)

Figure 5.18. Characteristics of a user interface.

facility? Menus? Graphics? Natural-language features? The answer to this question depends largely on the skill of the intended user and the user's familiarity with the program. If the system is intended for novices, the interface should probably assume nothing of the user and provide step-by-step instructions, perhaps even to the point of describing the location of the Escape key on the keyboard. You can imagine, however, that such an interface, though suitable for a neophyte, would quickly encumber the experienced PC user and be considered a hindrance to the system's performance. The ideal interface, then, permits users of different skill levels to choose their own degrees of instruction from the computer.

A good example of this is the TELE*ACCESS program implemented by the T. Rowe Price investment firm. An account holder interested in obtaining current prices of various T. Rowe Price Funds, current account balances, or related information, dials the TELE*ACCESS number and is informed by a recorded message how the system works. It involves entering a code by pressing certain numbers on the phone. For the first-time user, the instructional message is not only helpful, it is essential. The more experienced user, however, would find the message repetitious and a waste of time. TELE*ACCESS invites such a user to interrupt the message at any time by entering the code at will. In this way, the interface accommodates both those who need more assistance and those who know their way around the program.

An expert system can be made to function in a similar way. A developer can assume that end users know their way around the system but, just in case they don't, the system can incorporate various windowing techniques to provide the user with an explanation of an unfamiliar concept or to remind the user of the appropriate keys to press. Several examples that appear later in this chapter will illustrate this key idea.

Knowing the audience is an important first step in designing an interface. Developers cannot create an appropriate interface until they identify the range of experience of the users.

There are, however, some features which everyone, novice and professional alike, value in an interface. In fact, books have been written and courses taught on this very topic. We will not summarize these features here, but rather suggest four important guidelines:

1. Keep the screen content sparse. Nothing turns off users more quickly than 24 lines of single-spaced information on a screen. Such screens are intimidating to novices and boring to veterans.
2. Require as few keystrokes and the use of as few different keys as possible. Having to remember when to use the space bar or when to use the Return or Escape keys bewilders the inexperienced user and annoys the expert.
3. Use graphics whenever possible. Show an expert a collection of twenty rules, and he or she may or may not be able to make sense out of it; show that same expert a diagram depicting the same information as the rule set, and he or she will quickly grasp its content and meaning.
4. Use windows or hypertext for nonessential but relevant information. A good approach might be to assume that the user of the system is knowledgeable and requires neither extensive elaboration on the questions that the system is asking nor a blow-by-blow description of the keystrokes required to communicate with the system. But then offer these elaborations and descriptions in a collection of pull-down windows or in a hypertext format to the less knowledgeable user. In this way, the details are hidden until such time as a user may need to see them. Imaginative use of windows and hypertext allow the end users to essentially customize the interface for their own purposes.

One method that some employ during the development of an expert system is to include a member of the targeted user group on the development team. In this way, the developer will be mindful of the user as the system develops and will be able to take the user's suggestions and criticisms into account as he develops the interface. Other developers employ an elaborate validation process which involves the targeted users (see chapter 6 for a discussion of evaluation).

Explaining HOW

Suppose, at the end of a consultation session, the user asks the expert system how it reached its conclusions. Because a rule-based system keeps track of the fired rules of its knowledge base, it may list all such rules in the order in which they were fired, and in this way trace the logic leading to its conclusion. Though this method of explanation is often very meaningful to the developer, it tends to overwhelm the end user and may, consequently, be ineffective.

Another method that some inductive shells use to reveal their reasoning is to display the decision tree which they induced from the examples provided by the developer. Because of its graphic format, this manner of representation of logic tends to be more comprehensible to the users. A very large decision tree, however, may confuse the users and leave them dissatisfied with the system's justification of its conclusion.

A more sophisticated method of explaining reasoning is to use natural language. Some shells respond to HOW questions by presenting the rules which they have fired, but rather than displaying them in the a cryptic IF . . . THEN format, they first translate them into more fluid English. If, for a simple example, an expert system to classify vehicles contains the rules:

IF the vehicle travels on land THEN the vehicle is a motor vehicle and IF a motor vehicle has two wheels THEN the vehicle is a motorcycle,

and if the user volunteers that the vehicle travels on land and has two wheels, the system naturally concludes that the vehicle is a motorcycle. In response to the user's request for an explanation of its reasoning, a natural-language explanation facility, rather than merely displaying the pertinent rule, might rephrase it as follows:

"I concluded that the vehicle was a motorcycle because you said that the vehicle travels on land and has two wheels. Any vehicle that travels on land is a motor vehicle; any motor vehicle with two wheels is a motorcycle."

Natural language is more satisfying (and ultimately more convincing) than a mere display of rules.

Explaining WHY

HOW questions are generally asked after the system has reached its conclusions, that is, at the end of the session. WHY questions, in contrast, are asked in reaction to a question that the system poses to the user during the session. Returning to the vehicle classification problem, when the system asks the user:

"Does the vehicle travel
on land
on water
through the air,"

the user should be able to ask the system "Why?" The system, in turn, should be able to respond to the user's question either by displaying the rules that require this information before firing, by displaying its decision tree, or by using natural language. The ideal interface would respond to the user's query using words like these:

"I am asking this question in order to establish whether the vehicle is a motor vehicle, a boat, or an aircraft."

Implementing the User Interface

Most expert system development tools come equipped with explanation facilities. Some display rules, some trees, others use natural language or text windows. So, to an extent, when developers adopt a tool they simultaneously choose a method of explanation. If they are satisfied with the quality of explanation that the tool offers, they have little work to do in this stage of the development cycle. But, as described in chapter 4, most tools offer the feature of linkage to other programs, and, if so inclined, a developer can take advantage of this property to customize an interface. By hooking the expert system to, say, a window program, a developer can transcend the limitations of the shell and make the explanations not only convincing, but visually appealing as well.

The following examples suggest different approaches to designing an interface that will respond to the end user's WHY or HOW questions.

EXAMPLE 7: PC PLUS (courtesy of Texas Instruments, Inc.).

The Money Market Funds Advisor is a demonstration expert system produced by Texas Instruments, Inc., to demonstrate its Personal Consultant Plus development software. The intention of the advisor is to suggest either conservative or aggressive money market funds to a user based on (1) current interest rate movements, and (2) the amount of risk the user can afford to take. When users consult the system, they are first prompted for their names and ages; the session then continues:

PC PLUS: How much money can you invest?

USER: 2000

PC PLUS: Are you employed?

USER: Yes

PC PLUS: At retirement will you be eligible for government old-age assistance?
YES
NO

(At this question, the user, curious to know why this information is requested, asks the system WHY. The reason the question is being asked, of course, is to enable PC PLUS to fire a rule which contains this information in its IF part. So PC PLUS displays the pertinent rule and, because the developer earlier "translated" the names of the variables into English (see Example 1 above), the system prefaces the rule with an English explanation:

PC PLUS: Whether you are eligible for government old-age assistance is needed to determine the amount of risk you can accommodate in your investments.

RULE016
IF 1) you are employed, and
2) you are eligible for government old-age assistance and,
3) you do not have a good retirement plan at work, and
4) you do not have significant savings,
THEN it is definite (100%) that the amount of risk you can accommodate is LOW.

USER: (satisfied that the question is pertinent) NO

PC PLUS: Do you have a good retirement plan at work?
YES
NO

USER: YES

PC PLUS: Do you have significant savings?

USER: No

PC PLUS: What is the direction of short-term interest rate movements?

<—> . . . . UP
<—> . . . . FLAT
<—> . . . . DOWN

(Use an arrow key to indicate your degree of certainty)

USER: (positions cursor over the beginning of the line labelled FLAT and strikes the arrow key 7 times, indicating that he is 70 percent certain that the short-term rate movements have been flat.)

PC PLUS: The last time the central bank changed the discount rate, did the rate increase or decrease?
INCREASE
DECREASE
UNKNOWN

(Again the user is curious about the purpose of this question and so asks WHY. PC PLUS responds as below.)

PC PLUS: The direction of the most recent change in the discount rate is needed to determine if the central bank is making expansive moves—lowering the bank discount rate, decreasing reserve requirements, or lowering stock market margin requirements.
RULE022
IF the direction of the most recent change in the discount rate is DECREASE
THEN it is definite (100%) that the central bank is making expansive moves—lowering the bank discount rate, decreasing reserve requirements, or lowering stock market margin requirements.

USER: UNKNOWN

PC PLUS: Is the central bank making expansive moves, such as lowering the bank discount rate, decreasing reserve requirements, or lowering stock market margin requirements?
YES
NO

USER: NO

PC PLUS: My recommendation is as follows:
When interest rates are not falling, a money market fund is one of the best investments.
Since your risk profile indicates that you can accommodate a certain degree of risk in your investment strategy, invest in an aggressive money market fund. Select from those funds offering the highest yields.
   You can find a comparison of current yields in the Money Market Funds column of the *Wall Street Journal.*

So the technique PC PLUS uses to respond to the user's WHY questions, those questions that allow the user to understand why the system is asking for certain information, results in a display of an English-like version of the rule that the inference engine is attempting to fire.

We now turn to an example illustrating how an expert system might respond not only to a user's WHY question, but also to a user's request for a justification of the system's recommendation at the end of a session. Here the user wants to know HOW the system reached its conclusion.

EXAMPLE 8: VP EXPERT.

An independent agency has been hired by a local newspaper to rate films that are playing in town. The newspaper would like each film to be rated either G, PG, PG-13, or R depending on the following factors:

a. Does the film portray sexual situations?
b. Does the film contain violent scenes?
c. Does the film have an adult theme?
d. Is there any nudity in the film?
e. Is there any strong language in the film?

After consultation between the agency and the newspaper, eight rules were established for the rating system and entered into a knowledge base using Paperback Software's VP EXPERT shell as in Figure 5.19.

(As this example will demonstrate, the purpose of the BECAUSE clauses attached to each of these rules is to enable the system to respond to WHY questions.)

A member of the agency has just reviewed a film and consults the expert system for advice concerning the appropriate rating. Because he is using VP EXPERT, the reviewer first turns on the TRACE function and then begins the consultation:

VP EXPERT: Does the film portray sexual situations?
REVIEWER: No
VP EXPERT: Does the film contain violent scenes?

(Suppose at this point the reviewer asks VP EXPERT *why* it is asking this question. Because the system is deciding whether to fire Rule 2, it responds by displaying the text attached to the BECAUSE clause of this rule: "I am asking this question because a film containing both an adult theme and violent scenes is rated R." The reviewer then responds.

REVIEWER: No
VP EXPERT: Is there any nudity in the film?

(Suppose the reviewer again asks why this question is being asked. VP EXPERT is testing Rule 5 and so it responds: "I am asking this question because a film containing nudity but no violence is rated PG-13.", the BECAUSE clause of this rule.)

REVIEWER: Yes
VP EXPERT: The rating is PG-13

Before accepting this recommendation, the reviewer wants to examine the logic the system used to reach its conclusion. This he does by invoking VP EXPERT's TREE function. The reviewer is then given the option of examining the trace in text or in graphical form. If he chooses text form, VP EXPERT displays the screen in Figure 5.20.

The diagram indicates that the inference engine first tested Rule 1 by asking whether the film contained sexual situations. Since the reviewer responded "no"

ACTIONS
     FIND rating;

Rule 1
IF sexual = yes
THEN rating = R
BECAUSE " I am asking this question because an R rating is
automatically given to films depicting sexual situations."

Rule 2
IF violence = yes AND adult = yes
THEN rating = R
BECAUSE " I am asking this question because a film containing both
an adult theme and violent scenes is rated R.";

Rule 3
IF violence = yes AND nudity = yes
THEN rating = R
BECAUSE "I am asking this question because a film with both
violence and nudity is rated R.";

Rule 4
IF violence = yes AND adult = no AND nudity = no
THEN rating = PG-13
BECAUSE "I am asking this question because if the film does not
have an adult theme and does not contain any nudity, the violent
scenes result in a PG-13 rating.";

Rule 5
IF violence = no AND nudity = yes
THEN rating = PG-13
BECAUSE "I am asking this question because a film containing
nudity but no violence is rated PG-13.";

Rule 6
IF violence = no AND nudity = no AND adult = yes
THEN rating = PG
BECAUSE "I am asking this question because a film with an adult
theme but no violence or nudity is rate PG.";

Rule 7
IF violence = no AND nudity = no AND language = yes
THEN rating = PG
BECAUSE "I am asking this question because a film containing
strong language but no violence or nudity is rated PG.";

Rule 8
IF violence = no AND nudity = no AND adult = no AND language = no
THEN rating = G
BECAUSE "I am asking this question becasue a film with no
violence, nudity, strong language or adult theme gets a G rating.";

Figure 5.19. A Knowledge base in VP EXPERT.

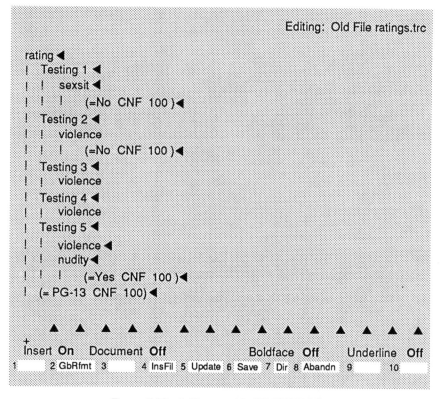

Figure 5.20. A Text tree in VP EXPERT.

to this question, the engine did not fire Rule 1 but went on to test Rule 2. When the reviewer responded that the film contained no violent scenes, the engine did not even ask about adult themes because it realized that in order to fire Rule 2, the answer concerning violence would have to be "yes." For the same reason, the system overlooks Rules 3 and 4. Rule 5, however, gets fired if the answer to violence is "no" and the answer to nudity is "yes." So VP EXPERT asks the nudity question and, when the reviewer replies "yes," Rule 5 fires, and the system concludes that the rating is PG-13.

Should the reviewer elect to examine the trace in *graphical* form, the screen would appear as in Figure 5.21.

Whether the reviewer elects to inspect the text or graphic format of the trace, he is presented with a clear indication of the path which VP EX-PERT's inference mechanism followed to reach its conclusion; he has learned HOW the system made its deduction. At the same time, by in-corporating BECAUSE clauses into the knowledge base, the developer

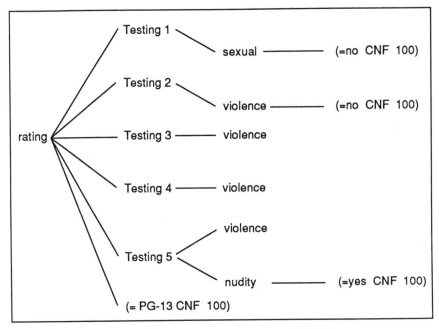

Figure 5.21. A graphical tree in VP EXPERT.

has allowed the user to ask **WHY** questions at any time during the consultation.

As another demonstration of explaining a system's reasoning, consider the method of directly attaching natural-language text passages to each of the expert system's recommendations as illustrated in example 9.

EXAMPLE 9: 1st-Class.

The Commission on Historic and Architectural Preservation in Liberty, Georgia, is responsible for designating certain buildings as historic landmarks. To ensure consistency in its decisions, the commission decides to build an expert system using the 1st-Class development software from 1st-Class Expert Systems, Inc.

In order for the commission to designate a structure as a landmark, the building must meet at least two of the following four criteria:

1. The building must have been designed by a prominent architect (one listed in *Who's Who of American Architects*).
2. The building must be architecturally significant.
3. The building must contribute in a positive way to its streetscape.
4. The building must reflect the lifestyle of its historical period.

After identifying these four critical factors and entering examples, the commission tests its expert system and finds that it works satisfactorily. But, so that future users will gain confidence in the system, the commission agrees that it is important that the expert system be able to explain its conclusions in plain English.

Using a wordprocessor, the commission creates a file called EXPLANATION which contains two sections: Section 1 explains why a building has been judged to be worthy of landmark designation and Section 2, why a building fails to be so designated. EXPLANATION appears in Figure 5.22.

Returning to the Definitions screen of 1st-Class, the commission attaches this text to the APPROVE result:

The building you have described should be designated a Liberty Historic Landmark. (Press F2 for an explanation)

{2:HELPW EXPLANATION 1}

Similarly, the commission links the following text to the DENY result:

The building you have described should not be designated a Liberty Historic Landmark. (Press F2 for an explanation)

{2:HELPW EXPLANATION 2}

Although the text in the curly brackets is not visible to the user of the system, 1st-Class interprets the information in the curly brackets to mean: If the F2 key is pressed, find the text file named EXPLANATION, pull down and open a text window, and display the specified section. After receiving the system's recommendation, the user, therefore, has the option of requesting an explanation of how the system reached its conclusion.

Attaching a natural-language explanation to each of an expert system's *recommendations* is a painstaking process, but it offers the most satisfying explanation of a system's reasoning to the end user. By attaching windowed text to the *questions* which the system asks, this natural-language technique also works for answering WHY questions.

The final example of this section demonstrates a sophisticated and effective means of communication between the expert system and the end user: the *hypertext* concept. Hypertext affords the developer the opportunity to accommodate end users of various levels of sophistication. As indicated in chapter 4, the basic idea behind hypertext is this: The developer notes any word or phrase which the system displays and which may need elaboration; such words or phrases are known as "buttons." The developer then attaches text to each of these buttons, text which the user can reveal simply be depressing one key. This explanatory text may *itself* contain buttons which can trigger the display of yet additional information. In this way, information can, in effect, be "layered" at different depths.

#1

According to guidelines, in order for a buidling to be registered as a historic landmark in Liberty, at least two of the following four criteria must be met:

(1) The building must have been designed by a prominent architect (one listed in *Who's Who of American Architects*).

(2) The building must be architecturally significant.

(3) The building must contribute in a positive way to its streetscape.

(4) The building must reflect the lifestyle of its historical period.

Since the building you have described meets at least two of these four criteria, it should be designated a Liberty Historic Landmark.

#2

According to guidelines, in order for a building to be registered as a historic landmark in Liberty, at least two of the following four criteria must be met:

(1) The building must have been designed by a prominent architect (one listed in *Who's Who of American Architects*).

(2) The building must be architecturally significant.

(3) The building must contribute in a positive way to its streetscape.

(4) The building must reflect the lifestyle of its historical period.

Since the building you have described fails to meet at least two of these four criteria, it should not be designated a Liberty Historic Landmark.

Figure 5.22. An explanation text file.

After the hypertext window opens, depressing another specified key closes the explanation window and returns the user to the previous screen.

EXAMPLE 10: KnowledgeMaker/KnowledgePro.

A developer using KnowledgePro has built an expert system to assist individuals in filing their 1987 Federal Income Tax forms. The knowledge base

includes a topic (called FILING) which addresses the question of whether an individual must file a return. One of the rules in this topic is:
If ?marital_status is single
and ?filing_status is headofhousehold
and ?age <65
and ?income > = 4400
then filing is yes.

In order to determine the values of the variables preceded by a question mark (marital_status, filing_status, age, income), the developer includes short topics for each. The topic "income," for example, may look like this:

topic income .
set_single_valued() .
ask('What was your gross income in 1987?' , income).
end. (*income*)

Most taxpayers using this system will understand the meaning of the phrase "gross income" in the "ask" statement of this topic. But to accommodate those who do not, the developer turns this phrase into a hypertext button. In KnowledgePro, this is a two- step process:

1. Sandwich the button in between a pair of "#m" symbols.
2. Write another topic that will display the text for this button.

So the topic "income" above will be modified to look like this:

topic income .
set_single_valued() .
ask('What was your #mgross income#m in 1987?' , income).
end. (*income*)

And the following topic will need to be added to the knowledge base:

topic 'gross income' .
window() .
say ('Gross income usually means money, goods, and property you received
    on which you must pay tax. It does not include non-taxable benefits (such
    as tax-exempt interest)').
close_window() .
end. (*'gross income'*)

When the "income" question is asked of the user, the phrase "gross income" will be highlighted on the screen. By pressing the F4 function key, the user activates the topic "gross income" and the system responds by opening a window on the screen and displaying the text contained in the "say" statement of this topic. The user reads the text and then returns to the topic "income" by pressing the space bar.

Hypertext is an effective means of accommodating users of different levels of sophistication. It can offer explicit information to less knowledgeable users while not encumbering the more advanced users of the system with superfluous text. Of all the tools discussed in this book, only KnowledgePro supports hypertext.

As the preceding examples have illustrated, a variety of methods exist for acquiring knowledge and building an effective user interface. The choice depends largely on the answer to these questions:

1. What development tool is being used?
2. Where does the knowledge to be incorporated into the system exist?
3. Who are the intended users of the completed system?

Let us return now to Z-EXPERT to examine how the knowledge was acquired and the interface developed for this particular expert system.

Z-EXPERT CASE STUDY — PART THREE
SYSTEM PROTOTYPING AND BUILDING

Prototyping

Since the developers of Z-EXPERT were to play the role of area experts in this project, the next step in building the system was to transfer their own knowledge and experience in configuring Zenith Data Systems (ZDS) packages into the 1st-Class development tool. The developers began by identifying all the possible results or recommendations that Z-EXPERT would ultimately offer to its users. Referring to the current ZDS product description sheets, which included information on the various basic systems as well as many of the options (for example, monitors, video cards, numeric coprocessors, etc.), was their means of ensuring that Z-EXPERT would contain the complete product line. The result was a collection of 72 different system configurations.

Having identified the results of the system, the developers turned their attention to an identification of the factors. It seemed that there were innumerable factors that the Z-EXPERT should consider before recommending a computer system: factors such as the type and size of disk drives, whether expansion slots were desirable or necessary, the type of video card and monitor, the intended application areas of the system, etc.

Though all of these factors (and more) would eventually have to be considered, for the purpose of building a prototype the developers made the two following assumptions:

— There would be only three factors: the *class* of the machine (8088, 8088e, 80286, and 80386), the type of *disk storage* (dual floppies, 20MB, 40MB, or 80MB hard disk), and the type of *video* (mono-cga, mono-ega, color-cga, color-ega, color-vga, or flat-tension monitor).
— The users of the system would be technically oriented and would know the differences among the various types of classes, drives, and video options.

The first of these assumptions allowed the developers to test the concept of Z-EXPERT without the complications that a more realistic set of factors would necessarily entail; the second assumption temporarily released Z-EXPERT from the requirement of having to explain the distinction, say, between color-vga and color-ega. At this point, then, the Definitions screen for Z-EXPERT's knowledge base took the form shown in Figure 5.23.

The corresponding decision tree appeared as in Figure 5.24.

The "#" preceding the names of the various classes in the RESULT column and the rule direct 1st-Class to branch to a knowledge base of that name. So, for example, if the user responded to the question, "What is the class of the machine you are interested in?" by selecting the value "8088," 1st-Class would then chain to the knowledge base named 8088. The same situation would be true if the user chose any of the other classes. Suppose that the user designated the 8088 as his choice for the class. In the 8088 class of ZDS systems, the 40MB and the 80MB hard disks are unavailable. The Definitions screen for 8088, therefore, looks like Figure 5.25.

The purpose of the EXPANSION factor is to determine whether the user anticipates requiring expansion slots in the system, while the DRV_TYPE factor answers the question of whether the user prefers 5.25-inch or 3.5-inch disk drives. The RESULT column lists the codes of all the ZDS configurations in the 8088 class.

For each of the 31 results in this knowledge base, the developers entered a descriptive example. To illustrate, the example associated with the result zsc157_2, one particular ZDS system configuration, was:

MONITOR	DISK	EXPANSION	DRVTYPE	RESULT
color_cga	dualflop	yes	five	zsc157_2.

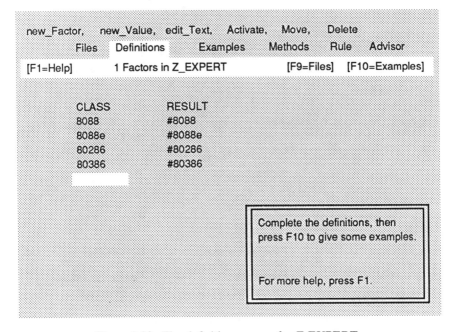

new_Factor,   new_Value,   edit_Text,   Activate,   Move,   Delete

Files   Definitions   Examples   Methods   Rule   Advisor

[F1=Help]   1 Factors in Z_EXPERT   [F9=Files]   [F10=Examples]

CLASS	RESULT
8088	#8088
8088e	#8088e
80286	#80286
80386	#80386

Complete the definitions, then press F10 to give some examples.

For more help, press F1.

Figure 5.23. The definitions screen for Z-EXPERT.

The decision tree that 1st-Class induced from this data is depicted in Figure 5.26.

To complete the prototype, a similar knowledge base was created for each of the other three classes of ZDS machines.

Expanding the Prototype

Encouraged by the performance of the prototype, and having achieved a "proof-of-concept," the developers next approached the task of building a full system which would not be restricted to a few factors and which was intended for a much less knowledgeable user.

Rather than Z-EXPERT asking users to identify the class of machine in which they were interested, the full system would have to ask fewer technical questions concerning intended application areas, and then *deduce* an appropriate class. The same was true for the monitor and disk selections.

Two compelling reasons suggested that Z-EXPERT be modularized by creating separate knowledge bases for the class, monitor, and disk options:

1. As indicated earlier, Z-EXPERT would contain 72 possible system configurations. Since the 1st-Class development tool allowed a max-

Edit_rule,   Mark!examples,   Print_rule,   Statistics_on/off   line: 2
      Files   Definitions   Examples   Methods   Rule   Advisor
[F1=Help]   File=Z-EXPERT   [F9=Methods]   [F10=Advisor]

— start of rule —
CLASS??
├ 8088: ————————————————————— #8088
├ 8088e: ———————————————————— #8088e
├ 80286: ———————————————————— #80286
└ 80386: ———————————————————— #80386
—— end of rule ——

Active examples:	4	Result's examples:	1	Examples:	1
Result frequency:	0.25	Result probability:	0.25	Relative probability:	1.00
Total weight:	4.00	Result weight	1.00	Average weight:	1.00

Figure 5.24. The decision tree for Z-EXPERT.

imum of 32 results per knowledge base, the developers would somehow need to partition the knowledge to accommodate this restriction.

2. Handling questions concerning class, monitor, and disk all in the
same knowledge base was very unwieldy. Too many possible com-
binations of these factors existed to make any sense out of a single
knowledge base.

Because 1st-Class has excellent chaining facilities which allow moving knowledge bases in and out of memory, modularization fit the situation very nicely and was adopted as a viable approach to developing
Z-EXPERT.

Class

After a great deal of discussion, the developers agreed upon a list of
factors which were pertinent in identifying an appropriate class of machine.
These factors included:

1. The primary types of applications (word processing, spreadsheet applications, database manipulations, graphics or design, programming,
statistical analysis, or any combination of these),

MONITOR	DISK	EXPANSION	DRV_TYPE	RESULT
mono_cga	dualflop	no	three	z157_2
mono_ega	20meg	yes	five	z157_3
color_cga				z157_12
color_ega				z157_13
color_vga				zsm157_2
ftm_vga				zsc157_2
				zsm157_3
				zsc157_3
				zsm159_2
				zsc159_2
				zsm159_3
				zsc159_3
				zsm15912
				zsc15912
				zsm15913
				zsc15913
				z157_2m
				z157_3m
				z159_12m
				z159_13m
				eazypc2
				z181
				eazypc20
				z183
				Ex2/181
				Ez20/183
				zf159f
				zw159f
				zc15912_
				zc15912v
				zc15913v.

Figure 5.25. The definitions screen for 8088.

2. The level (if any) at which word processing would be used (routine, sophisticated, desktop publishing),
3. The amount of computing power these applications require (average or above average),
4. Whether the intended applications were calculation-intensive,
5. Whether the system would serve as a multiuser workstation, and
6. Whether a RAM disk would be used.

A knowledge base called CLASS was constructed which included these factors as well as examples that the developers believed associated the

```
            Rule for knowledge base 8088
            ---- start of rule ----
   1:       video??
   2:       |mono_cga:disk??
   3:       |          |dualflop:drv_type??_____
   4:       |          |        |three:                    Ez2/181
   5:       |          |        |five:expansion??_____
   6:       |          |              |No:                 z157_2m
   7:       |          |              |Yes:                z157_2
   8:       |          |                  & _____ z157_2m
   9:       |          |20meg:drv_type??_____
  10:       |                   |three:                    Ez20/183
  11:       |                   |five:expansion??_____
  12:       |                         |No:                 z157_3m
  13:       |                         |Yes:                z157_3
  14:       |                             & _____ z157_3m
  15:       |mono_ega:disk??    _____
  16:       |          |dualflop:                         z159_12
  17:       |          |        & _____ zsm15912
  18:       |          |20meg:                            z159_13
  19:       |              & _____ zsm15913
  20:       |color_cga:disk??   _____
  21:       |          |dualflop:                         z157_2
  22:       |                   & _____ zsc157_2
  23:       |          |20meg:                            z157_3
  24:       |              & _____ zsc157_3
  25:       |color_ega:disk??   _____
  26:       |          |dualflop:                         z159_12
  27:       |          |        & _____ zsc15912
  28:       |          |20meg:                            z159_13
  29:       |              & _____ zsc15913
  30:       |color_vga:disk??   _____
  31:       |          |dualflop:                         z159_12
  32:       |          |        & _____ zc15912v
  33:       |          |20meg:                            z159_13
  34:       |              & _____ zc15913v
  35:       |ftm_vga:disk??     _____
  36:                  |dualflop:                         z159_12
  37:       |        & _____ zf159f
  38:                  |20meg:                            z159_13
  39:              & _____ zw159f
            ---- end of rule ----
```

Figure 5.26. The decision tree for the 8088 knowledge base.

factors with an appropriate class of machine. With the knowledge base CLASS, users would not be expected to specify whether they wanted an 8088, 8088e, 80286, or 80386 class machine; rather, they would respond to several questions concerning their intended applications, and 1st-Class would place them in an appropriate class of system as determined by the developers.

Monitor

In constructing the knowledge base called MONITOR, whose purpose was to determine which of the six available video options most closely matched the user's needs, the four factors that emerged as critical were:

1. Whether the user wanted a monochrome or a color monitor,
2. Whether the intended applications ɤ the computer system would generate graphics, and, if so,
3. Whether the applications would require high-resolution graphics,
4. Whether a flat-tension, glare-free monitor was desirable.

These factors were incorporated into a knowledge base with six possible results: monochrome cga, monochrome ega, color cga, color ega, color vga, and flat tension. By means of examples, the developers indicated which of these results best fit the values that users might supply to the four factors above, and then allowed 1st-Class to induce the corresponding decision tree. In this way, a user could be led to the most suitable video and monitor options without even knowing the difference among cga, ega, or vga.

Disk

The final knowledge base that needed to be developed was the one to determine which of four disk drive arrangements (dual floppy drives, or 20MB, 40MB, or 80MB hard drives) best matched the user's needs. Here, the developers identified four pertinent factors:

1. Whether the machine would be used as a network file server,
2. Whether the user's files tended to be "large",
3. Whether the user's applications included any "windowing" packages
4. Whether any of the user's applications came packaged on several diskettes.

After accepting the examples that reflected the developers' experiences on the subject of disk drive options, 1st-Class induced the decision tree that it would later use to assist users in determining the appropriate drive configuration for their purposes.

Z-EXPERT, then, eventually contained seven knowledge bases: CLASS, 8088, 8088e, 80286, 80386, MONITOR, and DRIVE, as illustrated in Figure 5.27.

When the system is run, Z-EXPERT invokes the knowledge base called CLASS, which asks questions to determine which one of the four knowledge bases (8088, 8088e, 80286, or 80386) it should chain to. Once in one of these four knowledge bases, MONITOR and DRIVE query the user, deduce from the user's answers the most appropriate video and drive options, and pass this information back to the appropriate class. Here, all the values are processed and the expert system displays its recommendation to the user. What began as a simple prototype evolved into a more complex system with several chained knowledge bases.

Developing the User Interface

At this point in the project, the developers were satisfied that Z-EXPERT performed well enough for them to start concentrating on the user interface. The development of the interface involved four different tasks:

— Making the system's questions as clear to the user as possible
— Making the system's recommendations as clear to the user as possible
— Explaining why the system was asking each question
— Explaining how the system reached its conclusion

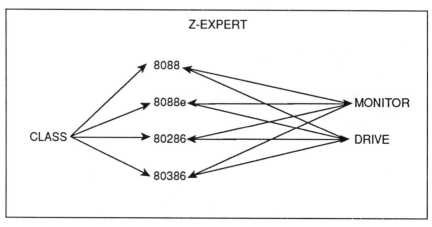

Figure 5.27. Relationship of knowledge bases in Z-EXPERT.

Clarifying the System's Questions

In 1st-Class, factor names and values are restricted to 11 characters, but a developer can associate as much text as desired with any *factor*, and up to one line of text can be associated with each *value* of a factor. Then, when the system needs to ask the end user a question, rather than display the 11-character word (which may have been perfectly acceptable to the developers but not to end users), it simply displays the text that the developer has linked to that factor and its values.

As an example, the knowledge base CLASS contains a factor named APPLICATION whose possible values appear in 1st-Class as follows:

> APPLICATION
> wp
> sp
> db
> graph
> prog
> stat
> combo

The idea behind this factor is to determine the users' primary area(s) of application for their computers. As they appear above, however, the values have no meaning to the end user. So, with the factor APPLICATION, the developer associates this text:

"Select your primary application from the list below. By indicating a primary category of use, you will not be excluding other uses for your system. If you will be using more than one application consistently, select the 'combination' option.

And with the values for this factor, the following text is linked:

wp — Word processing
sp — Spreadsheet applications
db — Database manipulation
graph — Graphics or design
prog — Programming
stat — Statistical analysis
combo — Any combination of the applications above

When Z-EXPERT needs to learn the user's primary areas of application, 1st-Class displays the screen depicted in Figure 5.28.

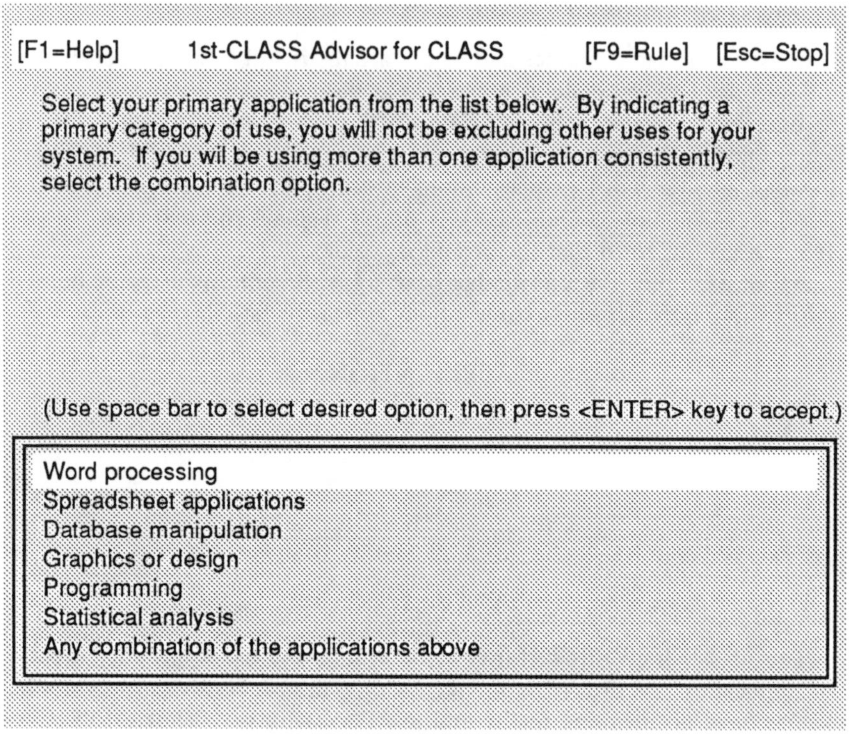

```
[F1=Help]       1st-CLASS Advisor for CLASS       [F9=Rule]   [Esc=Stop]

   Select your primary application from the list below.  By indicating a
   primary category of use, you will not be excluding other uses for your
   system.  If you will be using more than one application consistently,
   select the combination option.




   (Use space bar to select desired option, then press <ENTER> key to accept.)
 ┌──────────────────────────────────────────────────────────────────────┐
 │ Word processing                                                        │
 │ Spreadsheet applications                                               │
 │ Database manipulation                                                  │
 │ Graphics or design                                                     │
 │ Programming                                                            │
 │ Statistical analysis                                                   │
 │ Any combination of the applications above                              │
 └──────────────────────────────────────────────────────────────────────┘
```

Figure 5.28. The APPLICATIONS question in Z-EXPERT

This screen is effective in its format and its directions are explicit. By repeating this process of linking text with *each* factor and *each* value in Z-EXPERT, the developers were able to make this system as unintimidating as possible.

Clarifying the Results

As indicated above, the results in Z-EXPERT took the form of some code that represented possible ZDS configurations and whose meanings were known only to the developers of the system. Clearly, a recommendation to the end user such as "zsc15913" or "Ez2/181" would be meaningless.

However, in precisely the same manner as above, the developers associated with each of the 72 possible results in Z-EXPERT a screen of text which detailed the recommended computer system configuration. Consequently, if the user's responses to Z-EXPERT's questions led to result zsc15913, the expert system displayed the text linked to the recommendation shown in Figure 5.29.

Answering WHY Questions

What if an end user was curious as to why Z-EXPERT was asking a certain question? What if, for example, when the question concerning intended applications for the computer system was asked, the user wanted to know why this information was important. Not only could Z-EXPERT accommodate such requests, it actually invited the users to ask "Why" by allowing them to do so by a single keystroke. Here's how: To the text associated with the factor APPLICATION, the developers added two additional lines:

PRESS F2 FOR EXPLANATION OF QUESTION
{2: HELPW REASON 3 1 16 79 25}.

The text contained in the curly brackets is not displayed to the system's user, but is interpreted by 1st-Class to mean:
If the F2 key is pressed, open a window with upper left-hand corner at column 1 and row 16 of the screen, and lower right-hand corner at column 79 row 25. Then use the HELPW utility program to display in this

---

ZSC-159 Model 13   DESKTOP PC

        —   Easy to use, professional desktop PC
        —   0 Wait State 8088 microprocessor
        —   4.77/8 MHz switchable clock speed
        —   Single 5.25 inch (360K) floppy disk drive and controller
        —   20M hard disk
        —   768K RAM expandable to 1.2MB on main memory board
        —   Total system RAM expansion to 5MB
        —   Parallel port
        —   9-pin serial port
        —   Socket for 8087 numeric co-processor
        —   Three vacant expansion slots
        —   Professional detached keyboard
        —   EGA+ video card (640 X 480)
        —   ZVM-1380-c EGA color monitor (640 X 350 resolution)

Figure 5.29. Detailed text of result zsc15913.

window the text found in the third paragraph of the file named REA-SON.

The file REASON contained one paragraph for each factor in Z-EXPERT: Paragraph 1 corresponded to the first factor, paragraph 2 to the second, etc. Each of these paragraphs contained an explanation of why the particular factor was considered pertinent in recommending a computer system. The paragraph associated with the APPLICATION factor, for example, read:

"By asking you about your primary computing application, Z-EXPERT will be better able to infer an appropriate overall class of machine to meet your needs. You should not think, however, that by selecting any one application you will not be able to run other applications on your system. Other questions within Z-EXPERT are also used to help make this primary judgment."

This ability to link external files and programs to expert systems developed using 1st-Class greatly facilitates explaining both WHY a question is being asked and HOW the system reached its conclusion.

Explaining How

The last aspect of the user interface development involved explaining *how* Z-EXPERT reached its conclusions. The developers realized that a person using Z-EXPERT may well be suspicious of a ZDS computer making a recommendation concerning the purchase of another ZDS computer. Might not the expert system be written so that it tends to recommend those computer systems with the highest profit margin? In order to alleviate such skepticism, the developers went to great lengths to introduce an explanation facility into Z-EXPERT that would justify its recommendation. As in the case of responding to WHY questions, the developers relied on the ability of 1st-Class to "hook" an external file, in this case a Pascal program named EXPLAIN, for purposes of explaining *how* the system came to offer its advice.

Each time Z-EXPERT asked the end user a question relating to a factor, both the factor and its value were not only stored in the computer's memory, but were also written to an external file called ANSWERS using a file-writing utility in 1st-Class. So, by the time the session between the user and Z-EXPERT ended, ANSWERS contained the user's responses to each of Z-EXPERT's questions.

After Z-EXPERT listed its recommendation on the screen, it invited the user to examine its logic by pressing the F3 function key. Because the text of the recommendation contained the line:

{3: EXPLAIN ANSWERS},

pressing the F3 key invoked the Pascal program EXPLAIN, which accepted the file ANSWERS as a parameter. Each entry in ANSWERS was echoed by EXPLAIN along with an explanation of how that entry contributed to Z-EXPERT's recommendation. For example, had the user responded "Yes" to the question concerning the use of CAD/CAM, EXPLAIN would have output a message such as:

"You indicated that you would be doing some CAD/CAM on your system; for this reason, it is essential that you have a monitor and video card with very high resolution."

The result was a convincing argument that supported Z-EXPERT's recommendation. For reasons of improved efficiency, however, this particular method of explanation was later modified. Part 4 of the case study, which appears at the end of chapter 6, explains why.

6
Testing, Validation, and Maintenance

Once a PC-based expert system has been fully implemented, it can begin to be tested and validated. Afterwards, it will require maintenance, which can mean not only alteration, but enhancement and expansion of the system as well. These and other related issues are addressed in this chapter.

TESTING AND VALIDATION

Unlike the prototyping stage, when an expert system idea is being investigated to gain approval from those who have either the financial, technological, or human resources to commit to the project, the testing and validation stage seeks to demonstrate that the developed system has achieved its intended goal. That is, there is an overall shift from "proof-of-concept" of the system to its "performance." In effect, this stage attempts to answer this important yet basic question:

How does the system perform when compared to an expert?

This question can prompt a variety of responses, especially when looked at from the sometimes differing perspectives of the developer and the end user. In part, this difference stems from the expectations that are initially set for the performance of the expert system. The expert whom the system is attempting to replicate may seek absolute fidelity, and therefore find the automated version of his or her expertise incomplete and lacking in common sense. Users, however, might judge it differently: Automated expertise is better than none. But the system should behave in a way that fits the user's particular needs.

This problem of differing perspectives can, in part, be attributable to the fact that expert systems may not always be as good as real experts, though the systems may not be as likely to forget. So a compromise on the part of both user and developer may be required to accept the level of performance established for a particular expert system.

For these reasons, testing and validation should be done with specific performance criteria in mind.

We emphasize specificity here because we think that there is a danger in trying to oversell expert systems technology within an organization. Too often, what happens is that an expert system is developed in too large a domain and perhaps makes too many promises regarding its performance. So it is important to take a benefits-oriented approach when testing and validating a PC-based expert system. That is, it is better to focus specifically on:

— How useful the system is,
— How easily it can be integrated into traditional computing environments, and
— How it can be made as user-friendly as possible.

Seen from this perspective, expert systems stand a chance to extend greatly the productivity in an organization. With these basic goals in mind, we can identify six specific criteria for testing and validating a PC-based expert system:

1. Accuracy
2. Completeness
3. Reliability and consistency
4. Effective reasoning
5. User-friendliness
6. Run-time efficiency

Each of these criteria is discussed below.

Accuracy

Without question, an important criterion in judging an expert system is its accuracy. If expert systems are to be used as experts, or as expert *helpers*, then they must be able to perform as well as an expert in some instances. But just as we do not expect infallibility in our experts, so we cannot impose this constraint on an expert system. In fact, some might justifiably argued that the reason many expert system tools devote a fair amount of attention to uncertainty-handling is that it is a response to dealing with the accuracy problem.

So, when testing an expert system for completeness, the developer should first define the level of accuracy sought with the help of the area expert and then run enough sample cases through the system to test whether or not the system meets this minimal performance criterion for accuracy. It should be pointed out, however, that certainty factors are not a substitute for accuracy within a system. Rather, certainty or confidence factors should only express the real expert or user's level of confidence.

Completeness

Related to the idea of accuracy is completeness, for as an expert system grows in size and complexity, the more fallible it may become. Completeness in any problem-solving situation, which may be human- or machine-controlled, implies a thorough understanding of the present situation and a high degree of reasoning to work through a given problem. Such understanding and reasoning usually results from applying common sense knowledge to the problem at hand, which will, of course, leave the expert system solution at a great disadvantage since it cannot incorporate this kind of knowledge. So the more complete the expert system, the more complex it will necessarily become, with the chance for errors in its reasoning growing proportionally. Additionally, since some PC-based expert systems do not use high level structures for breaking down problems into discrete units or modules, the developer may be stuck with an inordinate amount of rules within a single knowledge base in order to achieve completeness. The more rules within a single knowledge base, the more chance for error.

A better strategy is to define completeness at the beginning of the development process in such a way that it would be acceptable to a user, though the system may not seem totally complete when compared to an expert. That is, the developer should set a carefully determined figure for what should be considered a "complete" system and then measure the developed system against this figure.

This strategy is, in fact, the one used at the Ford Motor Company for its expert system that diagnoses sick robots. You may recall from chapter 1 that the Ford expert system, with its small rule base, accounts for only 80 percent of the current problems in dealing with malfunctioning robots. Yet this system was considered highly successful, precisely because, given the amount of time and money invested in development, it had "enough" completeness to be useful to plant personnel. So successful was this approach that Ford did eventually plan to make the expert system even more complete in time.

It should also be pointed out that no expert system can ever be really "complete" if we accept the basic argument that knowledge is always changing and expanding. Indeed, when we call someone an expert, we are in part saying that this individual knows how to learn from continuing experiences. So any preestablished figure for system completeness will, of course, change over time. Better, then, to ask the key question:

How complete must the system be to be immediately useful to the user?

The developer will find that answering this question will facilitate the testing and validation process for system completeness.

Reliability and Consistency

Other than accuracy, if we expect anything of our experts, it is, justifiably, reliability and consistency. To say that someone is an expert implies that he or she is good at giving advice in almost all instances when confronting problems pertaining to a certain field of expertise; otherwise, we might call such individuals "experienced" or perhaps "amateur," but not "expert." So we are justified in wanting our expert systems to demonstrate the same kind of reliability and consistency; otherwise, we will not be able to rely on them and their usefulness will diminish.

The best way to test and validate an expert system for reliability and consistency is to simply measure it against a real expert. Sometimes this can be achieved in what is called the "telephone test," where an expert at a remote location is called and told of the same conditions that the user has input into the expert system. If the expert system gives similar advice to that of the expert on the telephone, then it may be said to be reliable. If this process is repeated and the expert system offers the same advice under the same conditions, then it can be said to be consistent as well.

But the telephone test might be a luxury in many situations, and may not even be possible when the developer and area expert are one and the same. So an alternative strategy for reliability and consistency testing is to run through as many sample consultations as possible and then query users with regard to this area of system performance. In effect, this test asks users if they were satisfied with the degree of reliability and consistency demonstrated by the system.

Another way to test for reliability and consistency is to "trace" the expert system's logic to the results or advice it will offer during consultations. However, this may not be easily done with a rule-based system that offers no visualization of the rule structure. But if a decision tree is provided, then tracing the various branches will offer an alternative to running several consultations in order to determine the overall reliability and consistency of the system. The precise procedure for performing this kind of trace is given below in the section dealing with effective reasoning.

Effective Reasoning

When most expert system developers think of "testing and validation," they focus primarily on system logic or the reasoning process, sometimes because this is often the most straightforward area of the system to test. But, unlike traditional programs, which depend on the programmer to control the logical processes within a system, expert systems rely on the structure of the rules and the input from the user to control the system. This means that at times the expert system might be "goal-driven" by a set of procedural statements, or "data-driven" by responses from the end user. Expert systems are often made even more complex when their behavior cannot be determined in advance, which is the case when system knowledge is highly complex. For example, when a user invokes a hypertext or chaining process within a system, the result might be an entirely new logical pathway through the expert system or a branch to an altogether new knowledge base. Furthermore, when large, complex expert systems are involved, it may be impossible to "play out" every possible path leading to a decision or recommendation. And uncertainty-handling makes the problem of testing system logic or reasoning even more difficult.

Still, on most small PC-based expert systems, logic or reasoning testing can be achieved in one of the two categories below:

— rule-base testing
— Decision tree testing.

Rule-base testing involves looking at a set of rules in order to determine if their relationships in fact represent correct procedural knowledge within the system. This process is sometimes referred to as "validating the rules." What is involved is using test or sample cases that represent "hypothetical" but likely situations. Then some type of trace, debugging, or reporting feature is used within the development tool to generate a listing that shows what rules were fired and what results or subgoals were reached. This information is then given to the expert, who is asked if he or she would have solved the problem the same way, given the same data or circumstances that the system worked with. In particular, what is sought is the validity of the result or recommendation and the order of the rules that were fired. This way, not only can the accuracy of the system be tested and improved, but system efficiency can also be judged.

Decision tree testing accomplishes much the same thing as rule-base testing, but by different means. A decision tree represents the logic or reasoning process of the system in a hierarchical diagram, which consists of "branches" and "nodes," as illustrated in Figure. 6.1.

So when the "tree" is tested, the developer or area expert is testing each one of the "branches" to see if an accurate and efficient pathway has been used to reach a valid conclusion or result. Note that, unless they exist within the same branch, branch elements have no explicit relationship to

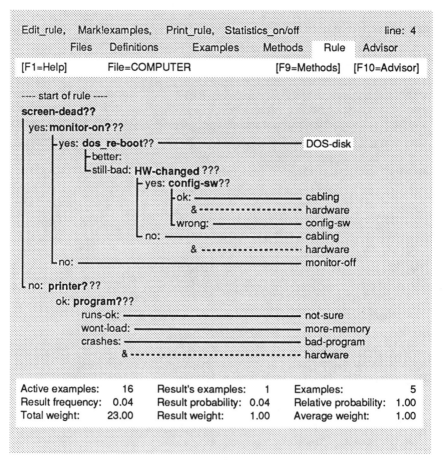

Figure 6.1. Sample decision tree from 1st-Class (Courtesy of 1st-Class Expert Systems, Inc.).

each other beyond the fact that they are part of the overall tree structure. Thus, decision trees are valuable in determining whether or not the branches need to be combined or separated, or if certain factors must be added or deleted within a given branch. Thus, decision-tree testing, like rule-based testing, offers a vehicle for improving system accuracy and performance.

User-Friendliness

As previously suggested, user-friendliness is often a key factor in the success of the expert system. No matter how accurate, complete, reliable, and consistent the system may seem from the developer's perspective, it may still be of little use to the user if it cannot convey its knowledge or expertise effectively. Rather than focusing on system reasoning or the validity of the knowledge represented, the user seeks trustworthy information that will solve the problem at hand. This means that the information conveyed must be clear and understandable and the user input and output formats optimal.

Several methods for improving user-friendliness were addressed in chapter 5 as they were associated with specific tools, so we will not discuss these features again here. Rather, we focus on the testing process itself for determining how user-friendly a system really is.

Basically, there are two types of tests for measuring user-friendliness: subjective and objective. Subjective tests involve a direct query of users once they have worked through one or more consultations with the expert system. In effect, the users are asked the following questions:

Was the recommendation correct?
Was the response format acceptable and efficient?
Were the system recommendations clear and useful?
Was the reasoning explained at a level that you could easily understand?

The answers to these and other questions are then interpreted by the developer and used to improve the user-friendliness of the system. For example, the *developer* may be satisfied with an accurate explanation of reasoning because it echoes the rules fired during a consultation. But the *user* may indicate that the revealed rules were not very useful in understanding how the system arrived at its conclusion. So the developer may infer that some type of graphical or natural-language approach to an explanation of reasoning might be needed.

Objective testing, on the other hand, does not query the user directly but rather involves close observation of users as they interact with the system. In such instances, the observer will focus on measurable factors such as those listed below:

— Response time to answer a question
— Number of keystrokes used to enter a response
— Number of times explanation of reasoning was used or a help facility invoked
— Degree of immediate productivity perceived on the part of the user after a consultation

Because of the human dynamics involved, testing and validation of system user-friendliness is often difficult. In fact, conducting thorough objective tests may require the skills of a psychologist trained in the area of software usability testing. For this reason, many expert systems are only tested subjectively, so the best safeguard against developing an unusable system is to keep the end user in mind throughout the system development process and to use as many tool features for screen design, on-line help, and explanation of reasoning as possible.

Run-Time Efficiency

Once the more important elements of an expert system have been tested and validated, run-time efficiency can then be assessed. It is conceivable that the most accurate, complete, reliable, and friendly expert system may still be of little use simply because users may choose not to use it. Such a case usually results for one of two reasons:

— The system is too slow to be effective
— The system cannot interact or communicate efficiently when accessing external programs or files.

Response time or system speed may be a result of hardware limitations, but, more often than not, system logic can greatly affect a program's run-time efficiency. If hardware seems a limitation, then a faster or more capable machine is needed. For example, the speed difference between an IBM PC XT system and a PS/2 class machine can be quite dramatic, though either system might have been used for expert system development.

If the hardware seems fast enough but the system still seems to run slowly, it could be that the knowledge base has not been built to run efficiently. Since most expert system tools depend on some type of search strategy to retrieve important system information, developers can use these searching techniques to their best advantage. For example, if a system that incorporates a decision tree uses a "bottom-up" search strategy, then it will be more efficient to place rules or data that are sought first at the bottom of the tree where they will be found most efficiently or quickly.

Assuming that the hardware and system design is optimal, the expert system still might run slowly simply because it must communicate or interact with other systems in order to achieve its goal. For example, each time an expert system must access a file or invoke an external program, its speed will be dramatically reduced by the operating system (DOS or OS/2) and the time it takes to open and close system files. Or, in another situation, when the expert system must communicate with another system to, say, get data from an external database, the rate of data transmission may reduce system response time, especially if such communication is achieved through the use of a serial device. This limiting speed factor in data communications may make the expert system ineffective for some real-time applications, as in the case where sensory data are used as responses to a system's questions.

In still other situations that involve graphics, system response time may be poor due to the time it takes to access graphic images in a file and then present them on the screen. For example, CGA graphic screens can take up to 16K of memory, and EGA screens might require up to 128K. So accessing a file with this much information and then drawing a complete screen may greatly reduce system performance.

Fortunately, there are at least a couple of ways to head off these kinds of system performance problems. The first way is to simply be aware of these problems and design around them. For instance, because file access operations are known to be slow, it may be better to include the information within the accessed file right into the expert system itself, provided this information is not too great in size. In other words, it simply does not make sense to read many disk files to retrieve just a few lines of information. Better to incorporate this information within a text screen in the expert system.

Conversely, incorporating too much information that is reference-oriented may slow an expert system down, and therefore such information would be more efficiently kept on disk. For example, on-line help or explanation information may not be used often, so it might slow down the system if it is kept in memory at all times. Hence, this kind of information should be retrieved from disk files only when needed.

When extensive file access seems to be the bottleneck in system performance, it may be possible to use a "RAM disk" to store file information in memory for quick retrieval. A RAM disk is simply additional system memory that is used to store information, much as a floppy or hard disk would. Since this information is not part of the expert system that is running, it does not slow the system down. Yet, when this information is called from the expert system, it will be retrieved quickly because it is in memory and not on disk. The PC operating system manual will give the necessary steps for installing a RAM disk. Caution should be taken when using RAM disks, however, since it is possible to actually reduce system performance by using up available memory for the RAM disk function. In such cases, you may be limiting the size of a knowledge base that can be loaded into memory or require more disk "swapping" than is necessary because of the limited memory size created by the RAM disk. The rule of thumb, therefore, is to know in advance how much memory can be allocated to a RAM disk without compromising system performance in other ways.

Summary

System testing and validation is an important step in the development of a useful expert system. Six areas can be examined in detail:

1. Accuracy
2. Completeness
3. Reliability and consistency
4. Effective reasoning
5. User-friendliness
6. Run-time efficiency.

In effect, what occurs at this stage of the development process is the overall verification that the system performs as intended. Strategies can be used to ensure that the system meets specific minimal standards set for performance. Furthermore, a consistent focus should be maintained on:

— How useful the system is
— How easily it can be integrated into traditional computing environments, and
— How it can be made as user-friendly as possible

MAINTENANCE ISSUES

Policy and Procedure

In order to effectively maintain an expert system, the developer must establish detailed criteria for modification and enhancement of the system. Unlike traditional programs, expert or "knowledge-based" systems are rarely ever complete: The knowledge they contain will constantly change over time, and procedures that may be currently effective may have to be modified as conditions change. This is especially true if the expert system is "event driven." Certain events may not only alter the values associated with factors within the system, but may also require the addition or deletion of factors altogether.

Thus expert system maintenance can only be effective when it is carried out according to a carefully conceived plan, preferably one that is reflected in a written *maintenance policy.*

A good starting point is to simply define when a completed system can be justifiably modified, though this is a highly subjective determination. We offer four instances when we think maintenance should be performed:

— When bugs or inaccuracies found in the program impair its performance significantly
— When new knowledge is essential to bring the system up-to-date or make it more useful
— When the logic or reasoning of the program no longer fits the situation and rules or examples must be changed
— When porting to another system is required

In each of these instances, the developer can justifiably generate a new version of the expert system since its overall success may be at stake. The intent of having a maintenance policy is to keep the expert system as useful as possible without allowing it to be modified so frequently that many versions of the program exist at one time.

In the early prototyping stage, it may be possible to have several versions of an expert system in the field at once as ideas are being tested and the overall technology is being sold. But formal software releases require significant resources that may not be initially considered by the developer. For example, during the development process, several versions of a system can be created by simply changing one or two factors. Because this occurs so rapidly and easily within an expert system tool, there exists a temptation to constantly "fiddle" with the system in an attempt to reach perfection. But, despite this fiddling, the ultimate difference to the end user may be negligible. Thus, the best maintenance policy is one that primarily takes into account the usefulness of the system.

Product Release and Tracking

Because of the great danger of having too many versions of an expert system in the field at one time, proper release and tracking procedures should accompany system distribution. When experienced programmers release a software product, they know that there exists at least two versions of their program: the source code version and the compiled run-time version. Hence, when they release the product, they know that their only avenue to maintenance and upgrading is through retaining a source code version that matches exactly the product that has been delivered. Furthermore, without the source code, no unauthorized individual can modify the program.

This is not always the case with fielded expert systems. In most instances, the expert system development tool will allow direct access to the rules or examples embedded within the delivered system. Though end users will not usually have this kind of access with the run-time version of the program, they can still modify it by obtaining a copy of the development tool.

In fact, with most of the lower priced expert system shells, it is generally expected that users will update or customize a system at will.

Thus, the only option a developer has in trying to consistently maintain and support a fielded system is through precise record-keeping. Records should minimally include the following items:

— Date of product release
— Product version number
— Author's name and title
— Version of development tool used, along with any copyright notices or restrictions
— Names and date stamps of all files associated with the developed system
— All factors and potential values
— All results or goals
— Type of inferencing or chaining method used
— Certainty formulas used
— Method of integration with other programs
— Known bugs or errors

Through careful record-keeping the expert system developer can hope to keep the product as current as possible with a minimal amount of frustration. Because development can occur so rapidly in an expert system environment, the more documentation that is attached to the system the better.

Z-EXPERT CASE STUDY — PART FOUR

Testing and Validation, and Maintenance

Accuracy

Once Z-EXPERT had been in the field awhile, the developers began to think about how the product could be made more accurate. In fact, accuracy considerations were a persistent issue throughout the development process. In part, this resulted from the simple fact that Zenith Data Systems (ZDS), in an attempt to keep current with the PC market, had to constantly change its product offerings and configurations; thus, Z-EXPERT had to reflect these changes as soon as possible to be kept accurate and up-to-date. At one point, the developers thought that pricing information could be included, but it soon became apparent that this was the one variable or factor that changed more than any other as ZDS sought to be price-competitive. The result? Pricing information was deliberately excluded.

A more tangible problem dealt with updating particular product configurations with respect to the class of system that was being recommended. When Z-EXPERT was first developed, a number of different video options were offered as well as a choice between 3.5- and 5.25-inch disk drives. Consequently, situations would arise where the user might need only minimal CPU power (say, a PC XT class machine), but a video or disk size selection would cause a much higher power (and expensive) system to be recommended. A trained ZDS representative in such circumstances might have said, "You really only need the low-power machine. Can you compromise on the drive size or video options, or get these items altered by a local dealer?" The expert system, however, could only pick from predefined bundles of systems. The result was that Z-EXPERT initially seemed to provide less satisfactory advice compared to the real expert who could use common sense to see the ridiculousness of recommending a higher level machine than a customer really needed.

This particular problem was solved by adding more custom system configurations to the knowledge base and by ZDS's own decision to (1) limit the number of system options, (2) provide a highly compatible video card in many of their PCs, and (3) offer more models with both 3.5- and 5.25-inch drive sizes.

Completeness

Actually, the problem of Z-EXPERT's accuracy cited above was closely related to the system's completeness. Since Z-EXPERT initially included mostly predefined "bundled" systems, its knowledge contained only a fraction of the systems that could result from custom configurations. This fact was made quite apparent via the development tool that was selected for the job. Because an induction tool was used to build Z-EXPERT, a number of "no-data" results were generated in earlier versions of the system, a situation which indicated that there were possible system configurations based on system options for which no examples existed.

So the next step was to "fill out" the example base in an attempt to not only rid the knowledge base of no-data results, but also to achieve custom system configurations that would give more accurate results during a consultation. A problem related to this action was that the text files that contained ZDS product information would either have to be updated or else new ones would have to be created. In all, as the system became more complete, it began to grow significantly to the extent that, at the end of the first development phase, the product barely fit onto one floppy disk.

Reliability and Consistency

Reliability and consistency also became significant issues in the Z-EX-PERT project because of the degree of overlap of ZDS products. That is, more than one system might fit a single user's needs, though differences may exist in some system options. For example, in some cases a user might respond to the system's questions in almost identical fashion to a previous user, and yet be recommended an entirely different class of machine. This problem was related to the situation described above, where a single factor could change the program's reasoning in such a dramatic way that the advice no longer seemed consistent from the user's perspective.

The "fix" for this particular problem (which was detected by a naive user working through the system) was to establish the "class" of ZDS system first before asking any questions regarding system options. Thus, users could no longer be given a recommendation for a system that was in too high a class for their primary application, though this meant some compromises on system options from time to time. This modification not only made the system more reliable and consistent, but also resulted in Z-EXPERT's recommending the lowest priced system for the user's needs. Consequently, the system was deemed more "useful" as a result of this one change.

Effective Reasoning

Throughout the building of Z-EXPERT, decision tree testing was used extensively. This process of validating system logic was made easier by the fact that one of the developers also functioned as the area expert. Since the program was built in a modular fashion, each knowledge base could be tested for accuracy and completeness before the entire system was tested. This meant that several smaller decision trees were validated first. This strategy supports the overall argument that modular systems are not only more easily maintained but easier to test as well.

The testing of Z-EXPERT's reasoning also had a valuable by-product in that it helped to visualize the logic of the system as a whole and reveal the underlying structure of its embedded knowledge. Because Z-EXPERT used an example approach and an inductive technique, the graphically-oriented decision tree was the first place that the structure of the knowledge was recognized. Each branch, because it revealed one possible pathway through the system, could be tested for accuracy and efficiency. In effect, using the decision tree method became the most expeditious way to test the system overall.

User-Friendliness

Without question, user-friendliness was a most important factor in Z-EXPERT for two reasons:

1. The system had to be easier to use than looking through ZDS product sheets.
2. Since the users did not yet own a ZDS system, they could not be assumed to have any knowledge about computers, including how to interact with them.

This last fact is critical, especially when we consider that people in the computer field often inaccurately judge the technical level of the end user. For example, it seems second nature to a PC user to hit the Return key to make something happen within a system (most often, to accept a response or continue with the program). But naive users may make a selection and then sit there looking at the screen wondering why nothing is happening. Fortunately, 1st-Class provided a "light bar" type of selection mechanism where only two keys had to be used to register a response: Space bar to select an option and Return key to accept this choice.

A more difficult problem involved the way the system's recommendation would be conveyed to the user of the system. At first, it was thought that a simple system configuration could be given on the screen or printer. But it became immediately apparent that users would not trust this type of approach in which they enter several responses and the system provides a single result with no explanation. A better strategy was to provide first an explanation that summarized the user responses into a "fact sheet" and showed the class of system needed, the type of video and disk options that would be required, the type of disk storage, and so on. Then, once this information was displayed, the user could press a function key to see the specific ZDS system recommendation.

The effect produced by this approach was dramatic. Instead of the system saying, "Here, buy this ZDS system," Z-EXPERT was, in effect, saying, "Here are the characteristics which describe a system that will fit your needs. Now press F2 to see the specific ZDS system recommended." The first screen is not vendor-specific and the second screen is simply tied to the established system characteristics. The user must even enter a keystroke to get to this information. This strategy actually draws on the standard technique of providing a HOW explanation within an expert system. The system will simply be more believable and user-friendly if the logic or reasoning of the program is provided as part of the overall recommendation.

WHY explanations were also important in the Z-EXPERT project, though they were not added until later. Once the system was tested for effective reasoning, it was then necessary to begin to think about how this logic could be conveyed to the user. The common strategy employed was simply attaching text comments to each of the questions using a window design. Thus, if users wanted to know why a question was being asked, they could press the F2 function key to get this information from disk. F2 was used not only for explanations but also for results or recommendations as a method of providing the least number of keys to remember and the most consistent interface possible. The text comments actually revealed the inference that would be established through the answer to a question. For example, if a user said that graphics would be used with a desired application, then the program would assume that minimal graphics capability was required. This type of conclusion, which would be included as the WHY text, reflects a use of "static" explanation techniques, rather than "dynamic." That is, there was no attempt to retrace system logic to the point at which the question was asked. Such information would be inappropriate to the targeted users of Z-EXPERT.

In the end, Z-EXPERT achieved a high degree of user-friendliness. In fact, because such great pains were taken to keep the program user-friendly and elementary, Z-EXPERT was not initially appropriate for individuals who had significant experience in a PC environment until more technical questions were added to the system. However, in order to avoid mixing audiences for the program, separate knowledge bases were added that were targeted solely at technical users. Consequently, the first question for each area-specific knowledge base inquired if the user was technically literate; if so, then the program branched to a totally new set of technically-oriented questions. By using such a strategy, the developers were able to achieve a system that was, in a sense, "friendly" to a diverse set of users.

Run-Time Efficiency.

Although run-time efficiency or speed was not initially a problem with Z-EXPERT, as the system began to grow, it tended to slow down proportionally. More knowledge bases simply meant more chaining as well as more modules being brought in and out of memory from disk. Each time a module of 20 to 30 kbytes was brought into memory, a few seconds delay would result. Not wanting to jeopardize the modular approach, the developers sought to make each of the system modules more compact. This was achieved in two ways.

First, the knowledge bases were "gutted" of their examples, since these were no longer needed for the 1st-Class system reasoning to work; the various decision trees would handle these functions. Secondly, the knowledge bases were not allowed to contain any reference-oriented information, such as explanations connected to WHY questions. This information was kept on disk and retrieved through window programs, which not only sped up the overall operation of the system but improved the user interface as well. Of course, when WHY questions were asked, the information would be brought to the screen somewhat slowly, but this explanation function was not invoked for every question, so the compromise was acceptable.

Another change in program design that dramatically improved system performance was the addition of a RAM disk. Using this standard DOS utility, the developers were able to load the various knowledge bases into memory prior to starting a consultation. The result is that when one knowledge base chained to another, this action appeared to occur almost instantly. One reason for adopting a RAM disk design is because Z-EXPERT would be used primarily in a floppy disk version. Consequently, if users got impatient waiting for one knowledge base to chain to another, they might hit the Return key several times thinking that the system was simply being inattentive. Then, once the program "recovered" from its internal operation of chaining, the user would be thrust perhaps four or five questions ahead into the next knowledge base by virtue of the repeated Return key presses. If a hard disk were used throughout for Z-EXPERT, it may have provided enough speed for chaining knowledge bases so as not to require the RAM disk installation.

A third strategy that improved Z-EXPERT's performance involved one of its explanation mechanisms. Early in the project, the developers thought that the best way to handle all explanation information was through external file-accessing processes, as in the case with WHY questions. However, using this strategy at the end of the program, when the user expects a system recommendation, was not effective because of the delay caused by having to run an external program from disk. So a better alternative was to scrap the earlier reasoning explanation approach and simply attach text to each of the system recommendations. These explanations would detail the specific system characteristics that would meet the user's needs. Though the knowledge bases grew in size by having this kind of redundant information attached to each recommendation, run-time performance was dramatically increased at a critical time in the program's execution.

So, through a number of combined strategies, the run-time performance of Z-EXPERT was greatly improved. The important thing to note is that the developers were not encumbered by performance issues at the time that they were trying to build a working prototype or a developed system. It was only after the first complete version of the system was built that this type of testing began.

Maintenance Issues

Maintenance Policy and Procedure

The maintenance policy for Z-EXPERT, though simple, was difficult to implement. If the product was to be used extensively in the field, then it would have to be as current as possible. Though unaware buyers may accept out-of-date product descriptions or price lists, they would surely be less patient with a program that recommended a system that was no longer available. In fact, it was thought early on that Z-EXPERT would generate product descriptions that could be sent directly to Zenith with a check to constitute an equipment order. If this seemed too ambitious, the program would at least do some of the redundant work of the ZDS sales representative. For this reason, the developers initiated a maintenance policy that would require Z-EXPERT to be updated when new product lists were issued from ZDS in hard-copy form. Additionally, dealers and other ZDS reps would be asked to use only the newest version of the program and to destroy or erase any earlier copies.

Aside from this automatic updating policy, Z-EXPERT would also be revised when new systems were added to the ZDS product list or old systems deleted. If the changes were minor, then only the text files would be changed. If a change in product produced a new category or class of system, then a logic upgrade was justified. Since the product list changed often enough, it would not be efficient to modify the program to improve only efficiency or correct minor errors.

Product Release and Tracking

Since the developers would maintain the program initially, they opted for a version-number tracking system, beginning with Release 1.0. Since the run-time version of Z-EXPERT did not contain examples, an exact copy of the "complete" program was kept by the developers for future upgrades. Simple modifications, however, could be achieved in 1st-Class through the customization feature. And, of course, text files containing ZDS product information could be altered anytime. Full documentation in printed form was also kept so that the system could be maintained by others, should ZDS decide to opt for this approach to maintenance.

One last point to mention about Z-EXPERT is that it was difficult to ensure that only one version of the system was being used at a time. Because there was a fair amount of "selling" involved in the Z-EXPERT project, several different prototype versions were passed around ZDS for approval. This meant that it was hard to tell what version of the software was being evaluated at any one time. From this experience, we recommend that even prototypes be treated as full working systems for the purpose of tracking.

Appendix A
Selected Tools, Prices, and Vendors

TOOL	PRICE	VENDOR
ESI	$ 495	Abacus Programming Corp. 14545 Victory Boulevard Van Nuys, CA 91411 (818) 785-8000
Xi Rule	$ 495	American Expertech Inc. P.O. Box AS Incline Village, NV 89450 (702) 831-0136
Arity	$ 295	Arity Corp. 30 Domino Drive Concord, MA 01742 (617) 371-1243
XSYS	$ 395	California Intelligence 912 Powell Stret, #8 San Francisco, CA 94108 (415) 391-4846
The Idea Generator	$ 195	Experience in Software Inc. 2039 Shattuck Avenue Suite 401 Berkeley, CA 94704 (415) 644-0694
ES/P	$ 895	Expert Systems International 1700 Walnut Street Philadelphia, PA 19103 (215) 735-8510
Exper OPS5 ExperFacts	$ 495 $ 495	ExperTelligence 559 San Ysidro Road Santa Barbara, CA 93108 (805) 969-7874

EXSYS	$ 295	EXSYS, Inc. P.O. Box 75158 Contra Station Albuquerque, NM 98194 (505) 836-6676
1st-Class FUSION	$ 495 $1295	1st-Class Expert Systems, Inc. 286 Boston Post Rd. Wayland, MA 01778 (617) 358-7722
Level5 Insight-2+	$ 685 $ 485	Information Builders, Inc. 1250 Broadway New York, NY 10001 (212) 736-4433
Auto Intelligence IXL Intelligence/ Compiler	$ 490 $ 490 $ 490	IntelligenceWare, Inc. 9800 S. Sepulveda Boulevard Suite 730 Los Angeles, CA 90045 (213) 417-8896
KDS	$ 795	KDS Corp. 934 Hunter Road Wilmette, IL 60091 (312) 256-4201
KnowledgeMaker KnowledgePro	$ 95 $ 495	Knowledge Garden, Inc. 473A Malden Bridge Road Nassau, NY 12123 (518) 766-3000
MicroExpert	$ 50	McGraw-Hill Book Co. Professional and Reference Division 11 W. 19th Street New York, NY 10011 (212) 2MC-GRAW
EST	$ 495	Mind Path Product Corp. 12700 Park Central Drive Suite 1801 Dallas, TX 75251 (214) 329-2142

Expert-2	$ 100	Mountain View Press, Inc. P.O. Box 4656 Mountain View, CA 94040 (415) 961-4103
VP-EXPERT	$ 99	Paperback Software, Inc. 2830 Ninth Street Berkeley, CA 94710 (415) 644-2116
Apes	$ 425	Programming Logic Systems, Inc. 31 Crescent Drive Milford, CT 06460 (203) 877-7988
RuleMaster 2/PC	$ 495	Radian Corp. 8501 Mo-Pac Boulevard P.O. Box 201088 Austin, TX 78720 (512) 454-4797
SuperExpert	$ 195	Softsync, Inc. 162 Madison Avenue New York, NY 10016 (212) 685-2080
PC EASY	$ 495	Texas Instruments, Inc. P.O. Box 809063 Dallas, TX 75380 (512) 250-6785
Smalltalk	$ 299	Xerox 250 North Halstead Street P.O. Box 7018 Pasadena, CA 91109 (818) 351-2351

Appendix B
Annotated Reading List

Historically, most books written on the subject of expert systems were written in technical terms and were of little benefit to the average PC user. Lately, however, with more and more expert systems being developed on personal computers, several books aimed at the nontechnical user have appeared. Below are descriptions of some of these.

Frenzel, Jr., L., *Understanding Expert Systems*, Howard W. Sams & Company, Indianapolis, (1987)

Using a step-by-step approach, *Understanding Expert Systems* explains what expert systems are, how they work, and where they find the greatest application. It also contains a comprehensive glossary, a list of expert system tool vendors, a bibliography, and a catalog of conferences, seminars, workshops, and courses related to expert systems. Unique is the inclusion of a short quiz at the end of each of the book's seven chapters. (Answers to the quiz questions appear in an appendix.)

Harmon, P., Maus, R., and Morrissey, W., *Expert Systems — Tools and Applications*, John Wiley & Sons, Inc., New York, (1988)

The authors state in the preface of *Expert Systems — Tools and Applications* their assumption that its readers (executives, middle managers, and computer systems personnel) are more sophisticated and concerned with more technical issues than they were in 1984, when Harmon and King wrote *Expert Systems: Artificial Intelligence in Business*. The four major sections of this book describe (1) the expert system market at the beginning of 1987, (2) expert system building tools of all sizes, (3) the expert system building process, and (4) fielded expert systems applications. Includes a glossary and a chapter-by-chapter bibliography.

Schoen, S. and Sykes, W., *Putting Artificial Intelligence to Work*, John Wiley & Sons, Inc., New York, (1987)

Though its title suggests a treatment of artificial intelligence at work, in reality, *Putting Artificial Intelligence to Work* deals only with expert systems and not with the other topics generally considered to be a part of artificial intelligence (robotics, natural-language processing, etc.). The point of view here is managerial: The preface of the book notes that its distinguishing feature ". . . is a discussion of the concept of knowledge as an organizational resource and how to manage it." The book addresses questions such as organizing and managing an expert systems project, determining return on investment, and selling an expert systems project. Included is a chapter-by-chapter bibliography and a glossary of terms.

Silverman, B., (Editor), *Expert Systems for Business*, Addison-Wesley Publishing Company, Reading, MA, (1987)
Representing the work of 31 contributors, *Expert System for Business* is a collection of 17 chapters dealing with topics as diverse as expert systems in management and accounting, modeling creativity, resource allocation by an expert system, and knowledge-based decision- support systems for military procurement. Not intended to be a "how-to" book, *Expert Systems for Business* provides a broad introduction to the applications of artificial intelligence in the private sector.

Van Horn, M., *Understanding Expert Systems*, Bantam Books, New York, (1986)
Understanding Expert Systems offers an overview of what expert systems are and how they work. It effectively defines and illustrates the basic notions of backward- and forward-chaining and describes some of the more prominent (non-PC-based) expert systems currently implemented (MYCIN, Dendral, R1). Only two pages, however, address microcomputer-based expert system development tools. This is not so much a "how-to" book as it is an expository treatment of expert systems technology. The book includes an extensive chapter-by-chapter bibliography.

Waterman, D., *A Guide to Expert Systems*, Addison-Wesley Publishing Company, Reading, MA, (1986)
Beginning with an overview of the field of expert systems, *A Guide to Expert Systems* goes on to discuss expert system tools, the expert system building process, and expert systems in the marketplace. Because the book was written before the popularity of microcomputer-based expert system shells, this aspect of expert systems is not emphasized. The book's strongest point is the extensive catalog and bibliography of expert systems in 16 specific areas ranging from agriculture to space technology. Also impressive is its catalogue of expert system development tools and list of companies engaged in expert systems work. Contains a glossary and bibliography.

Williamson, M., *Artificial Intelligence for Micro-Computers, The Guide for Business Decision Makers*, Brady Communications Company, Inc., New York, (1986)

The purpose of *Artificial Intelligence for Micro-Computers, The Guide for Business Decision Makers* is to teach the readers the jargon of artificial intelligence (AI) and to familiarize them with products relating to AI. An extremely readable and well-organized work, the book describes natural language inquiry systems, decision-support systems, artificial intelligence programming languages, and expert systems. A nice feature of the chapter on expert system shells is the author's collection of product "snapshots," two- to five-page descriptions of six expert system development tools (Expert-Ease, EXSYS, Insight, M.1, KDS, and KES) ranging in price from $95 to $10,000. A glossary and a short bibliography are included.

NEWSLETTERS

Several newsletters are devoted entirely to keeping readers informed of the most recent developments and trends in the area of expert systems. Though quite expensive, they do offer the most up-to-date information in the field.

Expert Systems Strategies	12 issues per year
Subscription Services	$297 per annual subscription
1100 Massachusetts Avenue	
Arlington, MA 02174	
AI Trends Newsletter	12 issues per year
DM Data, Inc.	$295 per annual subscription
6900 East Camelback Road	
Suite 1000	
Scottsdale, AZ 85251	

SPECIALIZED MAGAZINES

Several magazines carry articles on expert systems written for a non-technical audience. In fact, a few journals devoted entirely to this topic have recently appeared. Most include extensive advertising of expert systems products.

AI Expert	12 issues per year
Subscription Services	$3.50 per single issue
P.O. Box 10952	$39 annual subscription
Palo Alto, CA 94303-0968	

Calling itself "The Magazine for the Artificial Intelligence Community," *AI Expert* covers the gamut of AI applications but tends to emphasize expert systems. Among the topics you are likely to find in an issue: Intelligent Databases, Natural-Language Understanding, Knowledge Representation, Expert System Shells, Robotics, AI Workstations.

AI Magazine	4 issues per year
American Association for Artificial Intelligence	Subscription is a direct
445 Burgess Drive	benefit of membership in
Menlo Park, CA 94025	AAAI
	$25 annual membership

Though not written for the lay person, we include *AI Magazine* because of its stature in the AI community. Most of the articles appearing in this journal represent advancements in the field of artificial intelligence. Few, however, concern microcomputers.

PC AI	4 issues per year
3310 West Bell Road	$28 annual subscription
Suite 119	
Phoenix, AZ 85023	

The first magazine dedicated solely to artificial intelligence with personal computers, *PC AI* publishes items dealing with new artificial intelligence developments and applications, as well as future trends in artificial intelligence programming. Regular features include product updates and a description of a specific AI application. This magazine is a good source for product advertisements.

GENERAL MAGAZINES

A number of publications, though not dedicated to expert systems, do frequently carry articles (or even special issues) on this topic. Not appropriate, say, for a tutorial on expert systems, these magazines are an excellent means of keeping up with applications and news of expert systems products. The titles listed below can usually be found in most popular magazine outlets.

Byte	14 issues per year
Subscription Services	$3.50 per single issue
P.O. Box 6821	$22 annual subscription
Piscataway, NJ 08855	

Computerworld
Subscription Services
Box 9171
375 Cochituate Road
Framingham, MA 01701

52 issues per year
$2.00 per single issue
$44 annual subscription

PC Magazine
Subscription Services
P.O. Box 2443
Boulder, CO 80322

22 issues per year
$2.95 per single issue
$34.97 annual subscription

PC Week
Customer Service Department
P.O. Box 5970
Cherry Hill, NJ 08034

52 issues per year
$5.00 per single issue
$160 annual subscription

PC World
Subscription Services
P.O. Box 55029
Boulder, CO 80322

12 issues per year
$2.95 per single issue
$29.90 annual subscription

Index

About the Authors

Larry Bielawski is director of the Decker Center for Information Technology and co-director of the Artificial Intelligence Laboratory at Goucher College, Baltimore, Maryland. As a faculty member he has been actively involved in the development of expert systems technology at Goucher in a variety of areas. Working from his background as a technical writer and computer documentation specialist, he has also served as a teacher and consultant to many businesses and organizations nationwide. He has taught at the college level for eight years, has lectured on the topic of expert systems at national conventions, and is the author of *Organizational Writing*, published by Wadsworth, Inc.

Robert Lewand is professor of Mathematics and Computer Science as well as co-director of the Artificial Intelligence Laboratory at Goucher College in Baltimore, Maryland. For the past fifteen years he has taught college-level mathematics and computer science including courses in LISP and Artificial Intelligence. He has served as research scientist at The Johns Hopkins University School of Hygiene and Public Health and as research associate in the Department of Neurology at The University of Maryland School of Medicine. A popular teacher and speaker, Dr. Lewand has written papers on subjects ranging from abstract algebra to artificial intelligence, and has served as regional chairman of The Mathematical Association of America.

Mr. Bielawski and Dr. Lewand can be reached at the Artificial Intelligence Laboratory, Goucher College, Baltimore, Maryland (301) 337-6300.